Meyerhold at Work

MEYERHOLD AT WORK

Edited by Paul Schmidt

Translations by Paul Schmidt, Ilya Levin, and Vern McGee

 University of Texas Press

Requests for permission to reproduce material
from this work should be sent to
    Permissions
    University of Texas Press
    Post Office Box 7819
    Austin, Texas 78712

Some of the material in this book has previously
appeared in *October* 7 (Winter 1978)

Drawing of Meyerhold by Egan K. Sagik

Library of Congress Cataloging in Publication Data
Main entry under title:
Meyerhold at work.
    (University of Texas Press Slavic series; no. 2)
    1. Meierkhol'd, Vsevolod Emil'evich, 1874–1940.
2. Theatrical producers and directors—Russia—
Biography.
I. Schmidt, Paul, 1934–   II. Title.   III. Series.
PN2728.M4M4   792'.0233'0924 [B]   80-15265
ISBN 0-292-75058-7

For Robert Wilson and Timothy Mayer

◼ Contents

■ Introduction

It is the evening of December 17, 1898, the opening night of Chekhov's play *The Sea Gull* at the Moscow Art Theater. On stage, in the roles of the two opposed playwrights Treplyov and Trigorin, are Vsevolod Meyerhold and Konstantin Stanislavsky. "What we need is a new kind of theater," says the aspiring Treplyov/ Meyerhold. "We need new forms. . . ." And to Nina, when she complains that his play "has no living people in it," he replies: "Why should there be? I don't want to show life as it is, or the way it should be, but the way it is in dreams." Nina rejects Treplyov/Meyerhold and becomes the lover of Trigorin/Stanislavsky, who tells her: "I'd like to be in your shoes just for an hour, to see through your eyes and find out what you're thinking and what kind of person you are."

Like Nina, the October Revolution rejected Treplyov/ Meyerhold and chose Trigorin/Stanislavsky. It abandoned the openly revolutionary vision of "the way life is in dreams" and chose the prurient, petty desire, "to be in your shoes just for an hour, to see through your eyes and find out what you're thinking. . . ." The reasons for that choice are of less interest than the fact that a choice had indeed to be made; Chekhov had understood that as clearly as he understood most things. And the casting of his play for that evening seems an act of prophecy, for the choice must still be made today: in distinctions between the work of Stanislavsky and the work of Meyerhold is the definition of a modern theater to be found.

Stanislavsky's influence has been, and remains to this day, powerful, inside Russia as well as out. Yet the triumph of the Moscow Art Theater and the Stanislavsky system was a triumph of culmination, not of innovation. It marked the end of the nineteenth century, not the beginning of the twentieth. It was Meyerhold who brought theater into the twentieth century, yet he and his theater were obliterated, and he is still strange to us here in the West. How then can we distinguish Meyerhold's "new forms"?

We look in vain for some substantive text that will outline his method for us; he left none. Meyerhold wrote little. He did publish in 1912 a volume of essays in which he sketched out his earliest notions of theater and described some of his productions. But writing seemed to constrain him, and he did it less and less. What he did write was brief and polemical; he never attempted to turn his ideas into doctrine. He could not. His work was theater, and his clearest definition of that work leaves no room for writing. "The production of a play," he said, "is a conceptual task, which I accomplish physically using all the means that theater affords." To distinguish the theater of Meyerhold from the theater of Stanislavsky, then, we must seek something apart from language.

Let us return again to the evening of December 17, 1898, to the Moscow Art Theater, and to Stanislavsky and Meyerhold onstage. Both men were superb actors, but both men eventually left the stage in order to seek something beyond the role. Their vision of theater encompassed more than the introspective concerns of playing a part.

The actor is central to the theatrical enterprise. And yet the actor is always limited by his role and by the self-absorption he needs to perform it; he can never be anything but Hamlet or Boris Godunov. If we go merely to see him as Hamlet or Boris Godunov, we can never see the play _Hamlet_ or the play _Boris Godunov_. The director alone can perform the play for us. And in order for the director to do so he must first break through the willfulness of most actors, their overwhelming consciousness of self, their unawareness of their surroundings. He must teach them to hear not just their internal rhythm, but the rhythm of the whole.

All of Meyerhold's training devices, his "science" of biomechanics, were attempts to teach actors an externally controllable technique—but one that came, nevertheless, spontaneously and organically from the actor's gestalt.

Like Stanislavsky, Meyerhold knew that if we perceive in the actor's performance a split between mind and body, if we perceive the process of control of one over the other, we are distracted from the organic process of the performance as a whole. And yet he knew he could not as a director construct an elaborate whole, of which the actor was only one component, even though _primus_ *inter pares*, until he could rely with absolute assurance on the actor's sense of the whole.

The Stanislavskian actor is always idiosyncratic, autochthonous; Stanislavsky's drive was toward improvisation: acting "as if": as if it were spontaneous. Hence his acting is illusionary, subjective, conventional in the sense of stereotypical (since how else would we recognize it?). It is a concept of acting that rests ultimately on individual genius and denies the idea of any except supplementary training.

Hence any performance with such actors works best when the director simply provides a frame within which they are left to do what they do. The focus of attention in such productions is on the alchemical reaction between actor and actor. From this point of view we see that Stanislavsky was not a director, but a trainer of actors; his directorial impulse dissipated in the attempt to coordinate the individualities of his actors. Thus he was able to perceive the text only rudimentarily, only as an opportunity for the display of authentic emotion.

Meyerhold wanted his actors to express emotion, but he needed them also to fit into a larger pattern. He tried to systematize acting so it could be taught to all. His system of biomechanics was an elaboration of physical exercises which emphasized the actor's outward visualization of himself. It used the terms *risunok* (sketch, pose, outline) and *samozerkalenie* (self-mirroring) to force the actor's visual awareness of himself.

Meyerhold always tried to help his actors find the right pose, the right gesture or business, to figure forth their interior state as economically as possible. Through biomechanical exercises they were able to find the largest, most grandiose poses and gestures and then scale them down to precise measure. Meyerhold's system stressed the actor's dependence on the actors he played with; it changed him, that is, from a self-serving improviser to one who saw himself as a director would see him—as part of the whole.

Meyerhold's theater concentrated on the *act* of acting, not on acting as representing some kind of reality. Meyerhold's conception of acting totally denies the idea of "character," with its nineteenth-century overtones of bourgeois individualism: of private morality and personal motivation. And above all it attacked the Freudian notion of sexual individuality as a motivation for action. Freud's strange Viennese monodrama, the isolated individual talking in an endless attempt to reveal his intimate past to an invisible and unreacting audience—this was the image of the actor that Stanislavsky and his followers, willy-nilly, had installed at the heart of his theater. It is this image of the actor more than any other that has dominated the western stage for the last forty years. And it was this image that Meyerhold's theater was to deny above all else.

In Meyerhold's theater darkness is destroyed by light, the hidden chair of the analyst-observer-audience is discovered, made present; a passive, purely aural process is replaced by an active, physical transaction between two equal entities who occupy the same space. The idea of audience, those who hear, is replaced by the idea of spectators, those who see. The primacy of the actor as a speaker of words is denied for the sake of a text written in more than words. And the creation of this text is the task of the director.

Meyerhold was the first director to insist on the primacy of the director's role, indeed the first to conceive it as a role, something to be played out, performed—but a creative force as well, equal to the role of the playwright in shaping the theatrical experience, an experience considered different from the playtext, and not achieved merely by actors. Without the director as demiurge, henceforth, nothing theatrical would obtain. The role of the director is here perceived as an extension of the Romantic notion of the Interpreter, shifted away from the actor and the idea of character, from the mimetic impulse merely, to more complicated impulses.

Under Meyerhold's hand the whole of a performance became a crystallization of meaning. And the code of that meaning, beyond the language of the text, was _movement—gesture_ and the _reaction_ that gesture ineluctably calls forth. Only theater, by combining language with patterns of gesture and reaction, can encompass a future, and thus link the notion of probability to human behavior. It is in this sense that theater is always revolutionary. It points toward a future without having to present that future; rather, it shows us the virtualities contained within the present, and asks for response. Theater illuminates gesture and its source—the individual who makes it and the class it identifies: the class to which the gesture-maker belongs by virtue of having made the gesture. It traces the consequences of that gesture: it shows us Oedipus, blinded and setting out into exile; Hamlet, dying and yielding place to Fortinbras; Boris Godunov, dying and yielding place to the Pretender Dimitry.

The creative role of the director, then, as organizer of more than the actor's mimetic impulse, of more complicated impulses deriving from the already created playtext, is precisely to organize gesture into significant patterns. And in their conception of gesture Stanislavsky and Meyerhold differed greatly.

Stanislavsky conceived of gesture as movement that was neither presented nor arranged but that signified only accidentally, in reference to what he called "real life." Stanislavskian gesture is intended always to seem like movement observed unawares, and thus it implicitly reduces the spectator to an eye at a keyhole. Such gesture tends toward pornography, because it denies the possibility of the spectator's reaction and involvement.

Meyerhold structured gesture to present a possibility, a virtuality, an idea. This is a social act. It involves two gestures; the primary one is the gesture of presentation: the act which indicates and defines the gesture as gesture, and which demands from the spectator the gesture of response.

Stanislavsky was interested in gesture only as it served to reveal character. But the power of gesture, precisely, is that it can reveal human significance apart from individual personality. When an actor performs, as Meyerhold knew, only his gesture is real, not his "character." His gesture, and the things that surround him onstage. When these realities are arranged in patterns, carefully integrated with the language of the playtext, complex signification becomes possible. The uniqueness of Meyerhold's work resides in his investigations of these possibilities.

We observe in Meyerhold's work a constant breaking of the playtext into episodes which provided the framework for the staging, a constant use of "retard" and "reject" to slow the action, and a constant striving toward moments when the action onstage slows, freezes, stands still—a striving toward tableaux. Gesture was structured and presented in space, but in a moment removed from time. It seems to me that these are Meyerhold's attempts to make visible the *significant objectivity* of the world. Like a photographer, he attempted to make a past out of a present moment—but in that action, unlike a photographer, he also pointed the way toward a future. In Meyerhold's tableaux, in his episodes, temporality and causality in their traditional dramatic sense were removed: the time of the action as well as the time of the performance were both dissolved, the idea that x has caused y was suspended for a moment, and a situation (which may well have been contrived out of dramatic causality) was held up for observation and comment before the spectator. The line of causality was thereby removed from the dramatic frame and laid out along another axis—the line between stage and spectator. The tableau says to the spectator, in effect: "Consider this well: your own behavior is involved in this, may well be responsible for this. Now that you have seen this, what will you do in the future?"

Further, did not Meyerhold in his manipulation of time and space seek what Rimbaud has named as the goal of poetry, a moment of "essential desire and satisfaction"? His tableaux attempted to impose on the rigorous linear progression and causality of dramatic action the ambiguities of metaphor; they attempted to destroy "drama" and to substitute something richer and more flexible. His theater was polyphonic: complex rather than simple; it was polysemic: ambiguous rather than clear. It resembled a novel, in that plot and story became inseparable from staging; one could not distinguish plot from *mise en scène*.

The playtext on the page relies on linear causality; the director's task, as Meyerhold conceived it, is to reveal within the playtext a structural necessity. And since this directorial act is also a critical act, it can involve considerations not explicit in the playtext but which belong to the matrix which formed it, which derive from consideration of it as a political, economic, and ideological phenomenon. As a historical phenomenon, in other words.

In this modern conception of theater there is more to the playtext than actors or designers alone could convey. The text had to be revealed; it did not correspond to reality, it no longer held a mirror up to nature. In Mayakovsky's phrase, theater was "not a mirror but a magnifying glass." Meyerhold's was a modernist view of the complexity of the text, its need for elucidation. Meyerhold first of all directors operated on the playtext in the modern sense: he wrote the text anew. In Barthes' phrase, he "crossed its writing with a new inscription." And in this he reveals to us the only way in which a playtext can be "read" in the complex sense of the word *read* which Barthes intended: in the juxtaposition of text with historical time. Its performance ("reading") at any given moment is the measure of the time between its original writing and this new inscription. The author fixes the text in his own time, the director in his staging inscribes it in his, and in the inscription reveals history to us. It is in this sense that Meyerhold was a Marxist director: he knew that certain texts belonged to a past, and had to be reconstructed in a present with a sense of their implications for the future. Thus his responsibility to the text comprised his understanding of the time when it was first written, of the time in which he as director was to rewrite it, and of his vision of the future, which would determine the direction of his rewriting.

Meyerhold offers us theater as spectacle: a conception worked out in opposition to Stanislavsky's untenable notion of realism in theater, of "real life" upon the stage. To the idea of an art existing by itself and for itself, where the viewer is idealized and the author is absent, Meyerhold opposes an art whose very existence is the transaction between viewer and author. In his theater the viewer is made visible, and made to confront the author as director/inscriber, as presenter/commentator, as "author of the spectacle," as Meyerhold used to sign his productions. Meyerhold offers us a theater of the world, one that forces us to look at the world and our existence in it.

He offers us, in others words, a vision of community. And the work of theater—the arrangement of images in spectacles, where we spectators, as a group, can see ourselves as a group and can understand that the performance touches our behavior—is one of the truest expressions of community today, in that it attempts to rescue us from solitary slavery to the power of the written word, to the authority of the printed book. The struggle between authority and community is at the heart of the theatrical experience, for it is the struggle between the playtext and its staging.

To believe in books is to believe that things can last; to believe in theater is to know better. To contemplate performance is to understand with Heraclitus that all things flow and change, and no authority can stem that flow. All performance vanishes; only the idea of performance persists, in the memory and imagination of the community within which the performance took place—the community constituted, in fact, by the very performance.

It is in the memory of a community, then, that we must look for Meyerhold. We must seek his ideas in the realm in which he created them—beyond text, in imagination and in memory. We must find out how people remembered him, how he impressed them, how he left his mark. What did the people who knew him see? How much of him did they see? How close were they; how clear are the images in their memories? How well did they know him?

He wasn't easy to know. He dreamed a vision of community, but understood only authority. He talked of equality, but competed hierarchically, up or down, with his teacher Stanislavsky or his pupil Eisenstein. He imagined the Revolution, acted at it, but could not live it out. He delighted in the forms of disorder, but only insofar as they were raw material upon which he could impose his own sense of order. Like most directors, he was paternalistic, authoritarian.

Thus he was also lonely, like all lonely people he was difficult, and like lonely people of intelligence he surrounded himself with crowds, worked always in full view, in public. Yet those who surrounded him were followers, subordinates; they stood in the profoundly dependent position of actors before a director. He could not abide the only contemporary equal he had in his own world, Alexander Tairov, a director of equal imagination though infinitely less intelligence and vision.

Who then are the people who knew him and remembered him? Actors, directors, musicians, playwrights, poets—people who worked with him, who watched him work. People whose written texts, in fact, were largely dominated by the memory of Meyerhold and by the power of his image in their minds, images of working with him in the community of theater.

It is within that community that we must seek Meyerhold. And we confront him there cleanly, as we can never confront Stanislavsky, Brecht, or Artaud, because we have no canonical text to set between ourselves and him. We confront him in his work. We cannot monumentalize him on the shelf; he escapes our grasp, moving on ahead of us as he did in life, an image that beckons us to follow—sometimes as a pillar of cloud, sometimes as a pillar of fire.

Spectacles, we used to call the eyeglasses we interpose between our vision and the page, to make the page yield up its vision to our own. Let the pages that follow rather dissolve beneath the images of Meyerhold and of his spectacles, his theater, and so yield them up to us.

This book is intended to provide a view of Meyerhold at work on a few selected productions, as he was observed and remembered by those who worked with him, and to trace some patterns in the major events of his artistic life. I have tried to select and arrange the material so that Meyerhold's most important theoretical notions are clear, and so that something like a tone of voice can be heard. The focus of these materials is specifically Meyerhold's work onstage and the complicated personal relationships that were a constant part of that work, and not primarily the cultural and artistic context in which the work was produced. The majority of the texts included here do, in point of fact, situate the work historically, and for me one of the pleasures of reading these texts has been to piece together, from the random bits of information they contain, some of the power and passion of artistic creation during the Soviet twenties and early thirties. But my particular concern has been to find substantial texts by people associated with Meyerhold in the daily work of theater, texts in which the stuff of that work, the actual techniques of acting and staging, are discussed and made clear.

For this reason the book is unavoidably weighted in favor of later productions, for which more extensive material is available. Even so I have been highly selective, and the focus here is specifically on three productions: Crommelynck's *Magnanimous Cuckold* (1921), the unrealized production of Pushkin's *Boris Godunov* (1936), and Dumas fils' *Camille* (1934). In texts concerning these productions, I feel, we have a clear picture of Meyerhold at work, passionate and intense, with all the power of his experience behind him. For it is Meyerhold at work that we want. This book is meant as a source book for actors, directors, and designers; it was compiled with the needs of contemporary theater people in mind. They have studied long enough with Stanislavsky and Brecht.

I begin with a short biography of Meyerhold's life and career, with the dates of his major productions, and end with a glossary of the important Russian names in the text, including brief biographical details. The reader unfamiliar with the history of Russian theater would do well to refer to the glossary as these names turn up in the text.

Russian sources are given in scholarly transliteration following each separate text; newspaper articles are indicated in the text heading. Russian names in the text are given in more familiar, traditional form. All letters in this book are from *V. E. Meyerhold: Perepiska* (Moscow, 1976) and are indexed there by date.

Of recent books on Meyerhold available in English I recommend *Meyerhold on Theater* (New York: Hill & Wang, 1969) and *The Theater of Meyerhold* (New York: Drama Book Specialists, 1979), both by Edward Braun, and *Meyerhold: The Art of Conscious Theater* by Marjorie L. Hoover (Amherst: University of Massachusetts Press, 1974). These volumes are serious presentations and contain valuable material; I hope the present book will complement them. Hoover's book includes a complete list of Meyerhold's productions. More detailed information on selected productions can be found in my article "A Director Works with a Playwright: Meyerhold and Mayakovsky," _Educational Theater Journal_, vol. 29, no. 2, May 1977, pp. 214–220; and Nick Worrall, "Meyerhold Directs Gogol's 'Government Inspector'," _Theater Quarterly_, vol. II, no. 7, July–September 1972, pp. 75–95, and "Meyerhold's 'The Magnificent Cuckold'," _The Drama Review_, vol. 17, no. 1 (T-57), March 1973, pp. 14–34.

I am grateful to the following friends and colleagues: Ilya Levin, for his work on the texts by Pasternak, Sadovsky, Snezhnitsky, and Varpakhovsky; Vern McGee, for his work on the text by Zakhava; Gianna Kirtley and Rebecca Barker for their work on the manuscript; Kiril Taranovsky and especially Vsevolod Setchkarev, who guided my early research on Meyerhold.

A grant from the Ingraham Merrill Foundation allowed me time to work on this book.

My thanks to these friends for advice, encouragement, and hospitality: Lyn Austin, Stockard Channing, Robert Chapman, Leora Dana, Mike Holquist, Norris Houghton, Doug Kenney, Jay Leyda, Tim Mayer, Cynthia Merman, Annette Michelson, Honor Moore, Tim O'Malley, Victoria Rue, Egan Sagik, Margaret Sand, Michael Sand, George W. S. Trow, Victor Turner, Kathryn Walker, and Bob Wilson.

A Brief Chronology of Meyerhold's Life and Major Productions

Karl Theodore Kasimir Meyerhold was born in 1874 in Penza, southeast of Moscow. His parents were Lutherans and German citizens. When he was twenty-one he changed his name to Vsevolod, adopted Russian citizenship, and converted to Orthodoxy. A year later he married Olga Mikhailovna Munt.

Also in 1896, Meyerhold left his first-year studies at the Law School of Moscow University and joined the acting classes taught by Vladimir Nemirovich-Danchenko at the Moscow Philharmonia. He graduated in 1898, having won first prize for best actor, and joined the Moscow Art Theater, the new company that Nemirovich-Danchenko and Stanislavsky had just founded.

At the Art Theater Meyerhold created the roles of Treplyov in Chekhov's *Sea Gull* and Tusenbach in *Three Sisters*. Disagreements with Stanislavsky occurred. Meyerhold left the Art Theater and for two years directed his own company in the provincial cities of Kherson and Tiflis.

In 1904 Stanislavsky invited Meyerhold to direct his new experimental Theater-Studio. Meyerhold staged Maeterlinck's *Death of Tintagiles* and Hauptmann's *Schluck und Jau*. Stanislavsky was dissatisfied with the work, and neither production ever opened. Meyerhold returned to his provincial company.

In 1906 actress Vera Kommissarzhevskaya invited him to direct her new company in St. Petersburg. He staged significant productions of Ibsen's *Hedda Gabler*, Maeterlinck's *Sister Beatrice*, and Alexander Blok's *Balaganchik*. When disagreements with Kommissarzhevskaya arose, Meyerhold resigned as director.

In 1908, Meyerhold was invited to direct at the Imperial Theaters in St. Petersburg. There, over the next ten years, usually in collaboration with designer Alexander Golovin and choreographer Mikhail Fokine, Meyerhold directed notable productions of both operas and plays—Wagner's _Tristan und Isolde_ (1909), Molière's _Dom Juan_ (1910), Mussorgsky's _Boris Godunov_ (1911), Gluck's _Orpheus_ (1911), Strauss' _Elektra_ (1913), Lermontov's _Masquerade_ (1917), Stravinsky's _Nightingale_ (1918). The same ten years saw a production in Paris for Ida Rubinstein of D'Annunzio's _Pisanella_ designed by Bakst (1913); a film of Oscar Wilde's _The Picture of Dorian Gray_, in which Meyerhold also played Lord Henry (1915); and, under the pseudonym Doctor Dapertutto, numerous productions in various small experimental theaters in St. Petersburg.

In 1917 came the October Revolution. Meyerhold joined the Communist Party and threw himself into theatrical activity on behalf of the Revolution. He was arrested and imprisoned briefly by the Whites while in Southern Russia. In 1920, Commissar Anatoly Lunacharsky invited Meyerhold to become head of the Theater Division of his People's Commissariat of Education (TEO Narkompros in the Russian acronym). For the next three years Meyerhold taught acting and directing, and directed for a number of new theater groups in Moscow. His students included Sergei Eisenstein and Zinaida Raikh, whom he married in 1922, when he was forty-nine and she was twenty-eight. Among his notable productions were Verhaeren's _The Dawns_ (1920), Mayakovsky's _Mystery-Bouffe_ (1918, 1921), and Crommelynck's _Magnanimous Cuckold_ (1922).

In 1923, in the former Sohn Theater on Triumphal Square in Moscow, Meyerhold and a company made up largely of his students and former associates opened as the Meyerhold Theater. For the next fifteen years the company performed some of Meyerhold's greatest productions: Ostrovsky's _The Forest_ (1924); the agit-play _D. E._ (1924), based on material from Ilya Ehrenburg; Faiko's _Bubus the Teacher_ (1925); Nikolai Erdman's _Mandate_ (1925); Gogol's _Inspector General_ (1926); Griboyedov's _Woe from Wit_ (1928); Mayakovsky's _Bedbug_ (1929); Selvinsky's _Commander of the Second Army_ (1929); Mayakovsky's _Bathhouse_ (1930); Vishnevsky's _Last Decisive Battle_ (1931); Olesha's _List of Benefits_ (1931); and Dumas fils' _Camille_ (1934).

Criticism of Meyerhold and his work had been growing under Stalinism. His theater was closed by decree on January 8, 1938, and the theater building, then undergoing reconstruction, was converted into the present-day Tschaikovsky Hall. Stanislavsky immediately invited Meyerhold to direct the Stanislavsky Opera Theater. Meyerhold was arrested on June 20, 1939, and executed in prison on February 2, 1940.

Meyerhold at Work

I.

"...These Past Generations of Theater"

The story of a life begins in birth and parentage; that is the conventional, indeed the absolutely human, wisdom. Yet in the lives of artists a secondary parentage is often as important. Teachers and mentors, those who mold imagination: they are the parents-in-art, and they generate emotions as strong, relations as complicated, as those with parents of the blood.

The clearest view of Meyerhold's beginnings as an artist comes from someone who stood far away from them, but who succeeded him in the generation of the theater, his student Sergei Eisenstein. In the pages that follow Eisenstein discusses his relationship to Meyerhold as he understood Meyerhold's relationship to Stanislavsky: as one of succession, with the conflicting ideas of blessing and competition implicit in that fact.

A central motif of Meyerhold's life, as Eisenstein clearly notes, was the complicated pattern of rejection and love between father and son; in the image of their unaccomplished embrace we can see Meyerhold's stormy relations with Stanislavsky and with his own followers and disciples.

Meyerhold was able to express his love for Eisenstein: the inscription on a photograph of himself that Meyerhold sent to Eisenstein is quite specific: "I am proud of a student who has become a master. I love the master who has established a school. To that student, that master—Sergei Eisenstein—my congratulations. June 22, 1936."

But Stanislavsky seems never to have been able to offer such an acknowledgment to Meyerhold. Relations between them were touchy, marked by long periods of avoidance and moments of passionate regard. We have very little sense of Stanislavsky's own feelings; his lifelong search for "authentic emotions" onstage is a revelation, perhaps, of some profound lack he sensed offstage, in himself. There is a kind of divine fatuousness about Stanislavsky—his loftiness, his obtuseness, his perplexed seriousness, his often ruthless behavior. This was Meyerhold's artistic progenitor, and if Meyerhold's constant stance was rebellious, its very constancy at least testifies to the power of his feelings.

In some of the letters and jottings that follow we can see the young Meyerhold as an actor at the Moscow Art Theater, in conflict with Stanislavsky, "our director-in-chief," and although the conflict is phrased in terms of theater, the tone is one of emotional rebellion. The ties between teacher and student, between father and son, had to be broken. The pattern was clear to others as well—while they were students together in Meyerhold's workshops in 1921, Zinaida Raikh, soon to be Meyerhold's wife, scrawled this note to Eisenstein on an assignment sheet: "Seryozha—as soon as Meyerhold considered himself an independent artist, he left Stanislavsky." In order to accomplish his own work, Eisenstein, too, like Meyerhold before him, took the only possible course.

Eisenstein's affection for Meyerhold was profound, and his vision of "inheritance" was more than a mere metaphor: it was Eisenstein who rescued and kept Meyerhold's papers after his arrest, and so preserved for us much of the record of his artistic life. In these passages from his <u>Autobiographical Notes</u>, written in the early forties when Meyerhold was dead and had officially "never existed," Eisenstein has left us a moving testimony to Meyerhold's place in the generations of creativity.

The closing notes by Alexander Gladkov, one of Meyerhold's assistants, give us a few fragmentary images from Meyerhold's attempt to give form onstage to the idea of succession, of father and son. Meyerhold never staged <u>Hamlet</u>, no more than he did Pushkin's <u>Boris Godunov</u>. Yet both plays were linked in his imagination through the single resonant image of the embrace between father and son.

Sergei Eisenstein

It is time for me to confess that I have never loved, never worshiped, never adored anyone as much as I have my teacher.

Will any one of my students ever say as much about me? No. And it won't be because of my students' relationship with me. It will be because of my relationship with my teacher.

For I am not worthy to unloose the strap of his sandal—though he used to wear felt boots in the unheated director's studio on Novinsky Boulevard.

And for the rest of my days I will think myself unworthy to kiss the dust beneath his feet, although his mistakes as a human being have effaced from history, perhaps forever, all traces of his path as the greatest master of our theater.

And I cannot ever not love him, not worship him, not praise him, not honor him.

He was a staggering individual.

Living proof that genius and maliciousness can both abide within one human being.

Happy the person who knew him only as a magician, a theatrical wizard.

Woe to one who depended on him as a human being.

Happy the person who could learn from him by watching him.

Woe to one who went trustingly to ask him a question.

I went to him once, naively, to ask a few questions about some obscure problems.

And I saw his eagle face, with its piercing glance, its astonishingly outlined lips below a rapaciously curved nose, become suddenly the image of my father.

A smooth, cold, hard look, one that moves right and left and then becomes eternally alien, officially polite, mockingly sympathetic, ironically astonished; a look that looms over the phrase: "Really! How odd. . . ."

I know the precise meaning of the phrase "to spit in someone's eye."

It has no effect on love or adoration.

(The Buddhists spit chewed-up prayer papers on the carven images of their deities.)

The only thing is, it makes you feel sad.

I haven't had much luck with my fathers. . . .

His lectures were like the serpent's song.

Who hears those songs forgets all else. . . .

He seemed always accompanied by those two mythical birds of paradise—Sirin on his right, Alkonost on his left.

Meyerhold moves his hands. His bright eyes glitter. He holds a Javanese puppet.

The Master's golden hands move with the puppet's golden arms.

A white face with slanting eyes moves right and left.

And suddenly the puppet comes to life—and becomes Ida Rubinstein, with all the affectations we know from Serov's portrait.

It is no longer a puppet in Meyerhold's hands. It's Ida Rubinstein in *Pisanella*.

With a sharp gesture upward, Meyerhold calls down the cascades of shining fabrics that covered the stage of the Opera in Paris during the scene in the marketplace.

The hands stiffen in midair. . . .

And in a prophetic vision, we see the dumb scene at the end of Gogol's _Inspector General_.

A row of stuffed dolls, and beyond them in a savage dance disappear those who glittered in their image all evening on the stage.

The inimitable Master stands before us, like the shadow of Gogol.

Then suddenly the hands swoop downward. . . .

And we hear, very softly, drawn from kid gloves, the sound of applause: the approval of the guests at the end of Nina's song, in Lermontov's _Masquerade_, on the stage of the Alexandrinsky Theater, on the eve of the February revolution in 1917.

Suddenly the sorcerer rips the threads of his enchantment. His hands hold nothing more than a pair of gilded sticks and a painted rag.

The Elf King disappears.

Behind the tiny table sits the burnt-out archivist Lindhorst.

His lectures were mirages, and dreams.

Something was being described, feverishly.

But later, when we woke up and looked in our notebooks, all we found written was: "What the hell is he talking about?"

I can recall in precise detail how brilliantly Aksyonov analyzed the _The Merchant of Venice_ and _Bartholomew Fair_ and the triple plots of Elizabethan plays.

What Meyerhold said I can't remember. It was all incense, colors, sounds.

There was a golden haze over everything.

Elusiveness.

Impalpability.

Secret upon secret.

Veil upon veil.

Not just seven of them.

Eight, twelve, thirty, half a hundred.

In every color of the rainbow, they whirled about the secret in the sorcerer's hands.

Still—as the Romantic in us listened, enchanted, submerged, the Rational in us muttered dumbly. . . .

When would these "secrets" be revealed? When would we get down to methodology?

A winter of sweet delusions went by—and nothing remained. . . .

You can't eat reminiscences.

And everyone in the company wanted to eat.

But you don't eat unless you work.

And in the theater you don't eat unless you put on plays. (At least that's the way it used to be in the twenties.)

And *then*—with three rehearsals—we put on Ibsen's *Doll's House*.

I often ask myself: was it simply that Meyerhold was incapable of explaining things clearly?

Or was he unable himself to see clearly and to formulate?

Whatever the case was, what had remained an elusive secret all fall and all winter in our classes at the Novinsky studio turned out to be very smart that spring.

When you work, you can't keep things secret.

When you work, you can't be tricky.

When you work, you can't spin golden cobwebs out of ideas and turn them into dreams. When you work you have to *do something*.

And what had been carefully and provocatively hidden for two semesters was made triumphantly clear in three days of rehearsal.

Now, I have seen a few things in my time:

I've spent an afternoon at Yvette Guilbert's apartment, where she sang for me and talked about her art; I've spent days on a movie set with Charlie Chaplin. I have heard Chaliapin sing and watched Stanislavsky act. I've seen Ziegfeld spectaculars at the Admiral-Palast in Berlin; Mistinguette at the Casino de Paris; Katharine Cornell and Alfred Lunt and Lynn Fontanne; Alla Nazimova in a play by Eugene O'Neill and Mayakovsky at rehearsals for *Mystery-Bouffe*; I've discussed film with George Bernard Shaw and the meaning of theater with Luigi Pirandello; I've seen Raquel Müller in

Reinhardt's productions, rehearsals for the *Magnanimous Cuckold*, dress rehearsals of *The Dybbuk* and *Eric XIV*; I've seen Chekhov, Vakhtangov, Fokine's ballet "Jota de Aragón," and Karsavina dancing in "Les Sylphides"; I've seen Al Jolson, and George Gershwin playing "Rhapsody in Blue"; the three-ring circus of Barnum and Bailey and flea circuses in sideshows; I've seen Primo Canera knocked out of the ring by Max Schmelling with the Prince of Wales in a ringside seat; I've seen Mardi Gras in New Orleans. I've worked at Paramount Studios with Jackie Coogan; I've heard Yehudi Menuhin play at Tschaikovsky Hall; I've had dinner with Douglas Fairbanks in New York and lunch with Rin-Tin-Tin in Boston; I've heard Plevitskaya sing for the army; I used to do my morning exercises along with General Kuropatkin; I've watched Lloyd George speaking in Parliament for the recognition of the Soviet Union, and Tsar Nicholas II at the dedication of a monument to Peter the Great in Riga; I've photographed the Archbishop of Mexico and the papal tiara in the hands of the nuncio Rossas y Florez; I've gone car-racing with Greta Garbo and taken Marlene Dietrich to the bullfights.

But not a single one of these impressions can ever compare with the impressions made on me by those three days of rehearsal for *The Doll's House* in that hall on Novinsky Boulevard.

I remember shaking all the time.

It wasn't the cold, it was excitement, it was nerves stretched to the limit. . . .

Meyerhold!

A creative genius and a perfidious man.

The untold torments of those who loved him devotedly as I did.

The untold moments of triumph, watching the magic creativity of this inimitable theatrical wizard.

How many times his actor Ilyinsky left him!

How his actress Babanova suffered!

What torments—thank God they were short-lived!—did I go through, before I was thrown outside the gates of Paradise, out of the ranks of his theater, because I had "dared" acquire a collective of my own on the side—in the Proletkult.

He adored Ibsen's *Ghosts*.

He staged the play more than once.

He played Oswald numbers of times.

Many times, in moments of reverie, he used to show me how he played him, playing the piano.

He seemed to be fascinated by the theme of reoccurrence, of repetition, that so strongly permeates the story of Fru Alving and her son.

And how many times, repeatedly, insidiously, just like a director, creating unavoidable conditions and a *mise en scène*, did he recreate a page from the days of his own youthful creativity—his break with Stanislavsky.

His love and his admiration for Stanislavsky were amazing, even during the fiercest years of his fight against the Moscow Art Theater.

How often he spoke with affection of Stanislavsky, how highly he valued his talent and his knowledge!

Where was it—in some long poem, or a legend—that I read how Lucifer, the chief of all the angels, after he had rebelled against the Lord God and been cast out of heaven, continued to love him, and wept, not for his fall, not for his sin, but because he might never look upon the face of God again? . . .

Or was that the legend of the Wandering Jew?

There was something of both Lucifer and the Wandering Jew in the crumpled face of my teacher.

He was incommensurably more a genius than Stanislavsky, the canonized saint whom everyone adored, but he was absolutely unprovided with Stanislavsky's patriarchal, even temper—something we may take for harmony, but which is much closer to that philistinism which Goethe said was a necessary part of any creative personality.

Who better than that official of the court of Weimar? His own biography shows us that a certain share of philistinism ensures peace, stability, deep roots, and the sweetness of recognition, while its absence dooms a too-romantic nature to eternal dreaming and searching, to the rise and fall of fortune—and often to the fate of Icarus, to the final path of the Flying Dutchman.

In his longing for Stanislavsky, the patriarch warmed in the sunlight of second and third generations of admirers and enviers of his work, there was something of those tears of Lucifer, something of the ineffable longing of Vrubel's "Demon."

And I remember him at the end, at the moment of his reconciliation with Stanislavsky.

It was touching and pathetic to see the gradual reconciliation of those two old men.

I don't know how Stanislavsky felt in the last years of his life, betrayed by the artistic direction of his own theater—but he turned back to the eternally living sources of creativity, to the coming generation, bringing to them the vision of a genius eternally young.

I do remember the shining eyes of the "prodigal son" when he spoke of that reunion, of the two of them united again in a rejection of all those paths foreign to a true theater, from which the one had turned away on the threshold of the century to find his own creative way, and which the other had renounced decades later, when tendencies hostile to theater, fostered by the solicitous hand of Nemirovich-Danchenko himself, had begun to smother the very founder of the Art Theater.

The two were not united for very long.

But this time it was not discord between them that led to a break.

The tragic consequences of his own personal discord, arising from the same unbalanced disposition, brought one to the end of a fatal biography.

Death claimed the other. . . .

During those long years after I had already lived through my own trauma with Meyerhold, made my peace with him, and become friends once again, it invariably seemed that in his treatment of his students and followers he repeatedly played out the trauma of his own break with his own first teacher.

In those he antagonized he saw again his own gnawing bitterness, and in the act he became himself the tragic father Rustum striking Sohrab, as if seeking justification and fulfillment for a rejection he had received in his own youth, without any evil intent, from his "father"—a rejection that was the result only of the creative independence of spirit of the "haughty son."

That at least is the way I saw the drama.

Perhaps not objectively enough.

Perhaps not "historically" enough.

But for me it was all too close, too intimate, too much a part of my own family chronicle.

And perhaps through the inheritance of blessing, through the laying-on of hands, I am in some sense a son and a grandson in these past generations of theater.

Sergej Ejzenštejn, *Izbrannye proizvedenija v šesti tomax*, vol. 1 (Moscow, 1964), pp. 305 – 309, 418 – 420.

Meyerhold to Nemirovich-Danchenko

January 17, 1899

I was looking forward to taking part in the *discussion* on *Hedda Gabler* scheduled for today at our theater. There was, however, no discussion.

Talking about the social significance of the play, discussing the characters, discovering a tone for the play in the moods of the discussion—these are not the working principles of our director-in-chief.

What he prefers, as it turns out, is to read through the play himself, pausing as he goes to describe the set, explaining positions and crosses and marking pauses. In other words, our director-in-chief works on a play of social significance, a psychological play, a mood play, using techniques he worked out years ago and which he still uses to direct any play, whether a tendentious mood play or a period piece. I have no need to demonstrate that this is wrong.

Are we actors to do nothing but *act*? We want to be able to *think* while we act! We want to know *why* we are doing what we are doing, *what* it is we are acting, and *whom* we are instructing or criticizing.

That's why we want to know, why we must know and be able to make clear the social and psychological significance of the play; the characters—positive as well as negative; which social group the author sympathizes with, which he opposes. Only then will the actors, in a word, become conscious conveyers of the author's ideas, and only then will the public be able to relate consciously to the play as well.

It may be that the director-in-chief, thanks to his great artistic taste, will be able to stage the play without misrepresenting the author's intentions. I believe he will. But suppose he doesn't?

It is possible. Here are some examples of our director's literary preparedness, a couple of remarks made before the reading:

Maria Andreyeva: "I translated a few passages from a German article on *Hedda* that might interest us. I also found a Russian article."

Stanislavsky: "If it's anything like Lemaître's article, I don't want to read it. I only read criticism that expresses the same opinions as ours."

Maria Andreyeva: "The article is by Merezhkovsky."

Stanislavsky: "Well, I'll believe Merezhkovsky." (?)

Vishnevsky: "The play will be a great success."

Stanislavsky: "After seeing this play, society women will all be wearing dresses and hairdos like Maria Andreyeva!"

... Anyone who stages an Ibsen play for the sake of the roles it contains, and not its ideas, may leave the public with an impression diametrically opposite to the one its author intended.

Meyerhold to Stanislavsky

Moscow
January 6, 1902

Dear Konstantin Sergeevich:

In view of the *exceptional importance* for me of the interview I asked you for—of which you are aware from the calling card I left at your house on the evening of the fifth—I beg you to allow me to speak with you, in the presence of Saava Morozov and Maria Andreyeva.

V. Meyerhold

Meyerhold to Stanislavsky

Moscow
January 26, 1902

Dear Konstantin Sergeevich:
I have waited long enough. Three weeks have passed
since I begged you to let me come talk to you. You wrote me
that you do not have a single free moment, and yet you have
found it possible to see students from the school, of which I
am well aware.

I am in no mood to wait further. I expect to be admitted
to see you sometime during the next three days (the 28th,
29th, or 30th of January). I will not wait any further. Lack of
any response from you will give me the right first to resort to
correspondence, and then to consider myself free to act
otherwise.

V. Meyerhold

Stanislavsky to Meyerhold

Moscow
(after January 26, 1902)

I must ask you to spare me any future letters in the tone
of your last one, as well as your surveillance over those per-
sons I see fit to welcome to my house. I ask you as well to
abandon any further threats; they have little effect on me,
since where you are concerned my conscience is clear. I will
not answer such letters. You might perhaps find it sensible—
before resorting to threats—to acquaint me with the matter
that seems to have called forth such extreme measures on
your part. As for seeing you on the 28th, 29th, or 30th of January, which you demand in such an officious tone, please understand that I must refuse, in order not to appear a coward,
as well as to allow you the freedom to act.

If you really must see me, then it behooves you to write a
more suitable letter, and to realize as well that at present my

time is not my own, but is at the service of that enterprise of which you yourself are a part, and whose circumstances you are surely aware of.

                   K.S.S.

Meyerhold to Stanislavsky

Moscow
(the end of January 1902)

Dear Konstantin Sergeevich:

  My last letter to you was official, nothing more. It contained no threats. It was written in the same official tone as my first letter to you earlier this month.

  The reasons for such an official tone will be clear from what follows.

  You write: "wouldn't you find it natural first of all to acquaint me with the matter that has called forth such threats."

  I find it not only natural, but necessary. Otherwise I would never have made such efforts to see you during the course of an entire month. And if you still do not know the reasons for my persistent attempts to speak with you, then the fault is yours, not mine.

  On the fifth of January I left a calling card at your house, on which I asked you to see me *as soon as possible*. You refused to grant me this interview, explaining that you were very busy. Then I began to wait. I have waited *three weeks*. That will serve as evidence that I am aware of our social obligations.

  If I pointed out to you the contradiction between your words ("I am busy") and the facts (you found it possible to receive a delegation of students from the school), that does not mean that I am exercising any surveillance over those individuals you welcome to your house.

  If I set a fixed limit to the time beyond which I would not wait, that does not indicate an "officious" tone. Anyone in my position would have done the same, anyone who has been insulted, who demands satisfaction but who is being made a fool of, no matter for what reasons, lack of time or any other reasons.

Since, evidently, I will not be permitted to see you *personally*, I am left with the necessity of resorting to correspondence.

. . . .

Everybody in the company knows that *you*, on the first of January this year, at the theater, in conversation with several members of the company, *said* that I:

1. was an "intriguer" who had to be gotten rid of;
2. that I had admitted to the theater several individuals who hissed at the opening-night performance of Nemirovich-Danchenko's play;
3. that you had factual evidence in the form of letters signed by people you knew, that I had actually put someone up to hissing the author of *Dreaming*;
4. that I was "undermining the enterprise" of which I am a member.

I humbly beg you to corroborate these insulting remarks made behind my back, by repeating them directly to my face and saying simply "yes, you are guilty" or "no, you are not guilty."

If I do not receive a reply from you before the first of February I shall take that as an answer in the affirmative.

If the accusations made against me are based on signed letters, you are obliged to give me the names of those who signed them.

If you wish to hide those names, that will mean that you take full responsibility in this matter upon yourself.

Please do not hesitate to repeat what you have said.

I know perfectly well that outside of artistic matters your opinions are not always *your own* opinions. For that reason I wish to settle accounts not with you, but with those who have led you to believe as you do.

I expect an immediate reply.

In any case this matter must be made as public as possible, which I am not afraid of, since my conscience is clear.

I will stop at nothing to see the truth made plain.

V. Meyerhold

Meyerhold to Stanislavsky
**Draft of a note evidently meant to accompany a copy of
Meyerhold's essay Theater: History and Technique**

May–June 1907
Kuokkala

In this book (which is dedicated to you) you will find expressed an unfavorable attitude toward that school of theater of which you, in Russia, are the founder. I have intentionally emphasized only the negative aspects of that school. I had to do so. Perhaps I may write another book to accompany this one, in which I make clear the positive aspects of the school you founded. You have accomplished an enormous and necessary task. But it has long since passed into history. Such is the speed with which Russian art has advanced. There are new bridges to cross. That is why I have dared—while you are still alive—to write something that may cause you grief.

Alexander Gladkov

Dreams of staging *Hamlet* ran through Meyerhold's entire life. It was the play he loved most. More than once he scheduled it in his theater's repertory, and always something interfered.

One time he said: "Write on my gravestone: here lies an actor and director who never acted and never directed *Hamlet. . . .*"

A fragment of Hamlet was played at the Meyerhold Theater in Yury Olesha's play *A List of Benefits*, where the role of Hamlet is played by the heroine—actress Elena Goncharova. Zinaida Raikh played Goncharova. Meyerhold had thought of producing *Hamlet* with Raikh in the title role, but by the mid-thirties I no longer heard Vsevolod Emilievich speak of it, although we often talked about *Hamlet. . . .*

In February 1935, talking one time about the complex narrative scheme of a certain novel, where the hero is sometimes described in the third person and sometimes speaks of himself in the first person, Meyerhold suddenly said:

"At one time I dreamed of a production where Hamlet would be played by two actors: one vacillating, the other resolute. They would constantly replace each other, but while one was working, the other would not leave the stage, but would sit at his feet, and thus underline the tragic situation of two opposed temperaments. Sometimes the second one would even express his relation to the first and vice versa. He might even jump up at a certain point, knock the other out of the way, and take his place. Of course it's easier to imagine than to accomplish physically, since it would be hard to find two actors of equal physical gifts, and that's the whole point. . . ."

Vsevolod Emilievich already spoke of that idea in the past tense, so it's hard to say to which of his Hamlets the idea pertained; clearly, though, not to the "final" one, since in 1936 Meyerhold affirmed the idea of staging the classics without rewriting the text.

One time (in 1936) he was talking about *Hamlet*, and described how Laertes and the mob break into Elsinore; he added that the mob was all wet, that it had rained that day, and the water was glistening on boot-tops, on helmets and weapons.

"The only thing is," he said, "I don't know how to work it."

All those present vied with each other in trying to figure out various technical solutions to the problem of showing the effects of a rainstorm. I'm not sure that the rain would have remained in the production, but at the visionary stage he needed it.

After 1931 there seems to have been no real plan actually to stage *Hamlet* at Meyerhold's theater, but that does not mean that Meyerhold himself stopped dreaming about it and preparing for it. On the contrary, the idea of a production grew and ripened in his creative imagination, and by the middle of the thirties he was able to describe separate scenes from this production, that was never to see the light of day, with such brilliance and detail that people began to imagine that they had already seen the show on stage. . . .

In the fall of 1936, after his return from Paris, Meyerhold

told us that he had talked with Picasso about designing *Hamlet*. This was the last full, peaceful period of work in Meyerhold's life, the fall of 1936. Rehearsals for *Boris Godunov* were underway, and he had begun dreaming again of *Hamlet* in some not-too-distant future.

In 1936 the new building for the Meyerhold Theater seemed to be nearing completion (Meyerhold loved to take his friends over the construction site; he invited dignitaries at the International Theater Festival to see it, and showed it off himself, clambering around on the huge stone steps of the amphitheater), and Meyerhold indicated that he would open the new theater with a production of *Hamlet*.

He had a notion at that time of founding a special theater, in whose repertory there would be only a single play—*Hamlet*, in the various productions of different directors: Stanislavsky, Reinhardt, Gordon Craig, and himself. Occasionally, half-joking, he insisted that fragments of his future *Hamlet* were contained in all of his productions of the past twenty years. "But I've hidden them so cleverly," he said, "that nobody has noticed them. My *Hamlet* will be the summa of my work as a director. There you will find traces of it all."

What should be done, of course, is to question everyone to whom Meyerhold described scenes from *Hamlet* as they matured in his imagination, and try that way at least to make a literary reconstruction of the production. Especially since Meyerhold, as far as I can recall, when he was left in 1938 without his own theater, abandoned the idea of staging *Hamlet*, and thought of writing a book about that production: *Hamlet: The Story of a Director*. So that, as he put it, "someone, somewhere, sometime, for some anniversary or other of mine," would be able to stage the play according to his plans. (From my notes of a conversation on June 14, 1938.)

It was at that meeting that he told me he was about to write an opera libretto for Shostakovich based on Lermontov's *Hero of Our Time*—that period of his life was a time of literary imaginings.

Our conversation took place in curious circumstances. Meyerhold telephoned and asked me if I wanted to go for a walk with him. It was a hot summer day. We walked along the boulevards, then for some reason or other turned into the Hermitage garden and sat down. They were rehearsing a program in the outdoor theater. We could hear the music, and acrobats practicing. From somewhere or other came the click of billiard balls. Meyerhold talked about his literary plans, expressed his delight with the Belinsky essay on Lermontov he had recently reread, outlined plans for a Lermontov group at the Actor's Club, and told me about his book *Hamlet: The Story of a Director*. I believe it was that day he told me about the scene in his imagined production where Hamlet meets his father's ghost:

A leaden gray sea. The dim midnight sun through a thin shroud of clouds. Hamlet walks along the shore, wrapped in a black cloak. He sits down on a rock by the water and gazes into the watery distance. And then suddenly in that distance appears the figure of his father. A bearded warrior in silver armor walks across the water toward shore. He gets closer and closer. Hamlet stands up. His father reaches the shore, and Hamlet embraces him. He sits his father down on the rock, and then, so that he won't be cold, he takes off his cloak and wraps him in it. And beneath his cloak he has on silver armor identical with his father's. And they sit there side by side—the black figure of the father and Hamlet all in silver. . . .

I don't know whether that's theater or literature, but to me it seems true poetry, of the very highest order.

And it was thought up, not by a novelist, not by a poet, but by a theater director, one who knew how to calculate every last centimeter of a stage, and every precious second of playing time.

On that hot day, sitting with Meyerhold on a garden bench in the Hermitage, I felt more sharply than I have ever experienced it the fantastic power of his *directorial vision*.

Hamlet wraps his cloak around the ghost to keep him from the cold—

That one single touch of genius, which combines the tenderness of poetry and the reality of life, is worth a long judicious explanation with a raft of scholarly research and quotations.

Aleksandr Gladkov, "Master rabotaet," *Vstreči s Mejerxol'dom* (Moscow, 1967), pp. 500–502; "Iz vospominanij o Mejerxol'de," *Moskva Teatral'naja* (Moscow, 1960), pp. 365–366.

II.

Working with Actors

The memories of Meyerhold's actors are central to what we want to know, yet those memories present a complicated problem. For writers the process of recording memory on the page may be easy, but an actor's conception of what language is and how it works is very different. All an actor's powers of communication are developed for performance, for the word made flesh. An actor records memory upon the stage; an actor's memoirs—his memories of his own performances—are therefore memories of memories. An actor recalling his own performance cannot describe anything he saw, because he saw nothing. He feels everything; he cannot describe his own action, only his reaction.

The actor is the heart of the theatrical experience—without him it cannot exist. But no one can describe the moment of becoming, being, a character onstage. The moment is ineffable. Mikhail Sadovsky, one of Meyerhold's actors, relates later in this book: "What happened to me after this is difficult to comprehend and still more difficult to describe." Yet we are always avid to read the memoirs of actors, as we are avid to read the memoirs of politicians. And assuming we mean to go beyond mere prurient curiosity, then surely we read them for the same reasons: we hope to discover in them the power of performance, the mystery of the Act that seems to engender the Word, but that in fact is engendered by it.

In the texts that follow, Leonid Varpakhovsky, who later became academic secretary to the Meyerhold State Theater, describes for us the tryouts for admission to Meyerhold's theater workshops. Igor Ilyinsky describes rehearsals for what became Meyerhold's first great triumph after the Revolution, Crommelynck's <u>Magnanimous Cuckold</u>. Of all the actors who worked for Meyerhold after the Revolution, Igor Ilyinsky was the best known, possibly the best. He was nineteen when Meyerhold first directed him, in 1920, in <u>The Dawns</u>. He worked for Meyerhold on and off until 1935, later worked in films and as a director himself, and eventually became one of the most famous actors of Russia and was awarded the prestigious title People's Artist of the USSR. He wrote his memoirs after he had grown fat and famous and somewhat condescending, but through them we can perceive the energy and temperament that he brought to some of Meyerhold's productions.

Erast Garin began as a student in Meyerhold's workshop; he was still in classes while his colleague Ilyinsky, only a year older, had his triumph in The Magnanimous Cuckold. Garin's turn came when he created for Meyerhold two of the greatest parts in the Russian repertory—Chatsky in Griboyedov's Woe from Wit and Khlestakov in Gogol's Inspector General. He too left Meyerhold's company eventually, for film work and to work as a director. He was the best, perhaps, of the actors whom Meyerhold trained for his own purposes, and he affords us a careful look at the nature of that training.

Mikhail Sadovsky joined Meyerhold's company in 1934 and stayed with it until its liquidation. Sadovsky illustrates here Meyerhold's sensitivity to actors and rebuts the accusation that he reduced them to automatons.

Leonid Varpakhovsky

When I was a child I had dreamed of some day becoming an actor and a theater director, and I used to play for days with my puppet show. Later at school I played a number of roles in the school theater club, directed a few plays there, and as a result imagined myself as some sort of theoretician of the theater. Finally the time came to choose a profession and I decided without any hesitation to enter the real theater. In those days I thought the Meyerhold Theater was the best.

In the fall of 1925 I brought my application to the Admissions Office of GEKTEMAS (the State Experimental Theater Workshop, directed by Vsevolod Meyerhold). A large number of people of both sexes and of all age groups, different levels of education, and different social origins did the same. The weather was fine and clear. No less than a thousand applicants for twenty vacancies gathered in Aquarium Park. All of us strolled along the shady paths, glancing at each other and mentally comparing our chances with those of our future competitors. Suddenly there was some movement, a rumble of voices, and everybody rushed to the entrance of the Winter Theater. Meyerhold himself came to the examinations. He cast a cursory glance at the crowd of applicants and went inside the theater.

The bell rang. Timidly we entered the theater. Preparations for the examinations had already begun. Meyerhold, buried in some papers, was sitting at the center of a large table in the middle of the auditorium, while we examinees filled the orchestra and the balconies.

One of the directors, N. N. Butorin, unfolded the long list of applicants and called to the stage about forty people at once, all of whose names began with "A."

The examination started. I shall never forget it.

"Abrosimov!" announced Butorin, and a young, lean, bespectacled man of small stature emerged from the crowd huddling at the back of the stage.

"Your name?" Meyerhold called loudly from the auditorium in none too friendly a tone.

"Abrosimov," answered the examinee, gulping nervously.

"Louder!" shouted Meyerhold.

"Abrosimov!" he repeated louder, obviously scared to death.

"Still louder!" demanded Meyerhold.

"Abrosimov!" roared the poor fellow with all his strength.

"Dismissed! Next!" came the implacable response from the auditorium.

Meyerhold was conducting the examination at a very brisk tempo. A girl had just started to recite one of Blok's lyric poems when a voice came from the auditorium: "Recite a fable!"

"But I haven't prepared a fable."

"Next!"

The applicants whose names started with "A" were finished off pretty quickly. Almost the same story repeated itself with those who began with "B."

As a rule, Meyerhold would stop the examinees precisely at that point which they seemed to feel was the most impressive part of their piece. As soon as they would really get into the recitation came the merciless: "Dismissed!"

At this examination I recited Gorbunov's story "By the Cannon," and it happened that Meyerhold listened to all of my recitation. I was doing it loudly, with lots of "acting," like a genuine amateur, and for reasons that remained mysterious I wasn't stopped. I even managed to recite the concluding part of Mayakovsky's poem "A Cloud in Trousers."

In other words I was one of the lucky few selected for the second round of the examination. Everybody congratulated me and I was in a seventh heaven of happiness. As I returned home from the examination it seemed to me that everybody was looking at me and talking in whispers the way they do when a celebrity appears on the street.

My joy was premature. At the second round we were given skits to enact, and as I began to demonstrate how a man behaves beneath a heavy rain Meyerhold entered the auditorium. He cast a passing glance at our direction (at which moment I began to try really hard!), then looked through some papers, said something, and left. Our fate had been decided quicker than we realized. Alas, I turned out to be among the rejected ones. . . .

About a year later I happened to be present at a dress rehearsal of *The Inspector General* at the Meyerhold Theater. Among the actors who played the non-speaking parts of Hussars I recognized at once some former associates with whom I had taken the examinations and who had been accepted into the theater's school. Meyerhold was always obsessed with his current creative problem. At that period he had been totally absorbed in the staging of *The Inspector General* and I think that during the ill-fated examination he divided all the applicants, among other things, into Hussars and civilians. . . .

Leonid Varpaxovskij, "Zametki prošlyx let," *Vstrěci s Mejerxol'dom* (Moscow, 1967), pp. 462–464.

Erast Garin

Full of joyful excitement, we came out onto the square. It was still called Triumphal Square in those days. The lines of the famous "Jubilee"—Mayakovsky's conversation with Pushkin—hadn't yet been written:

> I'd like a monument
>> while I'm alive
>>> that suits my stature. . . .

The monument wasn't there then. No one had even thought of the pedestrian tunnel. It was just a silly little square.

We had just come from a celebration—a gala evening to celebrate the fifth anniversary of the Meyerhold Theater.

We had performed an extensive program:

The sixth episode of Verhaeren's play *The Dawns* (opened November 8, 1920);

The "Heaven" episode from Mayakovsky's play *Mystery-Bouffe* (opened May 7, 1921);

A scene from act two of Sukhovo-Kobylin's *Death of Tarelkin* (opened November 24, 1922);

The fourth episode from *The Earth Upside Down* by Martinet and Tretyakov (opened March 4, 1923);

Aksyusha and Peter's farewell scene from Ostrovsky's comedy *The Forest* (opened January 19, 1924);

Scenes from Faiko's *Bubus the Teacher* (opened January 20, 1925);

The reception of the electors from the play *D. E.* by Podgaetsky, after Ehrenburg and Kellerman (opened June 15, 1924);

A scene from act three of Erdman's comedy *The Mandate* (opened April 20, 1925).

I was very lucky and played three different parts that evening. At the end of the first section I played the clownish cook with the live rooster in *The Earth Upside Down*. We played the fourth episode, the "Black International." The Emperor had already fallen asleep in a sack and been wheeled off in a barrow. White Guards officers hauled him out of the sack, recognized him, and paid their homage.

Next was my entrance.

In a white jacket and hat, armed with a huge knife, I chase a live rooster in order to turn him into soup. I stumble and the rooster flies out of my hands. (He was tied by a long black string, since none of us quite trusted the way the rooster might develop his part.)

Then the chase begins; it was a comic improvisation. We were playing to a packed house. The space between the first row and the edge of the stage was full of folding chairs. The light from the stage illuminated the faces of the spectators. Out of the corner of my eye I caught a glimpse of Meyerhold's profile. He was sitting on a folding chair to the right of the stage.

The audience loved the chase. The rooster stopped, blinded by the lights, and looked around him. I gave a jerk in order to catch hold of him, but he pulled out of my hands, flapped his wings madly and flew right into the audience— the string had broken!

Shame, shame, misery, misery, I thought, my prop has walked out on me.

Suddenly Meyerhold leapt from his chair as if shot from a cannon, a look of grim heroism on his face. He caught the rooster by its leg in midair and tucked it under his arm. Then, with difficulty, but with the impassive gait of a stage attendant, he made his way through the spectators sitting around him, brought the rooster to the stage, and handed it to me.

I took it, tucked it under my own arm, and made my exit. Ovation.

Intermission.

Later I had to perform the reception of the electors, the quick-change scene from *D. E.* So that the audience would know that all seven electors were played by the same actor, Meyerhold had had them cut a big hole in one of the moving screens that served as the set for the play. That way the audience could watch all the mechanics of the quick change. The instant changes were effective, and when the seventh elector turned out to be a woman, the reaction was loud and hilarious.

Against that eventuality Meyerhold had taught me a circus bow. I ran out for the bow, hands raised, and turned first to the right boxes, then to the left.

Finally I had to play the third act of *The Mandate*. Now the challenges to my acting ability became complex. In the third act of Erdman's comedy Pavel Sergeyevich Gulyachkin gets a broad field for the display of his abilities at social mimicry, and for chameleonlike changes. At first he seems to be a quiet mama's boy, then he manipulates every event to his own interests, and passes to a moment of apotheosis as a scatterbrained exultant petty bourgeois, only to stop short after a moment to beg in a hurt tone: "I am, generally, a really multifaceted individual. . . ." A moment later, feeling the ground begin to slip from beneath his feet, he turns to the audience with the tragi-comic line: "How are we supposed to survive, Mama, if they won't even arrest us? How are we going to survive?"

The audience warmly applauded the theater company,

the playwrights, and the actors on this summation of our first five years.

So there we were, full of joyous excitement, on Sadovo-Triumphal Square. In my pocket was a diploma, and while it was true that in those days we no longer had much respect for "paperwork," it was still awfully nice to see the familiar signature—"V. Meyerhold, Rector"—as well as a signature that the office hadn't even expected, and so which wasn't printed on the paper but simply scrawled slantwise in red ink: "A. Lunacharsky, Commissar of Education."

Erast Garin, "O Mandate i o drugom," *Vstreči s Mejerxol'dom* (Moscow, 1967), pp. 309–311.

Igor Ilyinsky

Tikhon in Ostrovsky's *Storm* was my first really big success, and it inspired my work on *The Magnanimous Cuckold*, which was already in full rehearsal. Strange as it may seem, this was the first time I had ever observed Meyerhold actually direct his actors. Until that time, as I've said, I had known him mainly as the stager of spectacles. But this play, with the pauses and the unexpected shifts in mood so characteristic of the role of Bruno, was my first encounter with his demonstrations, his scrupulous attention to the interplay between actors, his search for the most varied actor's choices, the brilliance of his movements and his readings.

I had noticed that all Meyerhold's demonstrations were already psychologically "justified," to use Stanislavsky's terminology, and for that reason I kept trying to find the psychological sense of each of his demonstrations or directorial ideas, no matter what form they took. I tried to get at the root of each individual scene or individual moment. I liked the fact that Meyerhold did very little talking or explaining (I hate talkative directors), but always *did* a lot. But all the same an actor occasionally needs some kind of psychological prompting or directorial explanation. If he had had them in his earliest productions, there were practically none in his work now with the actors.

When I would try to stop, to argue or to ask him to explain some scene that wasn't clear to me, he would say: "You're not getting it because you're near-sighted. Watch me carefully and repeat what I do. Then you'll get it right."

I could not work that way. It was beneath my dignity as an actor. I was a young actor perhaps, but an actor all the same, and not a monkey. Besides, I had already learned the basics of the actor's art from my first teachers. For that reason, from the very moment I began to work for Meyerhold I would take all the lavish material he gave me as a director, pick it over and work it through my own internal filter, and, although Meyerhold never demanded this, I would always try to justify everything that I was supposed to do on stage.

Even in those days, no matter how delighted I was by one of Meyerhold's demonstrations, I would immediately and instinctively analyze it, try to find the essence, the zest, the "idea-thought," and try to give it back by means of my internal and external resources, without ever intending or trying to reproduce Meyerhold's demonstrations exactly and formally.

But even that wasn't enough. I had then to work that bit rhythmically and *organically* into the entire fabric of the part, to make it come alive for *my character* in the given instance.

Meyerhold was very different from me physically. He was slightly stooped, although tall. He had long legs. One time, while demonstrating something for me, he crossed his legs in such a way that he was able to wrap one foot yet again around the other leg. I would never have been able to do that, no matter how hard I practiced, because I have short legs. But I was able to express the "idea" of that leg-crossing differently, which indeed I did, crossing my legs with *my own* flourish. I mention this minor detail as an example of the way I worked with Meyerhold.

Meyerhold was angry with me at first because I did not always reproduce his demonstrations exactly; I even allowed myself to ignore them, if I did not especially like them (which, by the way, was not often). He subsequently understood correctly my striving to understand the root and essence of his directorial ideas or of a particular demonstration. And those roots were varied. Sometimes they had to do with rhythm, sometimes with mood, sometimes with attack, with the direction of energy.

I had to find those roots and work them over within myself as an artist. Meyerhold came to value my ability to accomplish his ideas physically, and so always appreciated my
work more than he would some dead, formalistic, but absolutely accurate copy of his sketch. Of course I was never free
from the form of the sketch, but I always tried to live onstage,
to be a living person, and not to reproduce mechanically, according to biomechanical laws, some emasculated directorial
outline.

I always tried to bring Meyerhold's tasks down to earth,
to make them—if only for myself—psychologically real. That
held even for the set constructions. For me they were absolutely real, not abstract constructions or meaningless platforms which simply served to display the actors, whether
posed or in motion.

In Lyubov Popova's construction for *Cuckold*, as far as I
was concerned, one platform was my room, another a room
that led to the bedroom, and the little bridge connecting
them was a hallway. The slide-chute down which the actors
slid standing or on their backsides, as I saw it, was the chute
for loading bags of flour, since the entire action of the play
took place in a mill. At the rear of the construction there were
large wheels and fanblades of different colors that were
vaguely reminiscent also of a mill. It's hard to say whether all
the spectators understood the set that way, or if all the actors
in the production did, but that is how I understood it, and I
tried to create for myself, out of all that conventionalized
conglomeration, a completely real stage world.

I have to say that I was far from elated by all the novel-
ties that Meyerhold displayed on his stage. In the beginning
at any rate I was not much taken by Popova's construction,
which so inspired Meyerhold. I was pleased with the magnificent and fascinating staging he worked out for us young actors from his acting workshop, the result of a mastery of
rhythm and bodily movement, harmonized perfectly in all
his demonstrations with interior emotion and with psychological truth. It was this in his work that was most useful for
his pupils, who greedily drank up all the wonderful variety of
their great teacher's mastery of the art of acting.

The costumes for all the actors in *The Magnanimous Cuckold* were identical: the so-called workclothes (*prozodezhda*) of
the young Meyerhold actors. This uniformity has been justi-

fied formally by saying that the young actors and students
were to be playing in a series of productions in student or
rehearsal workclothes and that there was no necessity for any
illusion or costume. Not at all! It was so that here, on the
bare platforms of the construction, in dark blue workclothes,
young actors without make-up could display their work
openly, so to speak, unaided by theatrical illusion.

However, this pedagogic purpose suddenly and unexpectedly—even for Meyerhold himself, to a degree—acquired additional significance. This particular production idea was
surprisingly successful for the odd Crommelynck tragi-farce.
There were *no* realistic details that might overshadow the
theme of jealousy. Actors in workclothes, in identical, somewhat severe outfits, were able to convey their human passions
and preoccupations more concentratedly and more pur-
posefully. It was the abstract theme of jealousy itself that we
played. Costumes, make-up, and realistic props might have
emphasized the farcical situations, made them more real or
naturalistic, and for that reason unbearable in view of their
extreme frankness. These conventionalized forms together
with an enormous dazzling energy and the actors' belief in
what was happening onstage were extremely persuasive, if
not the only correct way to stage Crommelynck's play. The
visual style of the production made it more innocent and free
from the farcical, vulgar touch.

Much time has passed, and it is now clear that Crommelynck's tragi-farce, despite all the talent it displayed, nevertheless contained many of the unhealthy traits of decadent
bourgeois art. I doubt whether the play could now be performed on the Soviet stage, even in Meyerhold's production.
But in those days many people were delighted by both the
play and the production. In vain did Lunacharsky in his review of the play complain: "I pity Ilyinsky, a wonderful actor,
contorting himself in a cheap imitation of a poor clown; I
pity all these young actors, muddled in their 'strivings.'
Shame on the audience that roared with laughter at slaps in
the face, pratfalls, and obscenities. Shame on people who
laughed like that not in some den barely tolerated by a Communist regime, but at a performance directed by a Communist director, openly praised to the skies by Communist
critics. . . . It is terrible enough to think that Western bourgeois civilization is sliding catastrophically along this path,

but when we ourselves descend into the same pit to the applause of a Communist audience, the matter becomes absolutely disgraceful. I consider it my duty to say as much."

In defense of the general admiration for the play I must make it clear that the young actors were not running any moral risks. Neither the performers nor the audience savored these situations nor played them up, but understood them as tragic, rather than farcical or scandalous. But still it is now clear that the hero Bruno could not avoid appearing a pathological figure, and his paradoxical behavior was the source of a certain unhealthy attempt to shock the audience.

As a participant, in rehearsal and then for many years in performance, I noticed none of this. I repeat, as many others have done, that at the time I was delighted by the play, by the part, and by Meyerhold's directorial concepts.

I was less taken with the models of the construction and the idea of the workclothes. At the time I think I merely made my peace with them, and never quite understood the special significance these innovations of Meyerhold's later acquired.

The proof that Meyerhold himself never fully realized why the visual style of *Cuckold* was such a hit can be seen in retrospect if we consider the workclothes and the constructions thought up as mobile furniture in his next production, *The Death of Tarelkin*. It was a complete directorial flop. The workclothes confused and blended all the characters into one: the policemen Shatala and Kachala, Raspluyev and Officer Okh. The circus furniture was badly constructed and never worked right but, mainly, it diverted the spectator's attention from the action and added nothing to the production except turmoil and confusion.

In *The Magnanimous Cuckold* both the construction and the workclothes supported the play and created an inimitable atmosphere for this particular production. Here the construction and the workclothes appeared more *functional*. And by themselves alone they produced an unexpected impression on the spectator; precisely, they caused an esthetic effect— one which was not a part of Meyerhold's plan, since the construction and the workclothes, in his view, were not meant to impress the public but on the contrary to fill an ancillary and pedagogic role.

Toward the end of the rehearsal period, when the play was almost in shape, we had yet another surprise: Meyerhold stripped the entire stage, removing all drops, flats, and wings. The acting construction for *Cuckold* was set up against the rear brick wall of the theater. I assumed that this bare stage was only temporary and that for the performances there would be some kind of backdrop and wings of some kind at the sides of the stage where the actors could wait for their cues and from which they would enter. I asked Meyerhold when they would be up. He told me that he was opposed to drops and wings and that everything would remain as it was for the performance. "There will be general lighting on the playing area," he explained. "The actors will be placed at the back of the stage or at the sides, depending where they enter from, at the very beginning of the play, beyond reach of the lights that light the playing area. They'll wait for their entrances there."

"But they'll still be in sight?" I asked.

"Yes. But barely. All the spectator's attention will be concentrated on the playing area, which will be brightly lit."

"But the stage manager keeps crossing the stage, and the canteen lady is always passing out tea and sandwiches. The way the theater is built there's no way to get across except by crossing the stage."

"That's all right, most of us will be wearing work-clothes," Meyerhold said. "It'll be interesting. The actors will be acting downstage, and upstage in the half-darkness, behind the construction, the tech crew and anyone else involved in the production can move around freely."

"But that many people walking around and talking, and the canteen lady bringing tea, it will distract the audience's attention."

"That's all right, that's all right. Let them drink their tea, it's interesting."

I was in despair. The production was full of delicate moments, nuances, and psychological pauses; it had a number of scenes that demanded the audience's concentrated attention.

I began to get mad. "Vsevolod Emilievich, it's impossible! All that is going to destroy everything you've been doing with us and building with such care. All the details and nuances will be lost. This way we'll have to act like street players."

Meyerhold flared up. "What an esthete, listen to him! If you want a lot of esthetic shtick, go see Sakhnovsky and

Rutz. What do you want me to do, hang up embroidered curtains and backdrops like Tairov?"

"I don't want any kind of estheticism," I declared. "I want you to do something. I don't want anybody interfering with my acting—nor with your direction. Hang something up behind the construction, Popova's old petticoats, I don't care. But I have to have something, some kind of screen around me, I don't care what it is, just so nobody interferes with me."

"Don't you dare talk like that about one of my fellow workers!" Meyerhold shouted.

I was so upset I began to cry, and went to hide in one of the boxes at the back of the auditorium.

Zinaida Raikh came to console me.

"Don't be angry, Ilyinsky. It'll all work itself out and it won't be so bad. Vsevolod Emilievich will back down somehow if it doesn't work. But what he wants to do is really interesting, and it's unusual. He doesn't want to ruin things for you or for himself. Trust him! You see he's working with you and he loves you."

We made peace. And in fact it didn't turn out so badly after all. There was no distracting crowd of people. We found places for the actors to wait for their entrances where they wouldn't be noticed by the audience. I even made use of the space behind the construction and the playing area. For my first entrance I ran all the way from backstage, from the dressing-room area. It was very effective. While I was still in the dressing room I began shouting Bruno's call: "Oho, ho, ho, ho! Stellums!" I used that shout to get me across the entire space of the stage from the brick wall and kept it up until I burst out onto the lighted playing area. It was indeed a much better effect than if I had appeared from the wings or from behind a backdrop.

I soon had occasion to regret it, in fact, because eventually a backdrop did appear. Other productions were brought into the theater, constructions for the new productions were leaned against the back brick wall since there was no other place for them, and in fact we found that the construction did not read well against the background of all that conglomeration. So Meyerhold had to hang up an old canvas to cover the construction parts and the brick wall, and that in effect became the backdrop. And in *Cuckold*, when I ran out from behind that drop, it was no longer so effective an entrance.

At the last dress rehearsals there was a feeling of uniformity, of leveling among all the characters dressed in workclothes. Sometimes at an entrance it was hard to tell which of the characters was which. Theatricality began to make its demands. I wanted to distinguish myself somehow from "all those people in workclothes." That's after all natural not only to an actor, but to anyone. But of course I wanted a distinction that corresponded to my character. I was aided by Popova herself, who had paid no attention to the petticoats, but gave me for the role of Bruno a pair of bright red pompoms to hang around my neck. They went surprisingly well with Bruno's poetic character, his childish spontaneity and mischievousness. Having indulged me, she then had to indulge the rest of the cast as well. It was decided to distinguish the burgomaster by having him wear a military belt and gaiters over his workclothes. The count got a stick and a monocle. Stella wore a pair of sheer stockings, which worked even better because the actress had to show off her foot during the action of the play. Besides the pompoms I sported a pair of boots.

We played without make-up. But street make-up wasn't forbidden, and so Babanova as Stella used a moderate amount of it. The others followed her example and made themselves up as well. In a word, the life of the theater reclaimed its own.

Sergei Eisenstein used to come to rehearsals for *Cuckold*, and also Levushka Sverdlin, who carefully and quietly watched Meyerhold at work, and who subsequently replaced me as Arkashka in *The Forest* quite successfully.

The opening night of *The Magnanimous Cuckold* was a smashing success. I have already done enough bragging when I talked about *The Storm*. But this success was more sensational and on a wider scale than that of *The Storm*. This was after all the first real success for Meyerhold as a director, for his new theater, his young actors, his new method of biomechanics. It was a success accompanied by heated debates, by elation or total rejection, and those are always the ringing, thunderous successes.

Many, many people loved the production. Mayakovsky

loved it, and Mayakovsky for me was always a crystal-clear and flawless standard, an unmasker of the least vulgarity. And once I read in *Theater* magazine fond memories of *The Magnanimous Cuckold* by Nikolai Aseyev.

The actors loved the play, and their delight in it did not go unnoticed by the audience. They were not only stunned by the production, but enchanted by it, by its freshness, spontaneity, and novelty, and by the energy of the acting.

If my success in *The Storm* was never to be repeated, so my success in *Cuckold* remains also unrepeated. There was no curtain, as everyone knows. So it is impossible to measure this success by the usual yardstick: "How many curtain calls did he get?" A storm of applause burst out, and then the audience, especially the students and young people, rushed up onstage and tossed us in the air, beginning with Meyerhold. I was never shaken more than that, even in Meyerhold's theater. The storm of clapping went on and on and eventually, staggering somewhat from success as much as from the tossing, I went out into the fresh spring air in Triumphal Square. Viktor Ardov and Kolya Khrushchev, who then worked in the administrative offices of the new theater, were waiting for me.

"Oho ho ho ho ho!" Ardov yelled in the middle of the square, imitating me in *Cuckold*. "Now *that's* really something! Come to a café with us and let's celebrate with some piroshki!"

"I can't, I haven't got any money," I said.

"Don't worry about that! Kolya and I did an enormous business in passes and house seats all day long, so we've got plenty for piroshki. Come on! You're the one who earned it."

Igor' Il'inskij, *Sam o sebe*, 2d ed. (Moscow, 1973), pp. 173–182.

Erast Garin

It was the Meyerhold Free Workshop production of *The Magnanimous Cuckold* by the Belgian playwright Crommelynck that marked the beginning of a serious method of study and training for the actor; in this production Meyerhold summed up and began to generalize his enormous experience.

Let me present some evidence; the schematic score for the actors' movements in a culminating scene from *The Magnanimous Cuckold* (the end of act two). Even a cursory acquaintance with this score makes it clear that it could not be played using acting techniques from either naturalistic, "drawing-room," conversational theater, or from balletic, mimed, harlequinade theater. The director granted the actor a freedom whose fundamental requirement presented the actor with new and complicated tasks.

The Constructivist set recalled the outlines of a windmill, but left the actor free to move about on the entire downstage area, which was completely bare of set and props. Stage right was a semicircular bench. The upstage area contained the construction, which consisted of two platforms at different levels connected by stairways, a bridge, and a slippery chute that might have been used for bags of flour. The platforms enabled the actor to move up and downstairs and to make use of doors and windows, but removed the narrative security of concrete naturalistic detail.

Bruno—beautifully played by Igor Ilyinsky—takes Petrus to his room. Petrus is his wife Stella's cousin who has just arrived for a visit. (Stella was marvellously played by Maria Babanova.) Petrus, Stella, and her old nurse are out of sight behind the door. Bruno is alone onstage. He watches them exit, then runs quickly after them. He goes up the stairs and stops at the door that conceals them. He ponders anxiously. He peers through the keyhole. He moves away, as if weighing his growing suspicion. He goes up to the top platform, glancing back from time to time at the door. He goes back down, constantly slowing his walk, turning over the fantasy that begins to fill his mind. He crosses to the bench, dulled by his complicated imaginings, and sits down astride it, lost in thought, his eyes straining at one spot, as if someone had scratched on the bench an answer to the question that torments him.

Enter the town clerk, Bruno's assistant, the taciturn Estrugo. (This role, practically wordless, was superbly played by the late Vasily Zaichikov.) He goes up to the door (it was a revolving door). Estrugo is afraid of the door's mechanism.

He opens it carefully a crack, to see if it's all right to come in, then thinks better of it and walks through the open space where the wall of the mill should have been. (There were no walls in the construction.)

Once on the other side of the door, he closes it apprehensively, afraid of pinching his fingers. Then he turns around and catches sight of Bruno, sunk in contemplation of something. What is he looking at? Estrugo approaches carefully and peers over Bruno's right shoulder. He can't see anything, and so he climbs onto the bench and looks over the top of the seated Bruno's head.

He has to get still closer. Estrugo climbs down and approaches Bruno from the other direction, head-on, still looking for what Bruno is staring at, but understanding nothing. Finally Bruno raises his eyes. They are face to face.

Bruno slaps the bench with the palm of his hand, inviting him to sit.

"Estrugo, sit down!"

Estrugo apprehensively puts a leg over and sits on the very edge of the bench.

"Closer!" Bruno says, moving away at the same time.

Estrugo moves closer.

"Closer!" Bruno repeats the same business.

"Closer!" The same business.

Bruno jumps up and threatens Estrugo with his fists; Estrugo gets frightened and falls face down on the bench and covers his head with his hands. Pause. Estrugo raises his head.

"Sshh! Just a minute! Sshh! Be quiet!"

Estrugo covers his head again, then raises it in order to look at Bruno.

"Will you be quiet?"

Estrugo hides his head again. Bruno grabs Estrugo's head, raises it and shouts:

"What do you think? Is Stella faithful to me, or isn't she?"

Estrugo tries to answer, but Bruno pushes him back down into his previous position, and says unexpectedly, in a totally reasonable tone of voice:

"The question (Bruno draws a question mark with his finger on Estrugo's back) has come up."

Bruno thinks a moment, then states decisively:

"She is faithful! (He slaps Estrugo's back with the palm of his hand.) Just as (another slap) the sky (another slap) is blue today (another slap), just as the world (another slap) is round. Yes!" (Another slap.)

Estrugo here raises his head. Bruno continues:

"I don't want comparisons, please! Yes or no? If she's faithful, prove it!"

Estrugo realizes the impossibility of proving anything (he doesn't understand what's going on anyway), and lies down again on the bench.

"You can't prove it!"

Estrugo raises his head.

"Are you ready to swear? Swear!"

Estrugo tries to get a word out.

"You don't dare?"

Something dawns on Bruno. He puts his hand over Estrugo's mouth; Estrugo still hasn't said a word.

"He knows, he knows, poor man! And if you don't know for sure, at least you realize it's possible."

Furiously he grabs Estrugo's head and pushes him down into his former position. Only Estrugo's arms are free. He waves them in protest. Bruno holds down his arms. Estrugo protests with his hands, which are still free. Bruno stops that movement as well and begins to think. . . .

This excerpt is made up almost totally of movement and pantomime, yet the mime here is not the conventional balletic kind, but purposeful, constructed on the basis of a concrete, realistic, playable situation. Estrugo's appearance on stage becomes a harlequinade: it conveys an ironic attitude toward the action. But that harlequinade is free of drawing-room comedy cheapness or mannered affectation, free of any of those features we have come to call "playing for laughs." . . .

It was about this time that Meyerhold enlarged his troupe with students from the school. He tested his experience as an artist, a director, against his experience as a pedagogue. Meyerhold proposed a new discipline for the education of actors: biomechanics. The goal of biomechanics was the comprehensive training of the actor; its techniques were opposed to the photographic naturalism of "slice of life" theater on the one hand, and to balletic estheticism on the other.

At the beginning of a lesson, Meyerhold often repeated the fundamental formula of the elder Coquelin concerning the actor's double nature, where A^1 is the idea, the intelligence, and A^2 is the material: the body, the voice, etc. Biomechanics was a system for training the actor's material. Let me use two biomechanical exercises as example.

The first position for the student about to perform an exercise, and the signal to begin, is two handclaps. These claps are brought down from above onto the palm; the motion then transfers itself into the trunk, imparting elasticity to the entire body; finally the feet too receive the motion begun by the hands. The feet are placed parallel, heels slightly raised, toes pointed in. The stance is reminiscent of a boxer's and opposed to the turned-out technique of classical posture exercises. Walking and running exercises give the student a fluid quality when moving, the ability, as it were, to carry a container of water in the hands or on the head and not spill a drop.

When he is able to perform these exercises easily, the student performs the étude called "Shooting the Bow," which is done without props. The left hand mimes the carrying of the bow. In motion, walking or running, the left shoulder leads. When the student sights the target his body comes to a stop with all the weight centered. The right hand moves in an arc to grasp the arrow, held against the back by an imaginary belt. The movement of the hand conveys itself to the entire body, moving the weight onto the back leg. The hand finds the arrow and places it against the bow. The weight is transferred to the front leg. The arrow is aimed. The imaginary bow is stretched and the weight is transferred to the back leg. The arrow is let fly and the exercise is completed with a leap and a shout.

Even this beginning exercise develops in the student the habit of sensing his body in space, the ability to align himself, to work on elasticity and balance, and the understanding that even the smallest gesture—of the hand, for example—resonates throughout the entire body, producing in it the so-called "reject sign." Thus the pre-gesture in this exercise, the "reject sign," is the arc of the hand reaching for the arrow. It is a sort of involuntary intake of breath, figuratively speaking, before the intended movement. Every pre-gesture, like every gesture itself, has an accompaniment played by the entire body. This exercise acquaints the student with the "acting chain," which consists of three elements: (1) intention; (2) execution; and (3) reaction. A succession of these "acting chains" thus eventually constitutes the process of acting.

When Meyerhold decided to introduce students to the complicated étude called "The Dagger Attack" he would do it for them first himself. He would choose a student with a strong build, show him how to support his body with his hands against a table behind him, and how to make his body as elastic as possible. He then acted out a pantomime of creeping up on the student and leapt upon his shoulders, with his right knee resting on the student's ribcage. With his right hand he drew the imaginary dagger from his belt, struck his partner in the neck, then leapt down. The wounded figure fell to the ground, while the figure of the attacker straightened up.

Meyerhold had adapted this exercise from the Italian actor Grasso. It always produced a tremendous effect upon the students. Vsevolod Meyerhold at that time was my father's age, and although my father was a hunter, I could never imagine him making such a leap.

After two weeks we were all able to do the exercise flawlessly. And the student who had the other student leap on him, the one who received the dagger blow, never had to lean on anything. The attacker always made the leap to the shoulders extremely lightly. Beyond mere physical complexity, this exercise taught the student how to coordinate himself with a partner.

The beginning exercises in biomechanics set the student a series of steps toward the complete mastery of an actor's material—his body. They required of us clarity, moving with an awareness of our center, awareness that gesture is a result of movement even in static positions.

They taught us to understand the power of impression, the strength of acting with poses. Take as an example those toy figures which can be made to seem happy, sad, etc., even though the facial features never change. The secret of their expressivity is in the change of pose.

They taught us how to master the art of wearing a costume. Meyerhold suggested that we not practice in tights. A loose-fitting outfit was best. Thus the student would get a sense of the line and folds of a costume.

We worked for a long time, painstakingly, on the expressivity of eyes and hands. (As examples Meyerhold used the acting of Duse and Stanislavsky.)

Meyerhold possessed perfect pitch and an outstanding musical memory; he played the violin, was a marvellous conductor, read scores fluently, and had a musical sense of the spoken word (poetry and prose) and of movement. He was well aware of the powerful possibilities for an actor in doing movement exercises to strict musical accompaniment.

Beginning with elementary exercises in metrical patterns, we progressed to more complicated tasks: mastery of free rhythmical movement against a metrical pattern and, finally, to mastery of free movement in an unrestricted counterpoint.

After this we easily grasped the tempi and nature of movement in music: legato, staccato, etc. And there was yet one more problem set for us, connected with movement to music: coordination of the self in time and space. This coordination demanded great exactness, an absolute sense of time, an ability to count exactly in fractions of a second. Subsequently we mastered coordination of the self with partners, with objects and props, and thus came in real earnest to the foundations of theatrical composition.

Meyerhold could not avoid a discipline so important for an actor as the pictorial arts. He could draw, had made a thorough study of painting (more than some professionals), he knew how it develops the eye. He knew that it provides the actor with iconographic information and for that reason he instilled in us a feeling for it, for the nature of movement and the originality of figures in the paintings of Fedotov, Daumier, Callot, and other remarkable artists.

He taught us to see and to understand the unsurpassed expressiveness of the movements of animals, their behavior, their habits, their strength and the precision of their reactions.

As a result of this careful study, as a result of continuous training in the elements of biomechanics, we began to perceive the patterns of an actor's physical expressivity.

Meyerhold introduced a new subject to theoretical studies, "scenometry," where questions of blocking, the actor's position on the stage, became enormously important. The exceptional talent for blocking we observed at rehearsals produced in us a distaste for "literature" on stage, that is, for a theater where action and physical expressiveness were made to yield to the literary-narrative passivity of conversational theater. This was the kind of theater with which our teacher constantly waged war.

Biomechanical training might be compared to a pianist's studies, to the practice of technique with Hanon exercises and Czerny études. Mastering the technical difficulties of the exercises and études does not provide the student with a prescription for the lyric energy necessary, let's say, for a Chopin nocturne (that is the sphere of Coquelin's A^1), yet he must master the techniques in order to master his art. Technique arms the imagination.

Biomechanics are Hanon exercises for actors.

Erast Garin, "O Mandate i o drugom," *Vstreči s Mejerxol'dom* (Moscow, 1967), pp. 315–317, 322–324; *S Mejerxol'dom* (Moscow, 1974), pp. 35–37.

Mikhail Sadovsky

With Meyerhold it was only a step from hate to love, or from love to hate. These shifts were always unexpected and were most often triggered by insignificant pretexts.

Here is an example, something that happened to Evgeny Samoilov.

At the Meyerhold Theater Samoilov for a long time played only one part, Peter in *The Forest*, and never rehearsed any new roles. Meyerhold paid no attention to him. Samoilov was hurt and suffered in silence. Then one day Klavdia Martynova, who was in charge of the costume section, had a birthday party. She had invited a lot of the actors, and among them were Meyerhold, Raikh, and Samoilov. Somewhere about the middle of the party, when everybody was in exceedingly good spirits, Samoilov decided to make use of the warm and informal atmosphere of the party to have a frank, heart-to-heart talk about his situation with Meyerhold. He filled his glass and positioned himself next to Vsevolod Emilievich, but couldn't seem to come up with an appropriate way to introduce the matter. Finally he could contain himself no longer, grabbed Meyerhold's head with both his hands, and began to shake it, his face close to Meyerhold's, and kept shouting: "Look, I want to act! Don't you understand? I want to act!"

Meyerhold, scared and disheveled, freed himself from Samoilov's clutches with great difficulty. The guests were just as astonished and frightened as Meyerhold himself. What would happen now? But there was no scandal. Meyerhold became suddenly aware of only one thing: Samoilov's great emotional power, his temperament. It was as if he were hearing his fine voice and seeing his flashing eyes for the first time. He was amazed by it, and began to see Samoilov in a different light. He sensed a good actor in him. That moment changed everything for Zhenia Samoilov. He became one of Meyerhold's favorite actors.

If Meyerhold hated somebody he could not, would not conceal it. He hated—vociferously! And if he loved somebody—that too was at the top of his voice. He was always looking for an occasion to make manifest his attitude toward a person. There was a period when he was very much taken by the pianist Sofronitsky, and when he produced *The Queen of Spades* at the Maly Opera Theater in Leningrad in 1935, the playbills announced quite plainly: "Meyerhold dedicates this production, his op. 110, to V. V. Sofronitsky."

Meyerhold's character was indeed complex and difficult. But working with him was nevertheless a great privilege. A privilege because he was a great theater director, and also because the artist in him always had the upper hand during any argument.

No theater director ever caused more heated disputes than Meyerhold. Everything was disputed: his theater, his productions. Large matters were disputed, and small ones: Realism and Formalism, individual scenes, *mises en scène*, and even single cues. Very often Meyerhold's followers were defeated in these disputes. Vsevolod Emilievich admitted his mistakes not infrequently himself. Mistakes were unavoidable. Meyerhold was searching and experimenting. His way in art lay not along the beaten path but on new, untrodden ways.

One theater critic even maintained that he had heard from Meyerhold himself that he needed no actors: all he needed was simply a number of men and women with different characteristics; given that, he could stage any production, he could train those people for any part just as gun dogs are trained for the hunt.

I doubt very much that Meyerhold could ever have said anything like that. Meyerhold esteemed actors very highly. And actors, in their turn, were grateful to him for involving them in his quest for the new, for the esthetic taste he nurtured in them, for the high esteem in which he held the individuality of each.

He needed Sergei Martinson precisely because of Martinson's individual qualities and he had no intention of changing Martinson, or of dominating him.

He was also very much attached to Erast Garin because Garin was unlike anyone else.

I doubt that any other theater director has nurtured such a great number of excellent actors, all brilliant and each different from the other. Look at the names of some of his disciples: Babanova, Ilyinsky, Garin, Zaichikov, Martinson, Bogoliubov, Sverdlin, Shtraukh, Tiapkina.

Nevertheless some people persist in considering those actors exceptions, and continue to assert that Meyerhold violated an actor's free will.

How did this assertion originate? There is, after all, no smoke without fire. Let me attempt to explain where, in my view, this acrid smoke comes from.

Meyerhold's demonstrations at rehearsals were invariably amazing and admirable. They never repressed an actor—on the contrary, they inspired him. The actors accepted these demonstrations eagerly and gratefully, then developed them through their creative initiative and enriched them through their skill and individuality.

But of course there were actors who were not only unable to develop what had been demonstrated, but unable even to repeat the demonstration more or less similarly. In these cases Meyerhold tried to simplify their task; he changed the *mise en scène*, thought up all kinds of new variants, each of which remained stimulating and interesting. He could never

stand the "academic" staging of an extra's entrance and exit:
a door opens, a man enters, puts a samovar on the table,
turns, and walks off. Meyerhold would unfailingly do something interesting with that samovar, but some actors simply
could not comprehend the "interesting" part, could not apply
their own fantasy to it, could not bring it to life. The only
thing they were able to do was to repeat the bare outline,
with difficulty. And it was only then, after a thousand variants had failed, that Meyerhold would become enraged and
turn into a dictator, an animal trainer. "Stand this way!" he
would say. "Put your foot there and your arm here. Speak all
the phrase in one tone! Close your eyes, they express nothing
anyway. Now turn your back and stand like this without
moving."

Actors who got into this embarrassing situation would
begin to say that Meyerhold gave them no chance to express
themselves, that he was stifling their individuality, that he
turned them into marionettes. Nonsense! These actors had no
individuality, there was nothing to stifle. These were the people who got into the theater by chance, who were totally
helpless where art was concerned. Being sore at life and at
Meyerhold they spread this lie everywhere. They were the
source of the acrid smoke.

Meyerhold gave Ilyinsky a wonderful demonstration for
Arkashka, in _The Forest_, fishing. He showed how Arkashka
cast the line, hooked the fish, took the fish off the hook, and
put it into a teapot. I know people from whose memory time
has erased the performance, but who still remember the fishing rod in Ilyinsky's hands, remember him placing the
quivering fish in the teapot. It should be noted here that not
only was there no fish, but the fishing rod itself had no line. It
was Ilyinsky's mastery, his skill in developing the demonstration, in working all the actions into the character of his
Arkashka, that made this scene such a great success. It was
Ilyinsky's talent and technique that made it possible for him
to act so brilliantly with these imaginary objects and that invariably called forth the applause.

Meyerhold needed good actors; he could not have existed
without them. . . .

I recall that we performed in Odessa in the summer of
1935. Meyerhold and most of the actors were staying at the
London Hotel (since renamed the Odessa Hotel). The hotel

had a cozy restaurant situated in the inner courtyard. The courtyard was covered with gravel, there was a fountain in the center, and the tables were placed in niches along the walls. In the corner there was a small stage where a string quartet played classical music. Meyerhold reserved a table in this restaurant for the whole period of the Odessa tour, and every evening supper was served at a fixed time. Meyerhold used to sit at this table until the small hours every evening after the performance, in the company of friends, different friends every evening. The soft music, the sound of the fountain, the intimate lighting in the niches, flowers, and wonderful fresh air gave the place a special charm, perfect for conversation.

I was invited to one of these suppers. The conversation was about famous provincial actors. Meyerhold told many funny and curious stories from the life of the provincial theater of the past. He recalled one funny, but at the same time very odd, peculiarity of the provincial theater—the actors' requests that playwrights write them something "for an exit"—some fine concluding phrase that would assure them a round of applause as they left the stage.

"If the playwright wouldn't write the phrase they wanted," Meyerhold said, "they used to think up something on their own, some gimmick which would result in the applause they wanted. No matter how many times they made an exit, each one of them tried to get applause with something spectacular and unexpected. It became a game of sorts: who would succeed at it in the most ingenious, most masterly manner. It's true, all sense of proportion was usually lost, and the whole thing sometimes used to reach a point of absurdity and incongruity, but there was a positive side to it. The actors knew how to get the audience's attention, they were in close contact with the spectators."

Meyerhold developed this idea, and expressed his admiration for actors who were good at improvising, who were able, as the saying goes, to "work the audience." He admired their ability to feel the audience and manipulate it.

"Those jokers," Meyerhold went on, "were talented actors with a lot of experience and a rich theatrical technique. And somehow it always happens that a talented actor gets a good audience." . . .

Naturally all theaters exist for the audience. All the concerns of the author, the director, the actors are centered on the audience. But for Meyerhold the audience occupied an exceptional position. The audience was his beacon, his compass, the thermometer without which he could not exist for a moment.

"Do not be concerned with the audience!" some directors say to the actors at a rehearsal. "Do not think about them! You must think about what you are doing at this moment on the stage, in this room, with whom you are talking, what your desires are, what you are afraid of. . . . The more you are absorbed in all of this, the more attention you will attract from the audience. Keep in mind—there are no footlights over there with an auditorium beyond them, but an imaginary fourth wall! A solid, impenetrable wall. You are in this room now completely by yourself, alone with your thoughts and actions. That is all there is to it."

Stanislavsky used to call this state of the actor "public solitude." Meyerhold never denied the concept of public solitude. But it was the "public" rather than the "solitude" that was more important for him in this formula.

Meyerhold often referred to talented circus clowns who were often able to work the ring in a state of public solitude that actors could only envy. At the same time, Meyerhold stressed, they remain in this state not only without a fourth wall but with no walls at all, and they never forget about the audience. They are aware of the audience at every second, at every step, with every turn of their bodies.

If Stanislavsky said that the soul of the theater was the actor, then Meyerhold's formula was: "The actor plus the spectator."

It was his desire to bring the actor and the audience together that prompted him to abolish the curtain, to destroy the so-called fourth wall. This orientation of Meyerhold's toward the audience, his desire to make the audience part of the performance, to merge audience and performer, led him still further. He dreamed of a new theater building where the three remaining walls would be abolished, where there would be no stage box and where all the action would take place directly in the auditorium. Meyerhold not only could not stand a quiet, indifferent audience, he was genuinely afraid of it, and was ready to go against any and all established conventions to excite the audience.

In his prologue to *Mystery-Bouffe* Mayakovsky writes:

> There are other theaters
> that dismiss imagination:
> for them
> the stage
> is a keyhole.
> You sit down calmly
> facing straight ahead or sideways
> and watch a slice of other people's lives. . . .

That is exactly what Meyerhold rebelled against. He aimed at wrenching the spectator out of the familiarity of everyday existence, attempted to rip off his comfortable "house slippers."

> We will show you true life too—
> but transformed
> by theater into extraordinary spectacle.

These words of Mayakovsky are a good illustration of Meyerhold's goal.

In the established practice of our theaters spectators are admitted only to the two concluding rehearsals, the so-called dress rehearsals, when the actors and the director need to test the performance on the audience. Not infrequently this test yields miserable results—the audience supplies corrections to such an extent that the performance has to be delayed for additional work.

Meyerhold based his productions on the audience, beginning practically with the very first rehearsal. There were always some twenty or thirty "unauthorized" people, usually his acquaintances, present at his rehearsals. The presence of spectators, far from discouraging Meyerhold or getting in his way, inspired him. Meyerhold was always on the move, darting between the stage and auditorium. He could often be seen bending over one of the seated spectators, asking him something. He used to ask questions of everybody. One of the janitors might be in the auditorium, taking a break from his work. Meyerhold would head in his direction and one could hear his questions: "How did you like it? Do you understand it? What is it you understand?" And the next minute he would be conferring with Yury Olesha. One could never say with certainty whose view he preferred—very probably the janitor's. Most of all, he simply needed to test the performance on someone.

During a rehearsal he would sometimes say: "At this point we may get some applause." Or: "You ought to get applause here. If you don't, you're doing something wrong!"

If somebody observed that applause during the action interfered with the actor, destroyed his circle of concentration, Meyerhold replied: "I don't see how it is possible to deprive the spectator of his initiative, to deprive him of the opportunity to express his emotions. How can you forbid him to laugh, to cry, or to applaud?"

Probably no other director relied so much on the eyes of the viewer as Meyerhold. It was in visual terms that he strove to convey his productions to the public. Theater is a spectacle. The spectators come to watch. In order to become familiar with a play one can read it oneself or listen to an intelligent reading. But it is only at the theater that one can see a spectacle. And Meyerhold had a very clear view of what he wanted the spectators to see.

I recall the third act of Griboyedov's *Woe to Wit*, the scene of the gossip about Chatsky's alleged "madness." The word, used accidentally by Sofia in her conversation with Mr. N, immediately spreads to every corner of Famusov's house and to all his guests.

How did Meyerhold stage these scenes? He discarded the idea of showing the audience the different rooms of Famusov's house with the characters of the play scurrying through them. In his view, this would have provided the audience only with superficial amusement and distracted its attention from the important element of the scene.

Meyerhold decided to gather in one place all these gossip-mongers, liars, fools, toadies, and grovelers, "growing decrepit in concoctions of nonsense," and put them on trial before the audience. Right at the footlights, across the entire length of the stage, stretching from the right wing to the left, he placed a long table covered with a white tablecloth and set for supper. At this table, facing the spectators, sat all those who had inflicted upon Chatsky his "million sufferings." A striking gallery of figures and characters was thus presented to the audience, as it were, in the docket. Here, at this table, the gossip was born. Here, the audience could see it grow, develop, and become "public opinion."

And when the discussion of the gossip, the general glee, the spiteful laughter, and mock sympathy were at their height, Chatsky appeared, and everything suddenly went quiet, the figures pulled sharply away from him and hid behind their napkins, and all that could be seen of them were their frightened eyes above the hems of the napkins. Chatsky walked to the middle of the table where Famusov and Khlestova were seated, stopped, spoke his lines:

> I can no longer stand it—a million sufferings;
> my soul from friends importunate,
> my feet from constant shuffling,
> my ears from exclamations,
> and most of all my head from endless nonsense. . . .

and then continued on his way along the table. This melancholy progression was accompanied by music. As he disappeared into the left wing the music stopped, and all the figures and all eyes turned after him. Then a gong sounded and the stage went dark. End of scene.

Mixail Sadovskij, "Teatral'nyj čarodej," *Vstreči s Mejerxol'dom* (Moscow, 1967), pp. 509–511, 518–519, 515–517.

III.
Shaping the October Revolution in Theater

The passion of opposition that we find in Meyerhold, the polemical tone of voice, made him a perfect revolutionary. A consuming sense of justice is the leitmotif of his early life, and when the Revolution came he embraced it with fervent delight. It provided him at last with a theater wide enough and public enough for his diapason. Meyerhold's revolutionary spirit was surely a natural part of his often fractious and aggressive personality: he was famous for it. He was a celebrity in the modern sense, stormy and controversial, "newsworthy" without any ideological justification. Leonid Varpakhovsky, his assistant for a number of years, testifies to the power of his image.

But he was a passionate ideologue, and committed to the Revolution. His actor Igor Ilyinsky gives us a clear picture of Meyerhold's serious and precise intention: to found the Theater of the Revolution. And for that he needed not merely new actors and a new theater building, but playwrights above all: Soviet playwrights. His relations with them were frequently stormy, but his desire to bring the October Revolution into the theater was sincere. Even Ilya Ehrenburg, that eternal ironist, testifies to the energy with which Meyerhold sought to midwife a new Soviet drama. He sought out young playwrights, brought them together with other artists, staged their plays, encouraged them in letters and in his friendship, and most fundamentally in the image of himself that he held out to them. It is literally an image, in fact, that Yury Olesha first remembers, in an article he wrote to celebrate Meyerhold's sixtieth birthday. That image may have been highly theatricalized—his actors Erast Garin and Igor Ilyinsky remember his appearance in 1920 as carefully contrived—yet his adherence to the Revolution was total and profound.

Leonid Varpakhovsky

Members of my generation who lived in Moscow during the first years of the Revolution had heard the name Meyerhold for the first time when they were still very young. There was something enigmatic, alluring, even legendary, in his name. And if you had been in love with the theater since your childhood and there were always lots of theater people visiting your home, then you heard the name Meyerhold all the time.

And what things you used to hear about him! Popular singers at the Hermitage Summer Park used to sing a song:

> Cows out on the ice get cold;
> They can't walk too well.
> I won't go watch Meyerhold;
> Let him scream and yell.

This was "anti-Meyerhold."

During the same period you could buy a comb at a street kiosk with just one word written on it: "Meyerhold." This, obviously, was "pro-Meyerhold." . . .

A book of short stories appeared by a beginning author, Mikhail Bulgakov. In his story "The Fatal Eggs," written in 1924, Bulgakov defied chronology by burying Meyerhold in 1927. He wrote: "A theater named after the late Vsevolod Meyerhold, who is known to have died in 1927 during a production of Pushkin's *Boris Godunov* when a trapeze full of naked boyars fell on him. . . ."

Bulgakov, alas, could not be said to be lacking in wit. In 1922 Meyerhold produced *The Death of Tarelkin* in an extremely eccentric way, replacing ordinary furniture with gymnastic gadgets that moved in all directions. And Sergei Eisenstein, who had studied under him at the producers' workshops, went even further when he transformed Ostrovsky's comedy *The Diary of a Scoundrel* into a "propaganda satire and clownery."

I should mention in passing that every time I spoke with Meyerhold afterward about his projected production of *Boris Godunov* he remembered Bulgakov's naked boyars—good-humoredly, but not without some irritation. In 1936/37 he began working on a production of *Boris Godunov*, but it was to remain unfinished. Bulgakov turned out to have been off by only ten years. . . .

Meyerhold's fame was especially great in the beginning of the twenties. I'll never forget the day when I was present in the Bolshoi Theater where Meyerhold was honored on the occasion of the twenty-fifth anniversary of his theatrical career. It was the second of April, 1923. Onstage marched soldiers of the Red Army, with the orchestra playing. Meyerhold was greeted by the infantry and artillery, by the air force and tank corps. "You are no stranger to the rifle of the proletariat!" the orator was saying. "You suffered captivity by the enemy! You bear honorably the proud name of Communist! During the first great days of the Revolution you courageously announced the slogan 'The October Revolution in Theater' and started a major shift in the routine and backwardness which had dominated the sphere of Russian art until your rebellious intrusion."

A greeting from the circus actors was read by the famous clown Vitaly Lazarenko, who walked onto the stage on enormous stilts ("Lazarenko, great in height, greets Meyerhold, great in talent"). Then the Proletkult actors appeared. They played a topical political farce, *Joffre s'en Va-t-en Guerre*, based on Ostrovsky's *Diary of a Scoundrel*. I no longer remember all the crazy stunts that Eisenstein invented for it, but I remember that at the end of the play Glumov, played by Grigory Alexandrov, took an umbrella and, balancing with it like a regular acrobat, walked a tightrope straight to a box in the third circle above the heads of the stunned spectators. This "leftist" interpretation of the classics was the way Sergei Eisenstein greeted his teacher. Nobody could predict yet that in just three years Eisenstein and Alexandrov would create their famous *Potemkin*, and Charlie Chaplin would hail this masterpiece of revolutionary art as "the best film in the world."

I remember that I was surprised when Meyerhold in his concluding address proposed to send a telegram to Konstantin Stanislavsky, to whom, he said, he was "very much indebted for the beginning of his artistic career." In those years I could find nothing in common between the creator of the Art Theater and the leader of the "Left Front." Decades were to go by until these two names became linked for me.

When I was thirteen, I would stand for a long time in front of a pink playbill on the wall of the former Sohn Theater on Sadovaya-Triumphal Street. Its text was mysterious, unusual, and totally alluring. It read: "At the Actors' Theater on Bolshaya Sadovaya Street (Streetcar Routes 6, 25, B) the Free Workshops of Vsevolod Meyerhold present a production dedicated to Molière: *The Magnanimous Cuckold*, a farce in three acts. By Crommelynck/Aksyonov. Construction by L. Popova. Directed by Master Director Meyerhold."

What are Free Workshops?

And what is a "construction"?

What does "master" mean?

I kept repeating to myself enchantedly: *"The Magnanimous Cuckold*—a farce in three acts!" but I could never bring myself actually to enter the ticket office and buy a ticket for the play. I was confused by the genre of the play and its title. It was only after many years that I was fortunate enough to see this amazing production.

Bolshaya Sadovaya Street, streetcar routes 6, 25, and B! I take the streetcar, route B, on Smolensk Square and ride in the direction of Samotyoka Street. On Novinsky Boulevard a man in his fifties enters the streetcar. He is wearing a leather overcoat and a peak-cap, his face is gray and tired, he has a Cyrano de Bergerac nose, a well-formed mouth and amazing steel-colored eyes that are impossible to forget. At one moment his eyes stare coldly into space and seem to express nothing, at another moment they are scrutinizing the people around him. The conductor announces the stop: "Triumphal Square." The man in the leather overcoat leaves the streetcar and with long strides, slightly stooping, walks to the former Sohn Theater. In the streetcar someone says: "Meyerhold!" And it really was him! He looked the way I always thought he would, from what I'd heard.

But how could I get another look at him, to see him better? When I learned from the playbill for the performance of *D. E.* that Meyerhold would perform the part of the Third Savage (only once) I managed to make it to the performance by hook or by crook. Near the end of the play, when the scene is supposed to take place in the mid-European desert, a motorcycle with a sidecar appeared all of a sudden on the empty stage. There was Meyerhold sitting beside the driver,

wearing the leather overcoat I had already seen. The motorcycle made two turns of the stage, producing a deafening
noise, then drove up to the footlights, very carefully drove
down into the auditorium, and stopped in the middle of it.
That was the cue for the Third Savage, Meyerhold. He rose
upright, announced in a rather muffled voice: "Citizens, do-
nate to MOPR!" and then rode out into the lobby, giving place
to the actors who immediately appeared in all the exits and
aisles of the auditorium with cups for donations in their
hands.

I was disappointed. It was clearly the same Meyerhold I
had seen the first time—but the only thing I had learned was
that Meyerhold always wore a leather overcoat, even when
playing the part of the Third Savage in the mid-European
desert.

My surprise then was all the greater when I saw Meyerhold for the third time. It was at one of the concerts in the
Grand Hall of the Conservatory. He was wearing a conventional gray suit—but what a drastic transformation! What
amazed me on this occasion was his exceptional elegance,
displayed not in the suit alone but in that stylish casualness
with which Meyerhold could wear clothes. Gone were the
sloppy gait, the head sunk deep into the shoulders, the stern
scrutinizing stare from beneath the eyebrows. It was, in
short, a different Meyerhold—no longer the Third Savage
from *D. E.* but rather a character from a play by Oscar Wilde.
And perhaps that's what he looked like when he played the
part of Lord Henry in the film version of Wilde's *Picture of
Dorian Gray*. During the intermission Meyerhold made social
small talk with a group that surrounded him and then, as if
to add to my stupefaction, began to demonstrate magic tricks
with matches!

After this meeting I realized that Meyerhold could be
very various indeed, and that both the outer and the inner
aspects of his personality changed depending on what he was
wearing—just as it is with actors onstage.

Leonid Varpaxovskij, "Zametki prošlyx let," *Vstreči s Mejerxol'dom*
(Moscow, 1967), pp. 459–462.

Igor Ilyinsky

Meyerhold appeared on the stage. He was wearing a military overcoat, and on the turned-up brim of his soldier's cap was a badge with a picture of Lenin. It seemed strange to me that a man with such a reputation as an esthete would show up in an outfit like that. In my mind's eye I could see the famous portrait by Boris Grigoryev, where Meyerhold was depicted in a rather affected pose, wearing tails and a top hat. I listened to his speech. In a slightly hoarse voice he urged us to bring our art to the people, to the new spectator, to the workers and peasants, and as well to found a new theater that would express the ideas of Communism, a theater for our new era, a theater for the great October Revolution. He suggested contemporary themes, themes for today, themes that would move the people who now had triumphed in Russia.

He spoke fairly simply, but with the surge of emotion that was typical of the time. And despite his apparent simplicity he seemed somewhat theatrical: the casually worn overcoat, the puttees and slippers, the cap with the turned-up brim and the portrait of Lenin, the dark red knit scarf—it was all quite casual, but nonetheless effective. Older actors and directors didn't usually dress like that. . . .

It was several years before I realized that the faint ambiguity, the paradox I felt in this first impression of Meyerhold was practically a crystallization of all my future hesitations over the contradictions in his creative personality and his art.

Igor' Il'inskij, *Sam o sebe*, 2d ed. (Moscow, 1973), pp. 124–125.

Erast Garin

Meyerhold often used to show up at the hall where we did our training in gymnastics, dancing, and acrobatics.

He would appear in the door with a green military overcoat thrown over his shoulders (one of the Allies had sent a lot of them to Russia before the Revolution). The room was always barely heated. We were all young, and doing strenuous exercises, so it didn't bother us. Meyerhold sat by the round, concave-tiled stove, took a drag on his cigarette, hand-rolled out of newspaper and cheap tobacco (he was the only one who was allowed to smoke), and looked at us all, as if studying each one of us.

That's how I remember him, sitting alone by the glazed-tile ᶜ'ove in the former private mansion of the former golden-tongued lawyer Plevako.

He was looking after his brood.

He was like a good-hearted old gray wolf. Gray eyes, gray hair, gray field jacket. His eyes studied us intently, kind but cold. . . .

Erast Garin, *S Mejerxol'dom* (Moscow, 1974), p. 35.

Ilya Ehrenburg

When I was a boy I saw Meyerhold on the stage of the Art Theater several times. I remember him as a crazy old man in the role of Ivan the Terrible and as an excitable, indignant young man in *The Sea Gull*.

Sitting in the Rotonde in Paris, I often remembered the words he spoke as Chekhov's hero Treplyov: "The curtain goes up and inside three walls, lit by artificial light, our famous stars, those high priests of art, parade about, showing us how to walk, eat, drink, love, and wear our clothes. And then the playwright tries to squeeze a moral out of it, some smug little moral, cheap, manufactured for home consumption, and each play repeats this formula again and again and again. That's why I have to run from them, the way Maupassant ran from the Eiffel Tower, knowing it would cheapen his mind. . . . What we need is a new kind of theater. We need new forms, and if we can't have them, let's have no theater at all." (Chekhov wrote *The Sea Gull* in 1896, Maupassant died in 1893, the Eiffel Tower was built in 1889. In 1913 we loved the tower and hated Maupassant; but the line about "new forms" seemed to me alive and meaningful.)

I missed a chance to make his acquaintance in 1913; he had been invited to Paris by Ida Rubinstein to direct, together with Fokine, D'Annunzio's *Pisanella*. I knew little then about Meyerhold's productions, but I did know that D'Annunzio was a phrasemonger and Ida Rubinstein was a wealthy lady who was after success in the theater. In Paris Meyerhold met Guillaume Apollinaire; they became friends. Apollinaire clearly understood at once that the heart of the matter lay not in D'Annunzio, not in Ida Rubinstein, not in Bakst's sets, but in the psychological perturbations of the young Petersburg director.

When I made Meyerhold's acquaintance in the fall of 1920 he was forty-six and already gray-haired: sharp-featured, with prominent bushy eyebrows and a very long aquiline nose that resembled a beak.

TEO (the theater section of the People's Commissariat of Education) was situated in a mansion opposite Alexandrovsky Park. Meyerhold was pacing up and down a large room— perhaps because he was cold, perhaps because he didn't feel comfortable sitting in a boss' armchair at the traditional desk with folders full of papers to be signed. He gave the impression of a bird screaming; he was saying that he liked my poetry, then all of a sudden he ran up to me, threw back his head, which looked something like a head of a heron or a condor, and announced: "Your place is here. The October Revolution in art! You'll be in charge of all the children's theaters of the republic." I tried to protest; I was no pedagogue, and didn't know the faintest thing about the art of theater. Meyerhold cut me short: "You are a poet, and children need poetry. Poetry and revolution! . . . To hell with the art of theater! We'll talk about that later. . . . And I've signed the order appointing you to this position. Come to work tomorrow."

At that time Meyerhold—like Mayakovsky—was an obsessive iconoclast. He was not heading a government office, he was fighting against the same esthetics and easy morality that the hero of *The Sea Gull* had spoken of.

Not long ago I appeared on television in Geneva. A young girl waylaid me and said that she had to make up my face. I protested: I was going to speak about the problem of malnutrition in underdeveloped countries, what did my looks have to do with it, and, besides, it did not befit my advanced age to powder my face for the first time in my life. The girl answered that those were the rules, everybody had to have make-up, and she smeared my face with a thin layer of yellowish cream. It occurred to me then that the light of memory is as glaring as the light of TV studios, and that I have been involuntarily putting a layer of cream over the sharp features of some of the people I talk about. But somehow I do not want to do that with Meyerhold; I'll attempt to describe him without smoothing over the details.

He had a difficult character, one which combined kindness with a quick temper, a sophisticated personality with fanaticism. Like some outstanding people whom I have met in my life, he suffered from morbid suspiciousness, was jealous without reason, suspected intrigues where there weren't any.

Our first quarrel was stormy but short. One member of the Navy brought me a play for children where all the characters were fish (the Menshevists were carps) and the play ended with the triumph of the "Soviet of Fish Commissars." I thought the play was awful and I turned it down. All of a sudden I was called to Meyerhold's office; he had the play on the desk in front of him. He asked me irritably why I turned the play down, and without waiting for me to finish my reply began to shout that I was against revolutionary propaganda, against the October Revolution in the theater. Then it was my turn to get angry; I called Meyerhold's words "demogoguery." Vsevolod Emilievich lost his temper, called the building superintendent and ordered: "Arrest Ehrenburg for sabotage." The superintendent refused to carry out the order and suggested Meyerhold get in touch with the Secret Police. I was furious and left, determined never again to set foot inside the TEO. The next morning I received a phone call from Vsevolod Emilievich: he absolutely had to see me, to talk over the Punch and Judy theaters. I went back to the TEO, and everything went on as if the scene of the previous day had never taken place. . . .

Vsevolod Emilievich became sick. I visited him a few times in the hospital—he lay there with his head covered in bandages. He talked to me about his plans, asked what was going on at the TEO, wondered if I had been attending the new performances. Perhaps a certain irony was evident in my replies, because Meyerhold sometimes chided me for lack of faith, even cynicism. Once, when I spoke about the gap between many of these projects and reality, he raised himself up and burst out laughing: "You, in the role of the man in charge of all the children's theaters of the republic! Even Dickens wouldn't have been able to imagine something better!" His bandages were like a turban and Vsevolod Emilievich, gaunt and long-nosed, looked like an Oriental magician. I laughed in turn and observed that it was not Dickens but Meyerhold who had signed my appointment.

I attended several performances of *The Dawns*. It was a poor play, and the production as well was fairly haphazard. Meyerhold was struggling against "the three walls" that Treplyov had spoken about, against footlights, against painted sets. He wanted to bring the stage closer to the audience. The theater itself was tasteless—it had been a famous café-chantant where Muscovites used to watch seminude "starlets," but it was in such condition by this time that its former glories were barely apparent. The theater was not heated and everyone sat there in military overcoats and sheepskin coats. From the lips of actors the most thunderous words burst forth accompanied by delicate clouds of vapor. Some actors had been placed among the audience, they unexpectedly darted onto the stage where there were gray cubes and, for some reason, ropes hanging. Sometimes spectators came to the stage as well: Red Army servicemen with a brass band, workers. (I remember that Meyerhold also wanted to place actors in one of the boxes; they were to play Menshevists and Socialist revolutionaries and respond with appropriate cues. Vsevolod Emilievich told me regretfully that he had had to abandon the idea—the spectators might think they were real counter-revolutionaries and a fight might ensue.) I was present at that performance when an actor solemnly read the latest news dispatch: the taking of Perekop by the Red Army. The reaction of the audience was beyond description. . . .

The production was attacked at the discussion that always followed: Mayakovsky defended Meyerhold. I don't really know what to say about the production: it was an organic part of that era, along with Mayakovsky's propaganda verses, with carnival processions organized by the "left" artists, with the climate of those years. Rehearsals for Mayakovsky's *Mystery-Bouffe* also seemed to me an event that expressed the spirit of the epoch. It was difficult to like the performance, but you wanted to defend and even to glorify it.

I wrote in 1921: "Meyerhold's productions are faulty in execution but splendid in conception: theatricality is not only to be compressed but also instantly to be done away with, so that the footlights disappear and the actors mingle with the spectators." And this is how Mayakovsky concluded his speech at the dispute about *The Dawns*: "Long live Meyerhold's theater, even though it has begun with a bad production!" . . .

In the summer of 1923 I was living in Berlin. Meyerhold arrived and we met. Vsevolod Emilievich suggested that I turn my novel *The D. E. Trust* into a play for his theater; he said that the play ought to be a mix of circus acts with an agitational apotheosis. I was not too taken with the idea of turning my novel into a play: I had started to cool off in regard to circus shows and to Constructivism as well; I was reading Dickens avidly and writing a sentimental novel with a complicated plot, *The Love of Jeanne Ney*. I knew, however, how hard it was to contradict Meyerhold, and I answered that I would think about his suggestion.

Shortly thereafter a theater magazine published by Meyerhold's followers ran an article in the form of a fantastic story about how I had been abducted by Tairov who had contracted me to turn my novel into a counter-revolutionary play.

(Many times in his life Meyerhold suspected Tairov, that kind and honest man, of a desire to liquidate him by whatever means. This was a part of that suspicious character of Meyerhold's which I have already mentioned. Tairov never planned to perform *The D. E. Trust*.)

When I returned to the Soviet Union I read that Meyerhold was working on a play called *The D. E. Trust*, written by a certain Podgaetsky "after the novels by Ehrenburg and Kellerman." I realized the only thing that would stop Meyerhold was to tell him that I myself wanted to prepare a theater or cinema version of my novel. I wrote him in March of 1924, addressing my letter to "Dear Vsevolod Emilievich" and concluding it by "cordially yours": "Our meeting last summer and especially our discussion of the possibility of my reworking *The D. E. Trust* gave me reason to believe that your attitude to my work was a friendly and considerate one. That is why I have decided first of all to ask you to renounce your production, assuming the newspaper article about it is correct. . . . After all, I am a living author and not a classic. . . ."

Meyerhold's answer was terrifying; his rage was perfectly expressed in it and I would never bring it up did I not love Meyerhold with all his excesses: "Citizen Ehrenburg! I do not understand by what right you ask me to 'give up the production' of Comrade Podgaetsky's play. Do you think that our talk in Berlin gives you this right? But that talk made it quite clear that even in case you decided to rework your novel you would write a play only fit to be performed in any city of the Entente states." . . .

I never saw the production. Judging from remarks by my friends and reviewers who were well disposed toward Meyerhold, Podgaetsky wrote a poor play. Vsevolod Emilievich made a very interesting production out of it: Europe perished noisily, the sets moved about all over the place, actors frantically changed their make-up, jazz roared. I received some unexpected support from Mayakovsky: when the production of *The D. E. Trust* was being discussed he said, "As a play *D. E.* is an absolute zero. . . . A piece of fiction can be turned into a play only by a writer who is superior to its authors—in this case somebody superior to Ehrenburg and Kellerman." However, the performance was quite a hit, and the Java tobacco factory even brought out a new brand of cigarettes called *D. E.* And because of this stupid incident I didn't see Meyerhold for over seven years. . . .

Whenever I was in Moscow I attended Meyerhold's productions: *The Magnanimous Cuckold, The Death of Tarelkin, The Forest*. I'd buy a ticket, scared that Vsevolod Emilievich might spot me in the audience. (It was hard to find any agitational apotheosis in these productions; they could have been performed in any city of the Entente states. Vsevolod Emilievich never stayed in the same spot long.)

Meyerhold never followed a straight path; he kept climbing mountains, he moved in detours. While his followers were still loudly announcing their aim of destroying theater, Vsevolod Emilievich was already working on his production of *The Forest*. Many people could not understand what they thought was the transformation of a furious iconoclast—why was he attracted to Ostrovsky, to the tragedy of art, to love? (In precisely the same way Mayakovsky's followers could not understand why in 1923 he wrote "About It" while shortly before he had condemned lyric poetry altogether. Interestingly, *The Forest* was produced shortly after the poem "About

It" was written. Mayakovsky the poet had already returned to poetry, whereas Mayakovsky the editor of *LEF* severely chastized Vsevolod Emilievich for his return to theater: "For me the production of *The Forest* is repulsive. . . .")

Paintings are displayed in museums, books are preserved in libraries, but the only thing we have of theater performances we never attended are dry newspaper reviews. It is easy to see the connection between "About It" and Mayakovsky's early poetry, between Picasso's "Guernica" and his paintings of the blue period. But it is difficult for me to perceive what carried over from Meyerhold's prerevolutionary performances to his *Forest* and *The Inspector General*. One thing is indisputable: whatever detours Meyerhold made in his creative development, his path was always the same.

The Forest was an excellent production and it moved its audience. Meyerhold made many discoveries in this play, expressed the tragedy of art in his own way. However, there was one detail in it that enraged Meyerhold's enemies (or, perhaps, made them happy): a green wig on one of the actors. The production ran for many years. Once, after it was shown in Leningrad, there was a public discussion. Vsevolod Emilievich received many questions: he was amused, he got angry, he cracked jokes. Finally came the question: "Would you please explain the meaning of the green wig?" He turned to the actors and asked: "As a matter of fact, what does it mean? Whose idea was it?" After this discussion the green wig disappeared. I do not know whether Meyerhold was playacting his amazement or whether he was genuinely surprised (which seems more plausible) because he had forgotten a detail invented, naturally, by no one else but himself. (I have often heard puzzled questions like: "Whose idea was it?"; and sometimes these questions referred to issues much more vital than this ill-fated wig.)

Meyerhold was regarded as a threat by people who were opposed to everything new; his very name entered the vocabulary. Some of his critics failed to observe (or did not want to observe) that Meyerhold kept moving ahead; they would attack him on a point he had by then forgotten.

Vsevolod Emilievich was not afraid to give up esthetic concepts that he had regarded as correct only a day earlier. In 1920, when he produced *The Dawns*, he broke away from

Soeur Beatrice and *Balaganchik*. Later he ridiculed the "bio-mechanics" that he himself had invented.

Treplyov says in the first act of *The Sea Gull* that it is new forms that are the important thing, and in the last act of the play before committing suicide he admits to himself: "I think more and more it's not a question of old or new forms—what matters is to write without thinking about any forms, and allowing whatever you write to come straight from the heart." In 1938 Vsevolod Emilievich said to me that the struggle was not between old and new art forms but between art and imitations of art.

He never renounced what he considered essential, he stepped over "isms," devices, esthetic canons, but he kept true to his understanding of what art is; he was constantly in rebellion, in the grip of inspiration, always aflame.

After all, what was so threatening in his production of Chekhov's vaudevilles? By that time everybody had forgotten about "left art." Mayakovsky had been solemnly proclaimed a poet of genius. But Meyerhold's production was attacked regardless of that. He could say the most ordinary things but there was something in his voice, his eyes, his smile that went against the grain of people who could not stand the creative fire of a true artist.

In the spring of 1930 in Paris I saw Meyerhold's *Inspector General*. It was in a small theater on the rue de la Gaîté, where cheap vaudevilles or heart-rending melodramas were usually performed for the inhabitants of this remote district. There was a small inconvenient stage and no foyer (at the intermission the spectators would go out into the street); in short, the place was totally inadequate. I was shaken by the performance. I had long before grown cool to the esthetic passions of my youth and I was reluctant to see the play—I loved Gogol too jealously. And then on stage I saw everything that magnetized me in Gogol: the acute anguish of the artist and the panorama of cruel and eternal vulgarity.

I know that Meyerhold was accused of distorting the text of the play, of sacrilege. True, this *Inspector General* did not resemble the performances of my childhood and my youth; the text had been broadened, as it were, yet it contained no interpolations, everything in it was Gogol's. Is it possible to believe for even a minute that the only message of Gogol's play lies in exposing provincial officials of the reign of Nicholas the First? For Gogol's contemporaries *The Inspector General* was indeed primarily a biting satire on the social system and mores, but like all great works of art it has survived the phase of contemporaneity. It moves people still, a hundred years after the town governors and postmasters of the era of Nicholas have vanished. Meyerhold widened the limits of *The Inspector General*. Is there any sacrilege in that? After all, stage versions of Tolstoy and Dostoevsky novels are considered noble pursuits, although they narrow the scope of the works. . . .

Andrey Biely not only loved Gogol, he was intoxicated by Gogol, and perhaps many of the artistic failings of the author of *The Silver Dove* and *Petersburg* can be explained by his inability to cast off Gogol's spell. And it was Andrey Biely, after he had seen Meyerhold's *Inspector General*, who came out in passionate defense of the production.

When the play was performed in Paris the audience was mostly French: theater directors, actors, theater buffs, writers, artists—it looked like a show of celebrities. Louis Jouvet was there, Picasso, Dullin, Cocteau, Eluard, Dérain, Gaston Baty. . . . And when the performance ended these people, who were reputedly satiated with art, who were usually chary of their approval, got to their feet and gave it a stormy ovation.

I found my way backstage. Vsevolod Emilievich, overcome with excitement, was standing in a small dressing room. His hair had turned more gray and his nose become still longer. Seven years had passed. . . . I said I could not bear it any longer and had come to thank him. He embraced me tightly.

After that there was never any strife or the slightest chill between us. We never talked about our stupid quarrel. We met in Paris, in Moscow, had long conversations and were sometimes silent—the way you can be silent when you are genuinely close to someone.

When Meyerhold decided to produce *The Inspector General* he said to the actors: "What you must see is an aquarium where the water has not been changed for a long time, a greenish water, where the fish move in circles and emit slow bubbles." And to me he said that when working on *The Inspector General* he often remembered his high-school days in Penza.

(In 1948 I was walking with Alexander Fadeyev along a street in Penza. Suddenly Fadeyev stopped. "That was Meyerhold's house." We stood for a while in silence, then Fadeyev uttered an anguished exclamation, made a waving motion with his hand, and began walking quickly back to the hotel.)

Meyerhold hated stale water, yawning, emptiness: he often resorted to masks precisely because he was terrified by them—and what he found terrifying in them was not some mystical fear of nonbeing, but the petrified vulgarity of everyday life. The concluding scene of *The Inspector General*, the long table in *Woe from Wit*, the characters of *The Mandate*, even the vaudevilles of Chekhov—all of these were the same battles of an artist against vulgarity.

It was no accident that he became a Communist—he knew quite clearly that the world needed to be changed. He always based his views on his own experience, not on someone else's arguments. He seemed an old man among us. Mayakovsky was born with the Revolution, but Meyerhold had trodden many paths by that time: Stanislavsky, Kommissarzhevskaya, the Petersburg symbolists, *Balaganchik*, Blok and his tortured snowstorms, *The Love for Three Oranges*, and much more. Back in the days when we sat in the Rotonde we used to wonder what the mysterious Doctor Dapertutto looked like. (That was Meyerhold's artistic pseudonym.)

Of all the people I have a right to call my friends, Vsevolod Emilievich was the oldest. I was merely born in the nineteenth century, whereas Meyerhold had actually lived in it; he had visited Chekhov, worked with Vera Kommissarzhevskaya, he knew Scriabin, Yermolova. . . . And the most surprising thing was that he stayed always young; he was always inventing something new, always roaring like a thunderstorm in May.

He was under attack all his life. In 1911 Menshikov, a journalist from *Novoe Vremya*, enraged by his production of Mussorgsky's *Boris Godunov*, wrote: "I suppose it was from his Jewish psyche that Mr. Meyerhold took the constables, not from Pushkin, who has neither constables nor knouts. . . ." The truth is that some articles written about Meyerhold a quarter of a century later were neither more respectable nor more just than this one. . . .

There was nothing of the martyr in him: he was passionately in love with life—children and noisy rallies, carnivals and Renoir's paintings, poetry and construction scaffolding. I was present a few times at rehearsals: Vsevolod Emilievich not only gave explanations, he also used to act himself. I remember the rehearsals for Chekhov's vaudevilles. Meyerhold was over sixty but he amazed his young actors by his stamina, the brilliance of his discoveries, by his enormous spiritual delight.

I have said already that theater performances disappear—cannot be resurrected. We know that André Chénier was a superb poet, but we can only take it for granted that his contemporary Talma was a great actor. In spite of this, creative work does not disappear—it may merely be invisible for a while like a river that goes underground. I watch a theater performance in Paris, everybody admires it—"How innovative!"—and I remember Meyerhold's productions. I remember them when I go to many theaters in Moscow as well. Vakhtangov wrote: "Meyerhold was creating the theater of the future—and it will be the future that will repay him." It was not Vakhtangov only who admired Meyerhold, but also Craig and Jouvet and many other great directors. Eisenstein said to me once that there would have been no Eisenstein without Meyerhold.

In August of 1930 he wrote to me: "The theater may perish. Its enemies are on the alert. Moscow is full of people for whom Meyerhold's theater is an eyesore. Ah, it's a long and boring story!"

Our last meetings were sad. I returned from Spain in December of 1937. In January a government decree was published which announced the closing of Meyerhold's theater because of its "alien" nature. Meyerhold's wife Zinaida Nikolaevna suffered an acute nervous breakdown. Vsevolod Emilievich behaved with fortitude, talked about art, poetry, reminisced about Paris. He continued to work—he was thinking about a production of *Hamlet* although he did not think he would ever be allowed to stage it. He said: "Now, it seems to me, I could do it. I couldn't have ventured it earlier. Even if all the plays in the world disappeared and only *Hamlet* remained, then theater would remain as well."

I used to meet Peter Konchalovsky at the Meyerholds'—he was then painting a portrait of Vsevolod Emilievich. Konchalovsky loved Meyerhold passionately, and his portrait expressed Meyerhold's inspiration, anxieties, spiritual beauty. During that same period I also used to meet the pianist Oborin there, and other young enthusiasts for whom Meyerhold remained the Master.

Stanislavsky also gave Meyerhold moral support, and often phoned him trying to cheer him up. The noose was tightening. . . .

I have to mention, too, that Meyerhold received enormous support during this hard period from Zinaida Nikolaevna. I have in front of me a copy of a letter that Vsevolod Emilievich wrote to his wife from Gorenki, a resort area, in October of 1938: "I came to Gorenki on the thirteenth, looked at the birchtrees and caught my breath. . . . I saw those leaves scattered in the air. Scattered, and still as if they were frozen. . . . Still, and yet they seemed to be expecting something. . . . How hopeless they seemed! I could count the last seconds of their life like the pulse of a dying man. Will I find them still alive when I come to Gorenki again—in a day, in an hour? As I stood that day looking at the golden fairy-tale world of autumn, at all those wonders, I kept whispering to myself: 'Zina, Zinochka, look at these wonders and do not leave me, I love you—you are my wife, my sister, my mother, my friend, my beloved, golden as this wonder-working nature!' Zina, do not leave me! There is nothing in the world more terrible than loneliness!"

We parted in the spring of 1938; I was going to Spain. It was a somber parting. I never saw him again: Meyerhold was arrested in June of 1939 in Leningrad; on February 1, 1940, he was sentenced to ten years of solitary confinement. His death certificate is dated February 2.

In 1955 a young state attorney who had never heard Meyerhold's name before told me how Vsevolod Emilievich had been slandered. He read me his declaration before the secret military tribunal that condemned him:

"I am sixty-six. I want my daughter and my friends to know some day that I remained an honest Communist until the end."

As the attorney read these words, he rose. I rose too.

Il'ja Erenburg, *Ljudi, gody, žizn'*, in *Sobranie sočinenij v devjati tomax*, vol. 8 (Moscow, 1966), pp. 333–343.

Meyerhold to Ilya Ehrenburg

Moscow
March 18, 1924

Citizen Ehrenburg:

I do not understand the basis for your request that I "renounce production" of Com. Podgaetsky's play.

On the basis of our conversation in Berlin?

Surely that conversation made it perfectly clear that even if you were to redo your novel you would write the kind of play that could be staged in any city of the Entente, while in my theater, which is and will remain at the service of the Revolution, we need tendentious plays, plays that have only one purpose: to serve the needs of the Revolution.

Let me remind you: you absolutely rejected the idea of any Communist purpose, referring to your lack of faith in the social revolution and your native pessimism.

During this entire season you never proposed sending me a play, nor in your letter of March 5 did you say anything about redoing your book for my theater.

Podgaetsky's play, which I accepted in November 1923, uses material from Kellerman, Sinclair, Amp, and Ehrenburg, but its agitational intent and its dramatic structure are original.

Meyerhold to the All-Russian Society of Dramatists

Moscow
January 7 and 10, 1931

Please note the following remarks regarding the authorship of *D. S. E.*

At the beginning of 1924 M. G. Podgaetsky delivered to the Meyerhold Theater some *draft* sketches for a rewriting of Ilya Ehrenburg's novel *The D. E. Trust* as a play. Previously to this I had talked with Ilya Ehrenburg (in Berlin, the summer of 1923) about the possibility of redoing *The D. E. Trust* as a play. But since Ehrenburg was unwilling to give the play the ideological framework I proposed to him, our discussions went no further. However, I kept in mind the possibility of redoing Ehrenburg's novel, so I eagerly agreed to listen to the draft sketches Comrade Podgaetsky proposed.

After hearing these sketches I and other members of the directorial board of the theater indicated to Com. Podgaetsky that the play should be conceived as a political revue, constantly subject to change depending on new events in international affairs. We gave him a basic political slant—in fact the entire framework of the revue—and suggested to him a series of scenes and plot situations; one of the members of the directorial board (Zinaida Raikh) even proposed a new story line to parallel the one in Ehrenburg's novel: the drilling of an underwater tunnel.

On the basis of these suggestions Com. Podgaetsky made a new variant of the play, which was read to an audience consisting of members of a military school who were doing political work with our theater collective. Their suggestions, as well as another discussion of the play by the directorial board, provided material for a reworking of the play by five students in the directing course at the Meyerhold workshops (B. Ivanter, L. Kritsberg, N. Loyter, Zinaida Raikh, N. Ekk) under my supervision. After this reworking we began rehearsals. During the rehearsals a number of changes were made in the text.

D. E. opened in Leningrad on June 15, 1924. The audience didn't like the finale of the play, and we were delighted to receive a proposal for rewriting the last two episodes from one of the members of the audience—a student at the Communist University. That proposal and a number of further corrections formed the basis for a new finale that I wrote myself. Before we opened the play in Moscow on June 30 there was a dress rehearsal; some party workers present at that rehearsal gave us a number of suggestions for changes in the text, which we in fact then made.

The changes made in the revue from performance to performance made it unrecognizable when compared to the first version. Very substantial changes were introduced at revivals of *D. E.* first in 1926, then in 1928. For that reason we in the theater more than once questioned whether we should leave Com. Podgaetsky's name in the program. We did leave it, taking into consideration his difficult material situation and his illness, despite the fact that nothing of his work remained in the production.

The new revue *D. S. E.* was commissioned by the theater from N. K. Mologin, one of our actors, and is fundamentally different from the revue *D. E.* It is no longer simply a variant of *D. E.* but a new work. Not only were entire episodes changed (as before), but the structure of the entire piece as well. The fantastic elements have been removed: the destruction of Europe has become its enslavement; the plot of the underwater tunnel has been completely discarded and a new situation introduced. A whole list of new themes has been added, which by their nature could not have existed earlier (the five-year plan, the shock-worker movement, the struggle against saboteurs, etc.). Nor did Com. Mologin use Com. Podgaetsky's text while working on this revue; he used my directorial score, Ehrenburg's novel *The D. E. Trust*, and material from recent newspapers and magazines.

The foregoing should suffice to prove that Com. Mologin is the author of *D. S. E.* and that Com. Podgaetsky's pretensions to authorship of the piece are groundless. If Com. Podgaetsky wishes to continue his claim, then an entire group of people who have worked on the play are willing to testify against him.

> Director
> People's Artist of the Republic
> V. Meyerhold

Yury Olesha

It was in Odessa. I was a high-school student. I was in a moviehouse, the Urania, watching *The Picture of Dorian Gray*. Meyerhold played a part in it. He was lean, sinuous, smoked a cigar, one eye was enlarged by a monocle whose cord hung across his face; he wore a tailcoat with an orchid in his lapel.

That was my first encounter with Meyerhold.

The second encounter took place in Moscow. I was standing on the corner of Tverskaya Street and Chernyshevsky Lane, by the Mossovet building. It was the anniversary of the October Revolution. Marchers were going past. Among them was Meyerhold, at the head of a group of actors. He was wearing a sheepskin coat, high boots, and a gray sheepskin cap tilted to the side.

"Meyerhold," I thought. *"The Death of Tarelkin.* The innovator. No curtain. An honorary Red Army soldier. How proudly he holds his head. Moscow. I'm in Moscow. October. It's October. Meyerhold is singing. The red banners of the marchers. Workers. Workers and actors. Moscow. There goes Meyerhold. What a nose he has. A strange nose. A big curved bony nose. Heroic noseness. Often the subject of fictions and falsehoods."

At the third encounter we met. After the opening of *A Conspiracy of Feelings* at the Vakhtangov Theater, Meyerhold gave his opinion of it to the actors, the producers, and me, the author of the play. That's a custom with the Vakhtangovites. After each new production they invite Meyerhold backstage and he tells them what he thinks of it.

After a while Meyerhold produced a play of mine. I am proud that my ideas found some resonance in this great artist. When he started working on the play I understood the main thing: he was a poet. During rehearsals he once whispered into my ear: "It's Cinderella." In other words, he saw in my play what kept eluding me—he saw what I intended to put into it but failed. As far as I am concerned, the play (*A List of Benefits*) was a failure. I made it very difficult for the actress who was to play the main part. Zinaida Raikh acted brilliantly, but I think that if I had realized earlier that the pattern underlying my play was, unconsciously, the pattern of the Cinderella story the play would probably have been better.

There exists a widespread notion that Meyerhold paid no attention to playwrights. I think that Meyerhold was such a discerning judge of what was good and what was bad in art that any author, even the most conceited one, could trust his judgment. I often felt like protesting his opinion, I had my doubts, but in the end I invariably told myself: "Yes, he is right, and I am probably mistaken."

I remember Mayakovsky's attitude toward Meyerhold.

"You aren't tired of it yet, Meyerhold?" he'd address the host when Meyerhold's guests asked Mayakovsky to recite his poems. He interrupted the reading several times. "You aren't tired yet?"

Once there was a conversation about Edgar Allan Poe. Somebody said that the American writer Treadwell had a play about Edgar Allan Poe. I asked about the title of the play. Nobody liked the title (I don't remember it now) and we began thinking up a new title for a play about Edgar Allan Poe. Meyerhold said simply: "Edgar." He said it with wonderful tenderness. "Edgar."

And I agreed with him. Only such a title, just his name, which sounded so tender and helpless, was appropriate for a play about that poet's sad life. One day Poe had a business appointment which could have resulted in great good fortune. He was on his way to the appointment when he saw a girl skipping rope. He began to skip rope with her and broke the heel of his shoe. It was unthinkable to show up at this business appointment with a broken heel, and so good fortune eluded him.

Meyerhold told us that.

Meyerhold would speak with the same tenderness about Lermontov. And yet, all the same, he was a crude person. In the enviable sense of the word. In the scene in *The Inspector General* when Khlestakov tells his lies, the light suddenly goes off. Exactly at that place when Marya Antonovna says that *Yuri Miloslavsky* was written by Zagoskin. I asked Meyerhold whether the light went off at that place because that was where a drop of exposure suddenly fell into the torrent of lies. In other words, did Meyerhold not introduce the theme of punishment, perhaps, by switching off the light in this scene? I thought I perceived in the sudden disappearance of light something mystical. Meyerhold got indignant, said that was all nonsense: "Look, he was just waving his arms about too energetically, and knocked over the lamp. . . ."

During rehearsals he takes off his jacket. All he wears is a striped jersey. His hair is all messed up. He goes to the far end of the hall and watches from there. If he likes what an actor does he shouts, "All right!"

He walks quickly out of the darkness to the footlights. He

gets up onto the stage and walks across it, bending slightly in the waist. Lean, in the striped jersey, he resembles the skipper of a boat.

Then he "demonstrates."

I think those Meyerholdian "demonstrations" were a theater in themselves, a thrilling, fantastic theater. If those rehearsals had been open to the public, people would have seen the greatest actor of our time.

In this theater—closed, unfortunately, to the general public—one heard a unique kind of applause. The director of the theater transforms himself for a moment into an actor. A dazzling actor. And the actor who is to play the role that for this moment is being performed by a fantastic director realizes that he will not be able to play it as well as the director does. Envy would be quite natural in such a case. But the actor rewards his rival with applause instead. Igor Ilyinsky said to me once: "Sometimes I disagree with this or that suggestion of Vsevolod Emilievich. I think it would be better to do not what he says but something else. I try something else. It turns out worse than what he suggested. And then I have to agree that he was right."

And it was Ilyinsky who said that!

Meyerhold's physical endurance is amazing. He is indefatigable. I saw him demonstrate the death of a sailor in Vishnevsky's play *The Last Decisive Battle*. The scene was like a dance. Meyerhold danced a strange dance, close to acrobatics, one which demanded a special grace and lightness. He repeated it several times. Then, as if nothing special had happened, he climbed down into the auditorium to watch the actor perform the same scene. He paced about the auditorium, moving close to the footlights and then away again, shouted: "All right!"—and again ran up onto the stage and demonstrated the scene.

Evenings, the theater director appears in the auditorium. The performance is on. The director stands by the door, leaning against the doorpost. The glow of light from the stage touches him somewhat. Elegant, masculine, he stands there with his profile to the public, arms folded. At times when he is particularly attentive he raises his chin so high that his head seems to be lying upon his shoulders. And yet he doesn't unfold his arms. This happens when the rhythm of what is happening on the stage enters into some harmony with the accompanying music, a harmony known to Meyerhold alone.

And if there is a friend of his seated nearby, Meyerhold turns to him afterward and winks an eye at him. It means; "Well, what do you think of that? All right, isn't it?"

I was once at a rehearsal at the Moscow Art Theater. Stanislavsky came into his box while the rehearsal was going on. He didn't want to cause the slightest disturbance by his presence. An enormously tall man, he began slowly, with great difficulty, folding himself up in order to sit down on the chair. Very slowly, with extreme care, afraid that the chair might squeak and, although the chair didn't, an expression of alarm never left his face until he was seated. And he sat down quietly and gently as a butterfly.

Then he turned his attention to the actors.

Every emotion the actors expressed registered itself on his face, instantly, like a grimace, the kind children make. You would have thought this great theatrical reformer was watching a play for the first time in his life. To be childlike is a necessary quality in a genuine artist. Meyerhold is full of that quality. Both teacher and pupil were equally pure, simply, and lofty.

Meyerhold is a connoisseur of music, painting, and architecture. He loves music passionately. He is the great friend of a number of young composers, many of whom were his protégés: Shostakovich, Shebalin, Gavrila Popov.

Meyerhold is very fond of young people. His unity with the younger generation was determined once and for all when he joined the ranks of revolutionaries. He is on a first-name basis with young people. He is enthusiastic about the exploits of young pilots and seamen.

You can spend a lot of time trying to think up ringing slogans in which you try to unite your own life with the life of the age. So, for instance, I can say about my childhood: the name of my childhood was the Wright brothers. When I was a child I never thought I would be a writer and that art would be my life's activity. But that's what happened. And I even understand the Wright brothers now as a function of art.

The name Meyerhold could serve as such a ringing slogan. If there is indeed a new art that came into existence after the October Revolution, an art that now amazes the world, a

Soviet art, then one can safely say that the first years of that art had a name. Meyerhold.

He invented everything that others now claim as their own. The whole style of contemporary Soviet theater derives from him.

He keeps on inventing, furious and indefatigable. It's strange to think that this man, arguing with a fireman about smoking during rehearsals, this joyous, youthful spirit, laughing together with a group of Comsomols, this artist, who can argue all night about art and head off to rehearsal in the morning as if it were nothing—that this man is sixty years old!

His youthfulness is one of the wonders of the Revolution. He dreams of a new theater. Let us wish for him, on his sixtieth birthday, that the theater he dreams of will soon be built. That the theater building now arising on Triumphal Square, with a new kind of stage space designed by Meyerhold, will soon be finished, and that this amazing individual will continue with his customary brilliance to affirm the glory of Soviet art.

Jurij Oleša, "Ljubov' k Mejerxol'du," *Večernjaja Moskva*, February 9, 1934, no page numbers.

Meyerhold to Lev Oborin

Vichy/Nice
October 19/24, 1928

Dear Lev Nikolaevich,

Reading your letter (October 8/28), I was so happy that your *emotional* outburst for a moment—while you were writing the letter—flashed so brilliantly that it gave me back my faith in you as a strong, forceful, healthy, *resolute* human being. I rejoiced, and forgot about my weak heart as I ran to send off a telegram, to let you know that "the incident has been liquidated."

Well! Let's shake hands. There. Never again will I "grudge you my grudges."

After a year's acquaintance, I must confess that there is a great deal I haven't learned about you, a great deal I never observed. You have never written me a word about the continuation of our friendship. And I do so hope for that continuation! The element of music so overwhelmingly unites me to you that our acquaintance can be a powerful impetus not only for me (a new surge of creativity) but for you as well.

Autumn is wonderful here just now. What strength and health it possesses! I observe it and think that my own autumn ought to be this way. I want it to be. But oh, what intriguing modulations we find in nature! In the soft rustle of yellow leaves I hear the music of spring—the spring that has just passed us, and the one that will return to us soon again. There is no distinct autumn, no distinct spring. It is all intertwined, like a garland of verses.

That is why I love young people so much. And why I love you, dear Lev Nikolaevich. Don't be angry, just write me a letter—dry, devoid of emotion if you like, but be sure to write.

What can I tell you about my heart? It's better!

I wrote Hesia Lokshina that Dürer's skeleton on horseback with the scythe over his shoulder had turned his horse from my door and stopped at some other. I've been granted a reprieve. My heart still beats, but from time to time my weak blood pressure makes me think: *memento mori*! Yet the sun pours down such marvellous colors that life seems everlasting. I would dance with pleasure, but let me have a first-class accompanist, I won't dance to the wrong music.

In a few days we are off to the south of France, to the seacoast. We'll spend about two weeks there. Then to Paris, a week there. Then to Moscow.

Write: 8, rue Martin Bernard, Mme. Olga Sossine, Paris XIII. They will forward your letter south to me immediately. I very much want another letter from you (better yet, two).

I'm not very happy with my work in the film. It's not at all what I can do as a film actor. What I did was the stupidest sort of faking. Monkey-like. But I intend to work again. You'll see—I'll get better.

Still, let me ask for your opinion of my acting.

Yours in friendship,

V.M.

p.s.: Send me the photographs and the reviews right away (how slow it is to type them!) so I can give them to Ansermet as soon as possible, and to the music journals in Paris. And I want to write an article about you myself for one of the magazines. By the way: did you get a copy of a music journal with an article by a certain Parnakh that mentions you? And did you get Josef Hofman's letter to me that I sent you for your archive? Write Hofman right away, and I'll write him. Only send me his address. I forgot to copy it off the letter before I sent it on to you.

Meyerhold to Lev Oborin

Moscow
August 13, 1929

Dear Lev Nikolaevich,
    Tomorrow, Wednesday, August 14, at six in the evening, S. Eisenstein will be showing us his new work *General Line* (at Sovkino, 7 Gnezdov St.). It's the same film I once told you about (he wanted to show it to us—remember?—but the showing never took place).
    Stop by our house (Brusov St.) tomorrow at five o'clock. We'll have a bite to fortify ourselves and then go see *General Line*. By the way, you should try to get to know the young poet Dolmatovsky; it seems to both of us that his poetry is exactly the sort you could set to music very interestingly.
    Be sure to come. Especially since on Friday the sixteenth we are leaving for Kiev (early in the morning). We absolutely must get together before I leave. We must decide finally once and for all which of the plays in our repertory you will write the music for.
    Very best,

V. Meyerhold

Meyerhold to Lev Oborin

Berlin (Barnowsky Theater, Strasemannstrasse, 57)
April 5, 1930

Dear Lev Nikolaevich,

We are sending you a pile of reviews from the opening night of our tour in Berlin (*The Inspector General*). After you've read them (you do read German, no?), please pass them on to Yury Olesha. I'm counting on your kindness in this matter for the following reason: it's crucial that I get you and Olesha together, since we've decided that you will do the music for his extraordinary play. Be sure to ask him to read you his play, no matter what shape it's in. Olesha doesn't have a phone. Drop him a postcard and ask him to call you. Arrange to meet. Say in the postcard that you have our reviews and that you must show them to him. After you and Olesha have read the reviews, be sure to leave them at our place, 12 Brusov St., apt. 11.

Write us as soon as you get this letter. Let us know that you have the reviews, and tell us how you are: your health, what you're doing, do you miss us, to what degree you've stopped loving us, are you doing any composing at all. . . . Don't be lazy, write. If they've started the airmail, write us "Luftpost." We'll be in Berlin until the seventeenth of this month. Write, they'll forward your letter if it misses us. I hope you'll answer *right away*, and we'll have the pleasure of reading sentences composed of words that are normally kept a careful distance apart: "dear" and "Meyerhold," for instance.

Warmest regards, dear boy.

Oh yes, I forgot the most important thing: Zinaida Raikh has taken Berlin by storm. Her Anna Andreevna had a terrific success. The press is competing to find phrases to describe her. She has won everyone's heart, enchanted them all. They all talk about her as an international-class actress.

Meyerhold to Yury Olesha

Paris
May 19, 1930

Dear Yury Karlovich,

We got your letter about Mayakovsky. Sorry that we haven't written you about it until now, or let you know how we are. Today we took a ride with the Dovgalevskys *ins Grüne*, stuck our noses to the ground, and smelled the lilies of the valley. In the car Zinaida Nikolaevna told the Dovgalevskys the plot of your new play *A List of Benefits* (what a splendid title). When we got home we said almost simultaneously (Zinaida Nikolaevna and I): "what a wonderful play!" And the Dovgalevskys were enchanted by it. They also liked *A Conspiracy of Feelings* very much. We're on shore waiting for the weather to change: will or will not Moscow let us play in Paris? The Parisians are filling the streets with love in honor of spring, while like Lermontov's hero "he, darkly brooding, seeks the storm, as if in storm he could find peace." Replace "he" with "we," and storm means our tour.

Your sailor.

Best from Zinaida Nikolaevna and myself to Olga Gustavovna and to Igor.

Meyerhold to Yury Olesha

Hendaye-Plage, Basse s-Pyrénées
France
August 6, 1930

Dear Yury Karlovich,

I had a letter from Moscow yesterday saying that you intend giving your play *A List of Benefits* to the Vakhtangov Theater. The reason, according to the letter: "Raikh doesn't like the play."

Dear Yury Karlovich, that information is untrue. I've been hopping around like an animal who's just been burned by a hot iron and is still being chased with it.

My dear fellow, what happened?

I have centered our entire repertory for 1930–1931 around your play. Traveling around Western Europe, with all the problems our tour has caused us, tired, nervous, sick, I've still found time to work on your play. I've thought up some splendid details for staging it. Two or three times while I've been talking about your play with friends of our theater here in the West, I realized that never before have I been so taken with a play as I am with *A List of Benefits*. What happened? Don't you trust me as a director? Was it the failure of *The Bathhouse*? Was that my fault? Zoshchenko's betrayal? Is his example catching? Did our office insult you in some way? Didn't they send the money I promised? I beg you to let me know immediately (by telegram, please): is the rumor true? Or is it gossip? And anyway, what nonsense, that Zinaida Nikolaevna didn't like the play. Who is trying to cause trouble between us? Zinaida Nikolaevna is even more enthusiastic about the play than I am. I have heard her explain the tragic scheme of your great new tragedy, and how taken she is by its lyric surge.

When I learned of Zoshchenko's betrayal I was upset, but I didn't suffer. Because Zoshchenko is only a casual guest in the theater. But you were created for the theater. And there are very few of those. They are unique. Mayakovsky is gone. Erdman is suffering from a depression. Selvinsky will come back to us, but who knows when?

My dear friend, think it over!

I await your telegram.

Very best to Olga Gustavovna and Igor from Zinaida Nikolaevna and myself.

V. Meyerhold

Telegram from Yury Olesha to Meyerhold

Dear Vsevolod Emilievich,

I think I've written a bad play. It has to be worked on, and I just haven't got the strength for it. If you mention Erdman's depression, then I've got a depression myself, just as bad as his. I have no intention of giving the play to anybody. I'm living in Odessa.

IV.
Meyerhold and Pushkin

There is often present in an artist's creative enterprise a distinct image or theme—sometimes it is an entire work—by which we recognize and understand his creation. It is occasionally even the precise absence of that image or incompleteness of that work that points to its importance.

A gesture of the hand, poised against a vista of rocks and hills, let's say, in Leonardo.

A plangent duet between a father and a daughter in Verdi's operas—a duet conspicuously avoided in his <u>Otello</u>.

The passage from the world of the present to the world of the future in the plays of Mayakovsky.

The unrealized plans for filming Marx's <u>Capital</u> in the work of Sergei Eisenstein.

In Meyerhold's work, two playtexts are associated: Pushkin's <u>Boris Godunov</u> and Shakespeare's <u>Hamlet</u>. The theme that unites them is clear: the legitimacy of succession, the ties between father and son. We have noted already the importance of the unachieved <u>Hamlet</u> in Meyerhold's imagination. He never succeeded in staging <u>Boris Godunov</u> either, but it is worth examining in some detail his work on the text, precisely because that work remained work only: it never came to fulfillment, thereby to pass out of his imagination. Once created, a theatrical spectacle endures briefly, changes rapidly, and then dies—of petrifaction or attrition. Meyerhold is unique among directors because he adhered constantly and defiantly to the idea of art as experiment, as a dialectic between form and ideology that could never be resolved. We observe this in all his mature work: a rapid switch from one perspective to another, from one set of emphases to another.

For a theater director the idea of perfection, of stasis, is usually unavoidable: after opening night the thing is finished, essentially. Few directors are able, like Meyerhold, to have four or five sequent redactions, restagings, of the same playtext. His productions were moments in a dialogue with his audience.

And what attracted him to <u>Boris Godunov</u>, what underlay much of his work on the play, was his understanding of Pushkin's dialogue with <u>his</u> audience—a dialogue carried out, much like Meyerhold's, in the face of envy, outrage, and opposition. The sense of being a public showman with yet a prophetic duty was clear in both Meyerhold and Pushkin. For Pushkin, under the direct and constant surveillance of Nicholas I, the Tsar-Father who opened his mail and censored his writings personally, the position was maddening. Only a constant, healthy irony kept him sane. "There's no way I can hide my ears completely beneath this jester's cap," he wrote to his friend Vyazemsky. "They stick out!"

Meyerhold's intention was to show us those ears.

He rehearsed two productions of Boris Godunov; first in 1925–1926 with the Vakhtangov Theater, and then in 1936 with his own company. Boris Zakhava, Meyerhold's assistant on the project with the Vakhtangovites, has recorded some of what he remembers. For the rehearsals with Meyerhold's company, we have the remembrances of Mikhail Sadovsky, as well as verbatim transcriptions of Meyerhold's remarks and notes. For these rehearsals, Meyerhold had had the poet Vladimir Pyast work out a "score" for the text, with musical notation, marking tempi, rhythm, and the character of each line and speech.

Pushkin's play concerns the young monk Grigory Otrepev, the pretender, who passes himself off as the murdered Tsarevich Dimitry, Ivan the Terrible's son, and claims the throne from Boris Godunov. Pushkin modeled his play on Shakespeare's histories, and certain parallels with Hamlet are also clear. Meyerhold and his actors rehearsed scenes five and seven of the play most thoroughly. (I have translated these scenes, together with the brief scene six, and included them here to make Meyerhold's references easier to follow.) Meyerhold seems to have planned to expand this section of the play by including two scenes which Pushkin had cut or never finished: the "scene with the monk" and a scene for Grigory alone on a road. Both of these scenes show details of Grigory's decision to take on the role of Dimitry and claim the throne, and were evidently to be included between scenes five and six.

In Meyerhold's discussion of the play we can see some of his intentions. Clearly he wanted to get rid of the sacrosanct atmosphere that had enveloped the play—obscured for the general public then, as it is for us still, by the purple shadow of Mussorgsky's opera. So, for instance, his debunking of stereotypes, his elaborate upstaging of one of the most famous soliloquies in Russian drama. And clearly this text calls from a director all of his intelligence, all of his resources. "My credo," said Meyerhold, "is a theatrical language, simple, laconic, that leads to complex associations. That is the way I would like to direct Boris Godunov and Hamlet." But what marks the high seriousness of Meyerhold's attention to Boris Godunov, and what makes it so powerful for our purposes, is the repetition in this text of a central motif of Meyerhold's life, the motif that Eisenstein has so clearly noted and shown us: the crucial image of father and son, of rejection or love.

The right of succession in generations, the right of the son to the father's world, is the theme of both Boris Godunov and Hamlet.

Meyerhold's vision of Pimen as Grigory's spiritual father—through his chronicles, through his embrace—confers on Grigory a legitimate succession. Here we see, in the art of Meyerhold, as in the art of Pushkin and Shakespeare, the perseverance of human history in human themes and images. As <u>Hamlet</u> looms larger than any play in the English repertory, so <u>Boris Godunov</u> in the Russian. And in that tangled fabric—the texts of Shakespeare, his Hamlet, Claudius, and ghost; of Pushkin, his Boris, pretender, and Pimen; and of Meyerhold and his vision of them all—we share in their humanity, in the central theme that threads them solidly together: love or rejection from the father, love or rejection from the fatherland.

From <u>Boris Godunov</u>:

SCENE FIVE.

Night. A Cell in the Chudov Monastery. 1603. Pimen, and Grigory asleep.

Pimen
(*writing by lamplight*)
Yet one final story—yet one more—
And then I end my chronicle.
My task will be accomplished, a task
That God had set me. It was His purpose
To make me his witness all these years,
To train me in the writer's careful art.
Someday another monk will come and find
My work, my ardent, nameless labor;
Then he will light his lamp as I have done
And blow the dust of centuries from my pages
To copy over all my true accounts
So that the Russian land will know,
In years to come, what went before.
Our tsars in this will be remembered—
For their glorious deeds, for golden benefactions,
And for their sins, their secret midnight deeds,
On which we beg our Savior's holy mercy.
     My old age seems to me another life:
The fleeting world now eddies past
As once it pounded madly, full of action,

Turbulent as some overpowering ocean.
The world seems silent to me now, and still.
Some faces linger dimly in my memory,
And some few phrases echo in my ears,
But all the rest is gone, irrevocably
Gone. . . . it's almost day. My lamp is dim. . . .
And yet one final story—yet one more.

               (*he writes*)

Grigory
       (*he awakens*)

That dream again! The same, again! Three times!
Accursed vision! See, the old man sits
Beside his lamp and writes—untouched, I know,
By drowsiness the whole night long.
I love to see his rapt, attentive face,
His soul engrossed by visions of the past,
Unrolling his chronicle. I often wonder—
What is he describing as I watch?
The dark days of the Tatar yoke?
The bloody punishments of Ivan
The Terrible? The stormy days of Novgorod?
Moments of glory? I cannot tell.
His brow is clear, his eyes reveal no trace
Of veiled thoughts, of hidden speculations.
The same calm face, the same composure always.
He seems a judge who sits all day at statutes
And looks alike at innocent and guilty,
On good and bad, dispassionately sifting
Without anger, without pity, without sorrow.

Pimen
Awake, my son?

Grigory
Your blessing, holy father.

Pimen
Bless him, oh Lord, asleep, awake, forever.

Grigory
You write and write, and never seem to sleep,
While devilish fantasies disturb my rest,
And visions from the fiend torment me.

I dreamed I climbed a crooked stair that led
Up to a tower, and there upon that height
I stood, where Moscow like an ant hill lay
Under my feet, and in the marketplace
The people stared and pointed at me laughing;
I felt ashamed, a trembling overcame me,
I fell headfirst, and in that fall I woke.
Three times now have I dreamed this dream.
Is that not strange?

Pimen

Your young blood burns;
Go cool yourself with fasting and with prayer.
Then will your dreams be full of ease.
If I myself in other days allowed
Involuntary slumber to overcome me
And so forgot the appointed midnight prayer,
My old dreams were unquiet still, and sinful.
I dreamed of noisy drunken feasts,
Of brawling troops and warlike fierce affrays,
The mad indulgences of younger days!

Grigory

What joyful times you had when you were young!
You fought beneath the ramparts of Kazan,
Served Shuisky in the Lithuanian wars,
And saw the orgies of Tsar Ivan's court!
But since my childhood I've been imprisoned
Behind these holy walls, a hapless monk!
Why should I not go fight as well as you?
Or drink as well at some imperial table?
Then would I come when I was old as you,
Leave all the troubles of the world behind,
Pronounce my monkish vows, and in some cell
Immure myself and exercise my art.

Pimen

Never regret, my son, that you have left
A sinful world, nor that the Almighty
Has kept you free from such temptation;
Believe me, glory, luxury, and woman's love
Are traps that keep us endlessly captive.
I have lived long, and lived indulgently,

But not until God brought me safely here
Have I enjoyed one night's tranquility.
Think, boy, upon the mighty tsars of Russia.
What power is higher? God's alone. Who dares
Oppose them? No one. And yet
The golden crown has often seemed a weight
Too great to bear: they change it for a cowl.
Tsar Ivan sought to soothe his conscience
In acts of cloistered contemplation.
His palace, full of haughty favorites,
Turned overnight into a monastery;
His hellish followers in robes of black
Became a troop of penitential monks
And the ruthless tsar himself their holy abbot.
. . . .

And his son Fyodor? Upon the throne
He sighed after tranquility, and wished
To be a monk. He turned his royal chambers
Into silent prayerful cells, and there
The painful sorrows of a monarch's life
No longer lacerated his soul.
Almighty God so loved this peaceful tsar,
Beneath his rule the Russian land grew calm.
And when at last he lay dying
An unheard wonder was accomplished.
To his pallet, seen by him alone,
A figure came, streaming with rays of light.
Then Fyodor smiled, began to speak with him,
Calling him Father, holy Patriarch. . . .
Then all around him were struck dumb
And understood he saw some holy vision—
Since at that time the patriarch himself
Was absent. And when at last he died
His rooms were filled with an unearthly fragrance
And his visage shone as radiant as the sun.
We shall not see a tsar like him again.
Oh frightful, unforeseen calamity!
Our sins are punished for offending God—
A regicide now reigns as Russia's tsar!

Grigory

Worthy father, for a long time I have wanted
To ask you about the death of the Tsarevich

Dimitry; I have heard you say that you
Were then in Uglich.

Pimen

Oh, I remember!
God made me witness to that evil deed,
That foul and bloody crime. I had been sent
To Uglich, on vague suspicion,
In the middle of the night. Next day
At matin prayers we heard a tolling bell,
The beating of alarms, and noise and cries.
The people ran to the tsarina's house.
I ran there too. All Uglich was assembled.
Upon the ground lay the young tsarevich:
His royal mother swooned beside his corpse,
His nurse wept in piteous anguish—
And there the angry people dragged the wretched
Waiting woman that betrayed him.
Among them Bityagovsky then appeared
Like wretched Judas, pale with his crime.
"Assassin" was the furious general cry,
And in an instant he was torn to pieces.
His three accomplices next tried to flee;
The cowardly villains all were bound and brought
Before the bleeding body of the child
Which—wondrous to relate!—began to tremble.
"Confess!" the people shouted, and beneath
The axe the wicked men confessed—
And swore it was Boris that set them on.

Grigory

How old was he? The murdered tsarevich?

Pimen

Why, seven years old, and now he'd be—
(It's now ten years since then—no, more;
Twelve years). He would have been your age
And would have ruled. But God willed otherwise.
This mournful story ends my chronicle;
My work is done. I have spent little time since
In the world's affairs. My son, Grigory—
I have taught you how to read and write.
I pass along my task to you. At night,

When all your holy duties are fulfilled,
Write down without concealment or pretense
What things you witness in the world:
War and peace, the laws of government,
The holy miracles of holy men,
All prophecies, all heavenly signs and portents.
My time has long since come—to rest, to rest,
And so put out my feeble lamp. . . . But matins
Sound. Thy blessings, Lord upon us
Thy humble servants. . . . Give me my crutch, Grigory.
(he exits)

Grigory

Boris, Boris! Before you all men tremble,
And no one dares recall
The massacre of that unhappy child.
And yet in this small room an old man writes
A terrible indictment. You shall not
Escape the judgment of this world,
Nor yet escape the awful wrath of God!

SCENE SIX.

The Palace of the Patriarch. The Patriarch, the Abbot of the
Chudov Monastery.

Patriarch

He ran away, father abbot?

Abbot

Away, your holiness. Three days ago.

Patriarch

Damned rascal! What was his background anyway?

Abbot

From the family of Otrepev, descendants of Galician boyars. He took his vows quite young, no one seems to know
where. He lived in Suzdal, at the Yefimov monastery, left
there, idled about in various habitations, finally came to my
brotherhood at Chudov, and I, seeing he was young and unwise in judgment, gave him to the care of Father Pimen, a
gentle, mild old man; he learned surprisingly, could read our
chronicles, wrote canons very piously—but his learning, as it
now appears, did not come from the Lord. . . .

Patriarch

The trouble these men of letters cause me! What further nonsense has he invented here? "I will be tsar of Muscovy!" Ah, vessel of Satan! And yet I think it would be unwise to show this to the tsar; why disturb our royal master? I will inform his secretaries: Smirnov or Yefimov, that's enough. . . . What heresy! "I will be tsar of Muscovy!" We must apprehend the rebellious slave, and send him to Solovetsky, there to repent eternally. Why abbot, this is heresy!

Abbot

Heresy, your holiness, heresy indeed.

SCENE SEVEN.

The tsar's palace. Two serving men, then Boris.

First

Where is the tsar?

Second

Within. In his bedchamber,
Locked up in consultation with sorcerers.

First

That's all the company he keeps of late:
Sorcerers, astrologers, magicians,
Guessing fortunes like a blushing bride.
And what do you suppose he'd like to know?

Second

He's coming. Why not go ask him yourself?

First

How grim he looks!

Boris

I have attained the highest power;
For six years I have ruled this land in peace.
Yet happiness escapes me. Is this not
What happens when we're young?
We look for love, we seek to quench desire,
But once appease the hunger of the heart
In a moment's feverish possession and
We cool, grow bored, and wonder why. . . .
In vain the sorcerers have promised me

Long life and years of easy rule—
My rule is joyless and my life is drear;
I fear the wrath of heaven, I fear doom.
Happiness escapes me. I had thought
To make my people happy, to secure
Their love by what I do for them,
But I counted on an empty consolation.
The mob despises powers of life. They love—
They *can* love—only those who die.
We are mad to let mere applause
Or the popular shout move our hearts!
God sent a famine on the Russian land:
The people starved, in agony they perished;
I opened up the granaries, scattered gold,
Set up commissions, found them work—
I was the one responsible, they said,
And cursed me! Their houses were destroyed by fire,
I built new houses for them all—
I was the one, they said, who set the fires!
The rabble's judgment. Love that if you can.
I turned to my family for relief
And hoped to see my daughter nobly wed—
Then death, like some black storm, took off
Her bridegroom, and the slanderous mob
Said I had made a widow of my child!
I! I! The miserable father!
Came death to anyone—I was the secret
Murderer. I hurried Fyodor to his grave;
His wife, his empress, my own sister,
That holy nun, they said I poisoned her!
Ah! Now I understand: nothing, nothing
Can bring us peace while we're alive
But only conscience. Only conscience can.
If conscience be clean, then we triumph
Over malice, slander, black envy;
Yet let one spot show there, one stain,
Just one, the merest accident,
And then, alas! The mind inflamed
With pestilential sores pours out
Its dreadful poison on our heart.
Dizzy, we stagger till we fall

And bloody children dance before our eyes
But when we turn to run—there's no escape.
Ah, woe to him, whose conscience is unclean!

Boris Zakhava

What I was getting from Meyerhold seemed to me so valuable and so important that I kept wanting to make the same sort of creative communication with him available to the entire collective of the Vakhtangov theater. In the end I succeeded: Meyerhold began to drop in from time to time at the pleasant green building on Arbat where the Third Studio was located. He was usually shown a scene from whatever play was in preparation, and by the end of rehearsal it would show clear traces of the master's experienced hand.

Meyerhold's attitude toward the Third Studio was truly touching. He seemed to feel a kind of moral obligation, a certain creative responsibility to Vakhtangov and his students. After the death of its leader Vakhtangov's studio had experienced an extremely difficult period. The production of Gogol's *Marriage* in 1924 was unsuccessful, and there was serious talk of disbanding. It was Meyerhold who actively helped the Vakhtangov group to defend their right to an independent existence.

It is interesting to remember in this connection that Meyerhold worked somewhat differently in the Vakhtangov studio than he did in his own theater. With us he felt like Vakhtangov's deputy, and so he tried to work not Meyerhold-style, but Vakhtangov-style. And he managed to do it. He almost never went up onto the stage. He did very little in the way of demonstrating. He kept his seat at the director's table in the auditorium and threw out his remarks and notes to the actors from there. Meyerhold could never have worked like that in his own theater; his actors had been trained differently. And to me, from the sidelines, it was quite clear that to be able to work this way, a way he wasn't used to, gave Meyerhold a good deal of satisfaction. The result was that a great creative friendliness developed between Meyerhold and

the Vakhtangov people, and when we found out that Meyerhold dreamed of directing Pushkin's *Boris Godunov*, it was
not hard to convince him to try to realize his dream with the
collective at the Third Studio. I was entrusted with the task
of working as Meyerhold's assistant.

Long before meeting with the actors, Meyerhold and I
had a number of discussions about plans for the production.
He began our first conversation immediately with the question of the design of the production. He took a scrap of paper
and sketched a diagram of the construction which in his
opinion should form the basis for the set design. He proposed
a construction consisting of two long, fairly narrow platforms, or "sidewalks," as he called them, located one behind
the other, parallel to the footlights. The first platform was to
be located a third of the way back on the stage and the second, considerably higher, two-thirds of the way back. The
space between the floor and the first sidewalk, and also between the sidewalks themselves, was to be filled by inclined
surfaces, variously treated, which were to play a purely deco-
rative role. The idea was that the action would take place
only on the sidewalks which could, in certain scenes, be connected by short flights of stairs placed against the inclined
surfaces, and in this way the characters could move from one
sidewalk to another. He further suggested leaving narrow
spaces between the sidewalks and the inclined surfaces, so
that pieces of architectural decor could be raised from below
for individual scenes—a wall, a fence, an arch, a door, windows, and so forth. He also intended to have people appear in
these narrow spaces as if in trenches, so that the spectators
would sometimes see them only down to the waist and sometimes even see only their heads. It was with this device that
Meyerhold intended to resolve the problem of presenting
mass scenes with a limited number of participants.

At a later date he told Sergei Isakov, who designed the
sets, that in this staging the characters would have the clarity
and expressiveness of figures in the etchings of Jacques Callot. Isakov suggested that the inclined surfaces between the
sidewalks might be covered with old parchment, and
Meyerhold agreed.

The idea was that the action of the play would be continuous, since the scene changes would be simple and could be
made right before the eyes of the audience, without lowering

the curtain. Meyerhold maintained that the directorial
failures that had inevitably marked previous productions of
Boris Godunov were mainly the fault of bulky and complicated naturalistic sets and staging, which always made the
performance drag incredibly, slowing down its tempo,
whereas the entire structure of Pushkin's tragedy, its style
and character, demanded unusual lightness and swiftness.

I have only short, summary notes of my preliminary conversations with Meyerhold. But they show clearly that
Meyerhold attached primary significance to the question of
rhythm in performance. He said that the rhythm in this production should be "rapid and impetuous," and he constantly
insisted that I pay careful attention to what he called the
"overall composition" of the play, or its "musical construction." He said: "Keep yourself from observing the static,
observe only the dynamic!" And he explained: "The only way
to master Pushkin's material is by seeking out its tempi."

Speaking about the creation of a directorial master-plan,
Meyerhold stated: "Before you let your fantasy run free, before you begin putting things together, you must narrow your
fantasy: the greatest danger for a director is to yield to ca-
price." He added: "You are responsible for your own self-
restraint, for the organization of a plan. To do this you have
to spend a certain amount of time groping around on various
possible paths before you have the right to say: 'Now I am
able to begin constructing.'"

To the question of what the artist needs before he can
finally begin practical work, Meyerhold answered briefly:
"The concept!" He said: "The director must give birth to a
concept." And he added in passing: "It's all nonsense when
people say: it's easy for him because he's talented! Inventions
are the result of training, skills, and practice. And the thing
that takes charge at the moment of organization of the work
(Meyerhold deliberately avoided the word "creation") is the
concept." And he exclaimed: "It's not that some people are
talented and others aren't, it's that some people are smart
and others are stupid! Scriabin's "Prometheus" is the fruit of
a concept in constant motion."

"Individual parts," according to Meyerhold, "produce an
impression only when they are welded together. What is the
glue? Again, the concept. And it's fine if the hidden concept is
laid bare." (When I heard this I thought: isn't he talking

about Stanislavsky's "subtext"? Or perhaps Nemirovich-Danchenko's "second plane"? I had heard the word "concept" most frequently from Vakhtangov, who used it when referring to Nemirovich-Danchenko.) "It is incorrect to begin with the parts," Meyerhold maintained. "You must first embrace the *whole*. You can ignore all the stage directions entirely, but you absolutely must know the construction of the play."

Meyerhold incessantly repeated: "Concept, program, idea, tendency. . . ." I also have this aphorism of his written in my notebook: "The production of a play is a conceptual task, which I accomplish physically using all the means that theater affords."

Concept and rhythm: these are the things that Meyerhold foregrounded. I saw here no contradiction with anything I had learned from Vakhtangov. But that was theory. Practice, on the other hand, did not fully coincide with it. I kept asking Meyerhold what concept was to underlie the production of *Boris Godunov*, but I never received a clear answer. I only felt that in Pushkin's tragedy he was most struck by the image of the pretender. He was enraptured with him not only as a great creation of Pushkin's genius, but considered him a positive character on the socio-historical plane. Beyond being a mere adventurer, the pretender seemed to him to be the bearer of a progressive historical mission. . . .

The first rehearsal lives clearly in my memory. The actors arranged themselves decorously at the long table. Behind them sat the actors who were not in the play. Meyerhold was at the head of the table.

The reading began. My God, what incredible tension there was! Whether it was because of fear of Meyerhold, worship of Pushkin, or timidity in the face of a poetic text, or a combination of these factors, the actors began to read so quietly, so indistinctly, so unintelligibly that nobody could understand a thing. Meyerhold held his patience for a while. Then he began making remarks about individual scenes of the tragedy, mainly critical of Pushkin: he noted places where he thought that the author had not been particularly successful. By doing this he wanted to get rid of the religious awe that was turning the reading of the play into some kind of semi-mystical experience.

Speaking with the actors about building their characters, Meyerhold advanced a principle that he called the "paradoxi-

cal approach." This consisted of making all kinds of suggestions about the characters or about individual scenes that
were in sharp contrast to generally accepted views or to
whatever seemed immediately obvious. In this Meyerhold
saw a means of overcoming routine reactions. He told the actors: "There is no need to be afraid of the conflict that ini-
tially arises between us and the text." (I wonder whether
there is not some similarity between Meyerhold's paradoxical
approach and Stanislavsky's principle: "If you want to play a
good man, look for the places where he is bad.")

Meyerhold sharply criticized the usual stage portrayals
of characters from Russian historical plays. He said that all
these tsars and boyars, as a rule, looked not like living people
but like dolls—their furs and caftans always seemed to have
grown to their bodies; there seemed no way to undress them
or to imagine them naked. "We should be able to spy on Boris
when he is taking a bath!" Meyerhold exclaimed. . . .

Meyerhold worked with great enthusiasm on the scene in
Pimen's cell in the Chudov Monastery. About Pimen he said:
"A mummy. A real sense of the skeleton within. Two burning
eyes. Rapid tempo." Meyerhold demanded that the actor develop Pimen "not as a talker, but as a doer." He maintained
that Pimen should speak distractedly. And since this was apparently not the first time he had talked about the murdered
child, Meyerhold gave the actor this note for the speech:
"with the usual tempi of a storyteller."

In general, Meyerhold worked out this entire scene on the
level of lifelike, day-to-day truthfulness. He spoke indignantly
about performances where "actors in costumes read poetry."
Therefore the characters of the play in Meyerhold's conception, when speaking the text, were to perform a whole
range of ordinary physical actions. Thus, for example, Grigory, when he wakes up after his dream and recites his
speech about Pimen, was supposed to be washing and tidying
himself up. The promptbook notes precisely at which words
he takes the tub and pitcher, at which words he pours water,
where he rolls up his sleeves, when he gets the towel, when
he dries his face, and when he pours water into the bucket.

And Pimen, while delivering his long speeches, according
to the director's notes, was first to rub his aching shoulder,
the yawn, then stretch the fingers of his right hand which
were tired from long writing, then listen to a mouse scratch-

ing, then clean off a smudge of ink that had gotten on the manuscript; and during his story about the murder of the tsarevich he was to take off and carefully darn his worn felt slippers. Meyerhold's note for Grigory's final speech in this scene ("Boris! Boris! Before you all men tremble. . . .") is also curious: "Lively. Like a hooligan. A kid with a rock in his hand."

About the tavern scene Meyerhold said: "Pushkin wrote it deliberately in such a way that its vulgarity would mark it off from the rest of the play." Therefore he thought it could be staged with some of the crude devices of popular street theater which, as we know, he had mastered to perfection. Thus, for example, he had the monks drink their wine from an enormous cup in which, Meyerhold assured us, a multitude of flies and spiders were floating. The monks had continuously to blow these insects toward the side of the cup so they wouldn't get into their mouths. But one fly nevertheless made its way into Varlaam's mouth and stuck in his throat; it caused him to choke desperately and hiccough loudly, producing a very funny sound which Meyerhold repeatedly demonstrated with apparent satisfaction. Osip Basov, when he rehearsed the part of Varlaam, was embarrassed to tears at having to imitate this sound, but Meyerhold was adamant and stubbornly insisted that what he had demonstrated be precisely reproduced. He kept encouraging Basov with the words: "Come on, be brave, be brave! . . ."

The entrance of the police officers was interestingly staged. Having declared that "a powerful effect needs a powerful premise," and that Grigory in this scene was to be like "a poisoned animal trying to recover its senses," Meyerhold introduced a sharp whistle that was repeated offstage five times throughout the scene just before the entrance of the police officers. Grigory was to react to each sound of the whistle. This created an atmosphere of alarm and contributed greatly to the growing nervous excitement of the pretender.

The finale of the tavern scene also remains in my memory. It's necessary to remember that Meyerhold conceived the hostess of the tavern as Grigory's accomplice, someone who understood the situation and voluntarily, without any collusion with the pretender, took on the task of helping him in his flight. The role was cast with this interpretation in mind, and given to Nina Rusinova. She was tall, round-faced, dark-browed, a typical Russian beauty—she was clearly a hostess who would easily win the viewers' sympathy. This conception of the role of the hostess was closely related to Meyerhold's idea for the finale of the scene.

First, a brief description of the set. It was very modest. Directly before the audience was a wall with a window. Under the window, a bench. In front of the bench, a table. That was all. Before the pretender leaps through the window, the characters were placed as follows: the monks and police officials downstage, left and right at the proscenium. The hostess to the left of the table. Grigory in front of the table center. After Varlaam's words "Isn't that you, friend?" when the police officers make a rush for the pretender, he draws a dagger. They move quickly away and he turns completely around; the hostess with a lightning-like movement pulls the table over against herself and thus clears the pretender's path to the window; he leaps through the window and the hostess immediately shoves the table back to its previous position. The police officers and monks who dash after the pretender run into the table and fall all over one another.

Meyerhold managed patiently so that all this was done in a single instant. The hostess was to make two movements in a row without the slightest pause between them: the table back, the table forward. "One, two!" commanded Meyerhold. He repeated this order endlessly, until Moskvin learned to jump through the window between the command "One!" and the command "Two!" And Meyerhold made no pause between them. "You've got to be fast!" he ordered the actor. "One, two!" And if Moskvin miscalculated and ran into the table, Meyerhold inexorably demanded: "Again!" And again came the same command, loud and sharp: "One, two!" Yet when the desired result was achieved, it was impossible not to experience a feeling of elation at an artistic triumph: the effect was astonishing!

All these recollections of Meyerhold's work on *Boris Godunov* live in my memory accompanied by a deep feeling of gratitude for everything I received from him. And I received a great deal; it was a wonderful school for me: I left each rehearsal with new understanding, with new discoveries in the art of directing. But my recollections of work on *Boris God-unov* involve not only joyous moments of creativity, but also a moment of great bitterness.

The cause of it was my work on the central scene of the tragedy, on the famous soliloquy of Tsar Boris: "I have attained the highest power. . . ." Meyerhold entrusted me with the rehearsals of this speech. Boris Shchukin, the actor who played Boris, worked with me in a friendly way, conscientiously and with immense enthusiasm. Finally the moment came when it began to seem to both of us that Boris was finally coming along, and we wanted to show our accomplishment to Meyerhold.

We knew that Meyerhold already had something in mind for this scene. He shared his idea with us and we were delighted by it. "In vain the sorcerers have promised me long life," says Boris in his speech. "That clearly means that he has consulted sorcerers before this point," said Meyerhold, "so why don't we show him in their company? Let them wail over him and whisper their incantations to him, let them hop and dance around him, let them concoct medicines for him and rub him with their ointments . . . it will be a marvellous scene!" And Meyerhold instructed me to search the Lenin Library for the texts of the ancient lamentations we needed, to choose actors for the scene and work with them on building their characters. I managed to accomplish a good deal of this as well. Finally came the day when I was to show Meyerhold the scene with the magicians and the speech itself.

Meyerhold listened to the speech and he seemed to be satisfied. Then he asked to see the magicians. And around Tsar Boris all those magicians and soothsayers, those lame and hunchbacked freaks, those ancient men and sinister old women began to prance, to jump and wail. I was convinced that Meyerhold would find some way to get this entire group offstage, and only then would Boris' speech begin. How great then was my surprise when in the very heat of this bacchanal of sorcerers Meyerhold suddenly called out to Shchukin: "The speech! Start the speech!" Shchukin began, but of course it was impossible to make out anything in all that confusion. No matter how hard Shchukin tried to outshout the sorcerers, one could make out only a couple of individual sentences of the entire text.

But to our common surprise Meyerhold was apparently

very satisfied. I could not restrain myself at that point and turned to him:

"But Vsevolod Emilievich! The speech is quite lost! It cannot be heard at all!"

"Never mind, it'll be all right," answered Meyerhold. It's one of Pushkin's unsuccessful speeches. . . ."

I was in complete despair. There was no way I could reconcile myself to that. I placated myself by saying that we would make a common effort and still get our own way at some point in the future, and save the speech somehow or other, but a breach nonetheless became apparent, and the Vakhtangov theater collective began to cool toward the production. So when other factors came into the picture—various difficulties with the organizational and financial policies and also Meyerhold's heavy work schedule in his own theater, whose collective on top of everything was jealous of their leader's work with the Vakhtangov studio—it all led to a situation where work on *Boris Godunov* slowed down until it was halted altogether. But what a pity! What a great pity! Now, when I think back, it becomes clear how interesting a work that production would have been, and how fruitful for the future of the theater if, despite all obstacles and difficulties, it had been seen through to the end.

Boris Zaxava, "Dva sezona," *Vstreči s Mejerxol'dom* (Moscow, 1967), pp. 278–289.

Mikhail Sadovsky

It was in the fall of 1936 that Meyerhold resumed his work on *Boris Godunov*. That was a wonderful period in the life of the Meyerhold State Theater. Meyerhold was all inspiration, and this inspiration gripped all the actors. As far as I remember, very little was actually staged. Several scenes were worked out, but only in rough-draft form. Nevertheless Vsevolod Emilievich's plans, his interpretation of particular episodes, and his general conception for the production were absolutely amazing.

Time has erased much of it from my memory, but the

most striking impressions have lasted. One of these impressions concerns Meyerhold's work on the episode "A Cell in the Chudov Monastery." It must be noted that when we found out Meyerhold was going to stage _Boris Godunov_, all the actors began to discuss the possible casting. We unanimously nominated Gennady Michurin for the role of Pimen. He had, we thought, all the necessary qualifications for the role: he was tall and had a rich and expressive bass voice. From the viewpoint of the tradition begun by Chaliapin's extraordinary performances, Michurin was, as it were, "a Pimen in the flesh." All he would have to do, it seemed to us, was put on a black cassock and glue a beard to his chin to become an unsurpassed Pimen.

It is hard to describe our surprise when we learned that the role of Pimen was assigned to Sergei Kiligin. Kiligin's qualifications were diametrically opposed to those of Michurin. Michurin at that time was playing the part of Neschastlivtsev in _The Forest_, the part of the elder Duval in _Camille_, and the part of Professor Kellberg in _Prelude_, whereas Kiligin, who had joined the theater only a short while ago, was to replace Igor Ilyinsky who had just left. Kiligin was preparing the part of Arkashka in _The Forest_. We could not imagine how this thin actor of medium height with his high-pitched voice could play the part of Pimen.

The rehearsals began. Meyerhold started by doing away with our notions of what Pimen's cell ought to be like. Of course we had all pictured the set for this scene as a large low-vaulted chamber like a dungeon, with the walls done in black and gray. Sometimes a diligent set designer even makes this cell into a cave of sorts, with a huge icon of the Savior hanging in a corner and a large red icon-lamp in front of it. "We'll have none of that," Vsevolod Emilievich said; "such cells never existed anywhere except in the theater."

He pictured Pimen's cell as very light and cheerful. Its main tones were to be white and yellow. The large icon of the Savior with the red icon-lamp gave way to a small icon with a small but very bright green icon-lamp.

"Now, about Pimen," Meyerhold went on. "Pimen is very old and worn-out—the result of his tumultuous life and, of course, his age. He himself describes his life in this way: 'I have lived long, and lived indulgently.'

"How old is he? He may be ninety or even a hundred. His

hands and his head tremble slightly from weakness. It is hard for him to write, to see, to breathe, but he has to overcome all that. . . . He has to overcome it in order to accomplish 'a task that God had set me'. Naturally, we won't have him in a cassock. After all, it's night and he's at home. He has taken off his cassock long ago, but this time he hasn't said 'the appointed midnight prayer'; he can't sleep, so he decides to sit and write.

"He is wearing a long linen nightshirt. He is bald. He has one of those nice pink bald heads, with a crown of short sparse white hair from one temple to the other, and the same kind of beard. We want him to be a very nice, very charming old fellow. His voice is weak and extremely high-pitched. It is hard for him to speak, and he is frequently out of breath; there must be pauses in his speech—he has to rest, to regain his breath. We shall arrange all these pauses and mark them down. They should not be logical—on the contrary, they should be alogical, they have to turn up when they are least expected.

"Pimen should be childishly naive, cosy, and kind. He has three dominant traits: intelligence, humor, and childishness.

"Pimen is old, but he should not give the impression that he is going to die any moment. On the contrary, he is quite a busy character, he has always written, he is writing at the moment, and he still has a great deal to write. This small wiry old man is full of energy. It isn't true that this is his 'final story'; he will always find something more to write about."

And evidently wishing to add the final touch to this debunking of the stately basso in a black cassock, he said:

"Pimen took part in many battles and he may have injured an arm or a leg. He limps. This idea is worth thinking over. Just look how many dangers he was subjected to. Pimen says:

> I dreamed of noisy drunken feasts,
> Of brawling troops and warlike fierce affrays.

And Grigory continues:

> What joyful times you had when you were young!
> You fought beneath the ramparts of Kazan,
> Served Shuisky in the Lithuanian wars. . . .

And Pimen concludes with: '. . . Give me my crutch, Grigory!' "

This passionate speech about a new Pimen lasted almost two hours, and all this time, as always, Vsevolod Emilievich had his jacket off, gesticulated, demonstrated, presented arguments, literally created his Pimen in front of us and made us believe in him totally.

During rehearsals the talented Kiligin rapidly absorbed all Meyerhold's instructions, and Meyerhold kept feeding new details to him all the time, making suggestions: what kind of a pen did Pimen have, how did he write with it, how did he dip it into the inkwell, did he get angry at the pen because it wrote badly.

I remember Meyerhold's demonstration of how Pimen, without interrupting his recital, straightened the wick of the smoking lamp. This operation was done with great accuracy and lasted a rather long time. Then Grigory began to wake up, and Meyerhold suggested that Grigory should wash himself. When this scene was demonstrated, the towel in Meyerhold's hands betrayed the nervousness in Grigory's hands, gave away Grigory's anxiety. I remember Meyerhold saying that the towel in Grigory's hands ought to resemble a snake which had coiled, as it were, around Grigory's neck, and that he was struggling with it.

Music was to be of extreme importance in this *Boris Godunov*—it was to depict the masses of the people, their anxieties, their indignation, their sorrow, their despair. In Meyerhold's conception, there would be no crowd either onstage or in the wings. Two orchestras were to be involved in the production, a symphony orchestra and an orchestra of folk instruments, predominantly Oriental. The score for Meyerhold's *Boris Godunov* was written by Prokofiev.

Everyone knows that *Boris Godunov* was never completed. Why? The question is difficult to answer. It would be wrong to assume, of course, that Meyerhold cooled toward the production, lost his interest in it, or became confused during the final stages of work on the play. What seems more likely to have been the case is that in the course of his work on the production it took on such vast dimensions that it simply became impossible to realize it on his small and poorly equipped stage. Meyerhold was looking forward to his new

theater in Mayakovsky Square, but construction was pro-
gressing very slowly. Meyerhold stopped working on *Boris
Godunov* and in the beginning of 1937 started on *Natasha*, by
Lydia Seifullina.

Mixail Sadovskij, "Teatral'nyj čarodej," *Vstreči s Mejerxol'dom*
(Moscow, 1967), pp. 522–524.

Vsevolod Meyerhold
Notes at a Read-through of <u>Boris Godunov</u>

April 4, 1936

We've got to use every means we have to make sure the audience feels the poetry as familiar. I'm going to insist on
every one of our markings so that the enchantment of this
poetry is understood. Usually it's just a pedagogic fiction. I'm
not saying that we'll have it all ready by August of this year,
but I am saying that we've got to set the retards now so that
we don't wind up with a carnival of verse à la Kirshon. What
I'm saying is that we have to learn right now how to care for
this absolutely marvellous text. We have to love every bit of
it, prose, verse, everything. If we don't do that, then I doubt
we'll be able to make them rejoice in the power of the poetry.
I think perhaps only three actors have been able to do that.
Belinsky talks about Mochalov that way. I've seen Lensky do
it. . . .

No matter how many times I read Pushkin's *Boris Godunov*, or any page of Pushkin, it moves me to heights of ecstasy. I practically want to get down on my knees in front of
his statue.

We have to remember that we're entering a competition.
We haven't signed any papers or anything with the Moscow
Art Theater, but that's the way things stand: we're getting a
production ready, and so are they. (*Voice from the group*: "So's
the Maly Theater.") The Maly Theater I don't know about
yet—but I don't think we'll have to take them too seriously.
Things are in a terrible mess over there at the moment. But a

competition with the Art Theater would be interesting, because they haven't yet tried to work on the poetry the way we have; we've been working on it for quite a while now. So we'd better remember that and try to keep ahead of them.

When we were doing our reading of *The Stone Guest* it became quite clear where the difficulty for the actor was. Lots of actors can read verse, and whether they're reading Mayakovsky, or Alexei Tolstoy, or reading contemporary poets—Prokofiev, Kornilov—as soon as they get up onstage for some reason the words go all greasy, oily—like a dolphin, you know, if you cut one, its oil oozes out. Terribly greasy words. When we were working on *The Stone Guest* for a long time we couldn't get Pushkin. And it became clear we weren't getting him because the words were all swollen.

It's very common, it's banal to use this truism when talking about Pushkin, to talk about his "transparency." You've all studied literature, you know what's-his-name, Nestor Kotlyarevesky, every time he wrote about Pushkin, he had to say he was transparent. Well, it's true. With Pushkin you feel some sort of air between the words, and the words themselves are somehow compressed by that air. The words are light. . . .

I propose that we don't read softly, but full voice, so that we get a very special sonority; transparency, not just in the way we say the words, but transparency in getting a good feeling from the sound of our own reading. When you read it out, you begin to feel much lighter. You can't do it the opposite way. Start reading softly, and eventually you'll make havoc out of your reading. You can't do it that way.

It's a different matter over at the Maly Theater, where Lensky and Ermolova used to say that you have to practice your part in a whisper. They were saving their strength, because they knew that later on they could give whatever they had to. They knew how to read beautifully, especially Lensky. He had the ability to deliver the text lightly. He used to show off at it. Whenever he did a big speech he would suddenly find a certain line and the tempo would turn *vivace* and the text would flow out of him wonderfully lightly. It was light and sonorous, especially if you remember him as Famusov. Of course that technique has disappeared now because, as Amaglobeli was saying, we've all gone off to the marketplace to observe life. But then what happens to our ability to read Schiller, Calderón, and tomorrow Pushkin? It's all lost.

Consequently, we have to work seriously at restoring that. It's not easy to restore, that's why I propose the opposite of the school of Lensky and Ermolova, I mean the whispering—let it be their privilege to work on their parts that way—but I propose that we work at letting our voices resound. I want to hear Sagal's voice, I don't want his words stuck in his throat, I want them—I want his words to get out onto his lips so I can hear them, so that the words are out here somewhere on his lips, and so the words can glide off and fly in the air, like a juggler's balls. It has to be fairly loud. But not yelling. . . . I'm not talking about loudness in the sense of a loudmouth, yelling and banging things. I want sonorousness. When a violinist is very good, he can play *pianissimo*, but at the same time the sound carries, sonorously. . . .

Vsevolod Meyerhold
Notes at a Rehearsal of <u>Boris Godunov</u>

August 4, 1936
Scene seven. The tsar's palace.

> That's all the company he keeps of late:
> Sorcerers, astrologers, magicians,
> Guessing fortunes like a blushing bride.
> And what do you suppose he'd like to know?

See how Pushkin does it: the first serving man, whispering about Boris in some corner, speaks about him with a certain irony—that's clear from these first four lines. "That's all the company he keeps of late, etc." There has to be a lot of hardness and emphasis in it, real emphasis on making fun of the tsar. The second serving man is scared stiff of the tsar—he'd probably whack you harder than Ivan the Terrible did. So the second serving man has got to be played as a coward, and spiteful. And the third (that's why I want to introduce a third one), the third sympathizes with the tsar: "How grim he looks!" It'll be better that way, if there's a bunch of them. Pushkin won't hate us if we bring on an extra serving man.

When the Moscow Art Theater first staged *Boris Godunov*, Nemirovich-Danchenko directed it. Stanislavsky never came to rehearsals. And later on, when the thing wasn't going too well for Nemirovich, he asked Stanislavsky to come and give notes, and perhaps give him some help. He didn't insist—they probably weren't getting on too well at the time, which often happened between Nemirovich-Danchenko and Stanislavsky—and he didn't want to come. Finally he did. And the first thing he said, when he saw Danchenko's work (this was characteristic of Stanislavsky) was "it's boring." They asked him to change it. He said: "there's no way to change it now"—he was afraid of ruining the whole thing if he made any corrections. He agreed to make some changes only in the Polish scenes. They describe in great detail the way he showed Germanova, who was playing Marina Mnishek, how Marina should sit in her armchair. In that one gesture he immediately revealed her as a proud Polish noblewoman. His remark "it's boring" was a fairly accurate forecast; later when the play went on and the production was a failure, it probably failed because it was, more than anything else, extremely boring.

That's the reason that the most difficult part in the play is the part of Boris Godunov himself, because it's easy to play Boris boringly. Look at Dimitry the Pretender: he comes on first as a monk, then there's his adventurous flight—we see him jump through a window, a flash of legs and the glitter of a knife. We see him at the Polish investiture, he reaches for the throne of Muscovy, in an instant he becomes an ardent, passionate lover; there's such a wealth of color scattered in it, that the part is practically boredom-proof.

With Boris it's completely different. Boris has one definite line. But how are the big speeches constructed? When I found out that Kachalov was going to play Boris in the Art Theater production I was a bit afraid because, despite the fact that he's a very great actor, and a very interesting, very intelligent actor, in the nature of his vocal apparatus there's this flaw— not for everyone, of course, a certain part of the audience always adores him. It's "honeyed velvet," that's the way his velvet voice works—but I know there are some people who say: "it's a very beautiful voice, but it gets boring very fast." He has a certain heaviness, he loves his own vocal effects. He never manages to make it *bewegt*. I dearly love Pyast's indications "*a tempo*," and it has to do not only with a return to tempo (in music the phrase indicates a return to the basic tempo of the piece), but sometimes I read to you *a tempo* with a touch of what Wagner introduces as *bewegt*, that is when the action, movement, can be heard in the verse itself. . . .

Tsar Boris, insofar as he comes out of a church, insofar as he is laden with the regalia, insofar as he summons the whole clergy when he's dying, insofar as he makes a solemn disposition—to that extent you feel here a certain element of churchiness. These elements drag around after Godunov because of certain traditions, but not from Pushkin, from theatrical tradition. It's because of these traditions that *Boris Godunov* is always full of heavy jeweled collars, heavy armchairs, heavy costumes.

I've already said that we have to see the child through the eyes of the painter Nesterov, in his painting "The Murdered Tsarevich." Often, as a matter of fact, we cannot see something ourselves and so we attempt to perceive a given object more clearly by putting on the eyeglasses that a painter can provide for us. For instance, I couldn't see *Camille* until I put on the eyeglasses of Renoir and Manet. We often see the world with the help of the glasses worn by this or that great painter.

And yet I am forced to say that we have no right to look at the role of Boris with the eyes of those painters who enveloped the role with religion.

One time the Alexandrinsky Theater commissioned sketches for Alexei Tolstoy's play *Tsar Fyodor Ivanovich* from the painter Stelletsky. And he saw the whole play through the eyes of an icon painter. Fyodor seemed to have stepped right out of an icon, all the rest of the characters were from icons, and the whole play seemed to take place in those old frescoes that used to cover the walls of churches in the eleventh century, and that are now being uncovered in a number of churches like Sofia Cathedral in Kiev. Of course that's an artist's privilege.

Will we look at *Boris Godunov* that way? I think not. Why? Because that's not the way Pushkin looked at him. When Pushkin wrote the play he was interested in other ideas, he was moved by other concerns.

You know that Pushkin had to go underground, so to speak; he was forced to conceal all his connections with friends of his who had been members of the Decembrists. Pushkin was tormented by having as his private censor Tsar Nicholas and the secret police. It tortured him, and when he sent off letters to his friends saying that he was working on *Boris Godunov*, then he leapt out of the underground, so to speak, he was in revolt, he tried to write a play where every line contained a piece of the rebel, the potential revolutionary. That's why when we come across a trifle like the four-line speech of the first serving man, we can see Pushkin himself peering out of it. There's even one of his letters where he writes plainly that there is more hidden in this play than appears. We have to remember the famous "jester's cap"—we must copy out that quotation word for word and learn it, it ought to be an epigraph for our production. . . .

Since he was a thoroughly contemporary individual and interested not in history, but in somehow smuggling through history his own part in it, that is, to put in what led to the Decembrist uprising, we must read differently a few of the things he has included. . . .

Here it's a matter of thesis and antithesis: Boris on the one side, the people on the other. Pushkin wants to involve the people on his side, so that he's not the only rebel in this play, but so that we can feel the rebellious spirit he shows with the people. Critics sometimes call me a fantasist: he invented such or such an approach to *Boris Godunov*! At the moment I am not inventing any approach to *Boris Godunov*. At the moment I am only trying to understand Pushkin— what it was he wanted to accomplish with this piece. His own letters and remarks on the drama and his magazine articles are filled with references to *Boris Godunov*. That's where I've gotten this information, and only this information is of use to me. I'm not interested in other information. . . .

Remember, this period is called the Time of Troubles. And that's the reason I try to imagine, try to figure out, how much he was imitating Shakespeare's histories. You remember that they are all based on extraordinary struggles and on the clash of passions. Take *Richard III*. Whenever I see that play and read through Shakespeare's text, I realize that Shakespeare's characters succeed because he doesn't show people against a calm background; his background is continually in an uproar. He doesn't conceive his hero's character without that sea of people. . . . What kind of play is *Boris Godunov*? It's the struggle of passions against the background of a stormy sea. . . .

Boris Godunov is in no sense a church-goer. He isn't, simply because he has no time for it. He makes the sign of the cross, he performs the rites, he may well be a deeply religious man, but Pushkin brought him into this play not in his quality as a religious man, but as a man struggling for power, and furthermore in a situation where he must confront a pretender to his throne.

Thus we have Boris Godunov in his quality as a warrior, and from that we derive his intonations. He jumps off a horse and says: "I have attained the highest power." He jumps off a horse, he doesn't get up from his prayers, that's how Boris is different from Ivan the Terrible, *he* was always getting up from his prayers—when he had reason to pray and when he didn't—he was always making the sign of the cross, over and over, and suddenly Bam! he kills this one and that one, and then makes a sign of the cross. This man is completely different, and intonations we could use for Ivan the Terrible are impossible here. The Art Theater portrayed Ivan the Terrible not as a *raisonneur*, but as a neurotic, and that's why it was hard for Stanislavsky to play the part and he soon gave it up, because it was too much of a strain on the quality of his voice. After that I got the part, and I and a whole group of actors like me played Ivan the Terrible as a neurotic, the kind who had epileptic fits and whose praying was always slightly monstrous. . . .

In the drafts of *Boris Godunov* this scene has a different title: not "in the tsar's palace," but "Boris and the sorcerers." Although I consider Pushkin a great director, he didn't know how to manage something like that on the stage. That's why what he did was not to bring the sorcerers onstage, but have the tsar shut himself up in his bedroom with some sorcerer, and then come onstage after getting rid of him, and then do his big speech.

I want to go back to the plan that Pushkin has indicated but that he couldn't carry out, given the technical limitations of his time. I intend to bring the sorcerers onstage, and the magicians and fortune-tellers, and Boris Godunov sits in the midst of these sorcerers and fortune-tellers. Prokofiev has helped me out, he has invented a kind of sixteenth-century jazz band made up of percussion instruments and other sound effects, where the sounds come from one sorcerer who grabs a rooster and tries to get him to eat grain, and the rooster protests when they squeeze him. They pour wax onto water and watch for letters to form ("On Twelfth Night eve the maidens once told fortunes. . . ."). All these devices are scattered here and there throughout and cause a lot of noise: the hiss of red-hot metal being thrust into water; there's a shaman of some kind who bangs a bell; the sound of domras. It's stuffy, hot, crowded; they've thrown a cloth over his head, some sorcerers come up to tell his fortune and from underneath a transparent silk cloth we hear the voice of Boris Godunov; a servant is kneeling beside him holding a large container of kvass, or perhaps beer or mead; in that heat he has to keep cooling himself off; tormented by sorcerers, magicians, etc. What kind of "blushing bride" is this? And at this point he does his big speech. He tries to get out of the clutches of this rabble that keeps getting in his way. Most of all are the fleas; you can't count them, they've brought in so many, but it all just creeps along; he scratches and drinks. It's a simple speech, but he speaks it terribly painfully, he speaks it in distressing circumstances. This is Boris in dishabille. No silk embroidered with gold, no jeweled collars—nothing of the kind. This is a warrior, a dirty warrior. Perhaps in other circumstances, not during the Time of Troubles, he'd take a bath every day, but now where can he find the time to take a bath? They keep bringing him news that the Poles are attacking. . . . I've taken a trip up the Volga and seen those spaces that even today stretch from one district to another. The monasteries there are surrounded by walls, and the monks there had to be warriors, because the monasteries were built like fortresses, the distances are enormous. Hordes of Tatars plundering, organizing massacres. A turbulent life, terrible!

That's the reason there's no way you can speak this text calmly, it all has to be passionate, *bewegt*. . . .

You absolutely must read *Richard III*, you absolutely must read Shakespeare's history plays, because his favorite devices are self-flagellation; individuals torment themselves, scourge themselves. Remember the famous scene in *Hamlet*, where King Claudius kneels down and tries to pray, and Hamlet watches from behind a curtain.

Vsevolod Meyerhold
Notes at a Rehearsal of <u>Boris Godunov</u>

December 22, 1936
Scene eleven. Krakow. Wiśniewecki's house.

The pretender is a romantic. Nervous, distracted, what later
generations would call neurotic. Gawky. Outbursts. His
part might be indicated in the text by a line of dashes. He
should remind us of a young animal. In the scene in the inn,
his animal leap, that leap out the window, is preposterous,
like the one in Blok's *Balaganchik*.

There's a certain quality of paradox to it. Why does he
get attached to those two monks? And he falls in love on the
very eve of his moment of decision. He's by that fountain, instead of at the head of his troops. Pushkin drags him through
the play for a long while, but his big moment doesn't come
until scene thirteen, by the fountain (Boris Godunov's big moment comes in scene seven). Very little ink for a hundred
sheets of paper. The charm of Hamlet, really, may be that he
goes for a long time before he works himself up. Only Italians
(especially men) know how to play that—they know the secret of reticence. Germans and Russians find it totally foreign. Retards, veiling. Holding back like that. We brought
that off in *Woe to Wit*. A slow unwinding, and then such
strength accumulated by the last act; no one had ever gotten
it like that before.

Sobinov to the third power. Polish clothes, very tight at
the waist. He splutters with the flame of love. Then when he
has to wear chain mail he feels uncomfortable.

The pretender's line goes up, then down. The high point
is the scene by the fountain. It has to be done at the height of
passion. Everything that goes on in the scene at "Krakow,
Wiśniewecki's house" is slightly funny. Laughable. Least of
all in the pretender is there anything of Napoleon, of the as-
ceticism of a soldier. But what is astonishing is that he suddenly starts to sing about love like a nightingale.

Vsevolod Meyerhold
Notes at a Rehearsal of Boris Godunov

November 16, 1936
Scene five. Night. A cell in the Chudov Monastery.

One thing is absolutely clear: there is one indispensible condition for the part of Pimen. Actors in the old days—and they were absolutely right—kept strictly to the essentials of their type. They knew that all parts were first of all strictly divided according to type. So now we have to decide to what type the part of Pimen belongs. Without that we can't even begin. I'm not going to go through all the various theatrical types from the heyday of melodrama, but Belisarius, Tiresias, they're part of it. In Pushkin's day actors knew those things. *La Tour, The Doctor.* . . . Karatygin played versions of Calderón's plays. The Western European influence was generally pretty strong, and even though Pushkin was a reformer of the dramatic system and the Russian stage, he too came under that influence.

But Pushkin uses an unusual tone. Look at the way he begins this scene: "Night. A cell in the Chudov Monastery. Pimen is writing by lamplight." Korenev was right when he began the rehearsal and said: "We'll be reading 'Night'. . . ." We want a sense of the total atmosphere in which the actors find themselves: "Night . . . writing by lamplight." There is a kind of haste that reads as nervousness. We don't want the entire role to sound buoyant and youthful. Not at all. *Ausgeschlossen!*

I was twenty-four or twenty-six when I played Tiresias in *Antigone*. I struggled for a long time to make my young voice sound darker, and I was helped by the fact that I've always had a somewhat husky voice. When I played Treplyov I tried to change that huskiness, but for Tiresias I tried to accentuate it. Talking about the timbre of the voice is talking about type. To read Pimen in a young voice is nothing but rhetoric. He has his rhetorical moments, but as soon as they become apparent, we must immediately read in a whisper.

Samoilov has gotten Grigory very well, except for a few places. He gave us a real feeling of nighttime. In places where he might have spoken loudly, he spoke in a whisper. But where Pimen is concerned, we have to get rid of any echoes of the *raisonneur*. He's not a *raisonneur*. These are agitated, nervous lines. The verse has to flow, there has to be some kind of impetuosity in it. . . .

In Pimen's big speech there's the phrase "the furious general cry." Pushkin always puts his adjectives in the main position, not secondary. For instance, he could have written "the general cry," but he says "the furious general cry." Pushkin strengthens the modifier, the word that details the description, so that it always sounds as if it formed a single word with the main word. We have to pay special attention to that. It occurs a lot. Pushkin's lines absolutely require restraint. Pushkin is afraid of overemphasizing beautiful words, because in his case the beautiful parts are in the pauses, in his rhythms.

Pushkin always has wonderful endings. He keeps something marvellous in readiness. That's why it works the wrong way when actors try to drop the end of a line or phrase. That doesn't work anywhere. Pushkin doesn't need those drop-offs. . . . It's almost as if he were constantly breathing, and that keeps the line ascending. But ascending here doesn't mean being overemotional. I would say that this part all has to be in a monotone. . . .

We're keeping the scene with the monk, to follow "Night." Between the scene "Night" and the scene with the monk a certain time has passed, during which Grigory, as we know from researchers interested in his character, liked to change his address. He's by nature a wanderer. It may be this characteristic alone that led him to take on the mask of Dimitry. He was a servant of Wiśniewecki. Wiśniewecki not only employed him as a servant, he entrusted him with commissions of various kinds. And now he's back in a monastery.

Working on the character of Grigory, it was easy for me to work out a scenario in my head. When I was in prison in Novorossisk I had a little volume of Pushkin with notes by the historian Polivanov, and while I was there I worked out this scenario, which I later proposed to Esenin. I told him I'd give him a scenario and he was to use it as the basis for a drama in verse.

It's possible that at the time the Tsarevich Dimitry was murdered, Grigory might have been in Uglich. And that Grigory and Dimitry met. He was thirteen or fourteen at the time. Here we'd have to stretch one side or the other a little. Make Grigory a little younger, or Dimitry a little older.

Why am I saying all this? I'm saying it so that the scene that follows "A Cell in the Chudov Monastery" comes out sounding this way. Grigory leaves Pimen not because he was angry at Pimen, but because the place was getting on his nerves: black cockroaches crawling across the table, black monks' robes. He goes away, and the scene must definitely take place somewhere on the road. Once again, a road and a rock, just like in the old melodramas. It's a tradition that opera has preserved. And then we have a scene in pantomime: he's shivering, it's obvious he's running a fever, he collapses near the rock, falls asleep, and has a dream. At the moment he collapses we can make a switch, so that someone else falls asleep. And he has the dream. Some tree or something, a wall (_this section of the transcript missing_). That's why the rhythm changes. Now we can understand why the rest of the play is spoken in one rhythm, and here it's another. If the actor playing Grigory sings, then it's better if he does the recitative as an aside, very, very measured, like in _Don Giovanni_. Prokofiev liked that idea very much. He gave me his word that he would write the music for this scene while he was on the ocean liner, the way he wrote the score for his opera _Love for Three Oranges_. In this part we will hear leitmotifs from the ball scene and other bits. We will get Grigory's dream.

Korenev was right when he said that with this scene the exposition is over and the tragedy begins. And let's remember that we have no right to cut up the first scenes, because the exposition has to be heard in detail and with extreme simplicity. The tragedy starts later. Up to this point things are being marked out: Boris, the boyars, the pretender, and so on. We can't cut it. And then the tragedy starts. Look. We see Grigory's first dream. We see his second dream. Two dreams. Then his first words in the scene with the monk: "What does it mean?" He says that as Grigory Otrepev. Then he has another dream. He wakes up again and says: "That's it! I am Dimitry, the tsarevich!" And that's where the play begins. Up till then it's been only approaches to the play. . . .

Pushkin's fabric has been overlaid with too many heavinesses, and it needs transparency. And so at this point Pimen and Grigory have got to make us think of children. Naive

children. It's a bit strange, though, that a tragedy like this
is all born out of a dream, isn't it? And we have to preserve
the naiveté, fix it, so that the aura of this naiveté lies over
everything.

Pushkin wrote in the spirit of Shakespeare, but he was
better than Shakespeare; he's more fragrant, more limpid,
lighter. After all, why is it so hard to translate Shakespeare?
Because he's long-winded, and Pushkin isn't. He goes on
and on.

You just heard today the success Prokofiev had with the
battle scene. Why do you think he succeeded? Because he approached that scene with Pushkin's naiveté. Here you have a
group of Western warriors imported by Grigory, a group of
Asiatic warriors imported by Boris Godunov, and some Germans. He portrays this battle naively. That way the scene between Rosen, Margeret, and the Russians makes sense. It's a
cacophony of three languages—Russian, German, and
French. And so Prokofiev's music provides a cacophony. The
passage is a terrific success.

Pimen has to have the same naiveté. Pimen as a philosopher—it won't work at all. And that's the reason I suggested
he wipe his penpoints and rearrange his parchment scrolls.
You can't sit him down at a table and dress him in a black
cassock and even a surplice. He has to have a shirt mouldy
with age and stained from lampsmoke. He doesn't sit motionless, he shifts things around on his desk, parchments. Anything so long as he doesn't just walk around making the sign
of the cross all the time. No. He's a professional writer, he
knows all about manuscripts.

He works like an experienced writer. It was hard for Leo
Tolstoy because he had to make things up as he went, but a
historian only has to write things down. His material flows
through his hands. He can talk about anything he likes and
still keep writing. He can stick something under his chair,
then straighten up, look around, take a piece of parchment
out of a niche in the wall, and keep his monologue going
(*Meyerhold demonstrates*). But not like this: he can't sit down
like an opera singer and boil up a monologue (*Meyerhold demonstrates*). That's very hard to listen to. It won't do. If you
keep on doing something, then what's important in the
speech will get across to the spectator. . . .

After all, Grigory really loves the old man, he's like a father to him. He acts a bit infantile in this scene, but that's not
important. When we first wake up we're all like children. . . .

Grigory stops right next to him, but he doesn't look at
him. He looks only when he says: "You write and write, and
never seem to sleep." But then he forgets about him right
away and does his speech (*Meyerhold reads*). He doesn't even
notice whether Pimen is listening, he just leans on his table.
And that little old man keeps on working and half listens to
what Grigory is saying, and he still keeps on working when
he answers him, when he says:

> Your young blood burns;
> Go cool yourself with fasting and with prayer.
> Then will your dreams be full of ease.

Try it again.

(*Samoilov*: "You write and write, and never seem to
sleep. . . .")

That speech should be a little faster. This is a man who's
somewhat perturbed: he's just had a powerful dream. Don't
forget, he's a writer himself. He files books in the library, he's
read them, he's interested in books. He found a library by accident, almost the way Lermontov found his grandmother's.
"What's Mishka doing?" He's in the library. And he gets something out of it. So that these images flow rather easily from
him. You remember the scene with the poet? We have to repeat it. That's how he gets these images:

> . . . where Moscow like an ant hill lay
> Under my feet, and in the marketplace
> ·
> Is that not strange?

Ok, let's go on. (*Loginov*: "Your young blood burns. . . .") No,
those lines have to be read with a certain humor. (*Meyerhold
reads in an old man's voice, with a smile. Laughter. Applause.*)
It's a humorous bit. He's a little old vaudeville hoofer. And
you know Pushkin was laughing when he wrote: "Go cool
yourself with fasting and with prayer." (*Meyerhold reads, with
an old man's chuckle in places.*) "The mad indulgences of
younger days."

"Of younger days." He stands up, as if to show that just
for a moment his own young blood was stirring. We have to

get that across, that way it won't be dead, that way Grigory's next line makes sense: "What joyful times you had when you were young!" That way all of a sudden we have two young men: Grigory and this naive old man. That's when Grigory understands what kind of man this is. After all, Pimen has a very long, complicated biography. . . .

Pimen's monologue begins like this: "Never regret, my son, that you have left. . . ." (*Meyerhold reads the speech very softly, like an old man. Before "And his visage shone as radiant as the sun" he weeps. And at the final words "Our sins are punished for offending God—A regicide now reigns as Russia's tsar!" he shouts and pounds the table.*)

That's revolt. That's when Grigory understands who it is he's dealing with. He can say anything now. And that's when he begins:

Worthy father, for a long time I have wanted
To ask you about the death of the Tsarevich
Dimitry; I have heard you say that you
Were then in Uglich."

Then Pimen reacts to Grigory's speech right away and the tempo of his speech increases. (*Meyerhold reads at a rapid tempo.*) And then quietly, cautiously (*trembling*):

. . . Before the bleeding body of the child
Which—wondrous to relate!—began to tremble.
"Confess!" the people shouted, and beneath
The axe the wicked men confessed—
And swore it was Boris that set them on.
Grigory: How old was he? The murdered tsarevich?

It's a scene right out of Dostoevsky. And of course Dostoevsky is rooted in Pushkin. Read his speeches, throw away all the political nonsense, throw away his reactionary position, and then it's clear—this is the ground out of which Dostoevsky springs. I'll bet that even in the conversation between Alyosha and Dmitry Karamazov you'll find these same tones. . . .

Grigory is left alone. Pimen has had a great effect on him. He says (*Meyerhold reads, shaking all over*):

Boris, Boris! Before you all men tremble. . . .
(*very loudly*)

... You shall not
Escape the judgment of this world,
Nor yet escape the awful wrath of God!

See, this is the executioner talking. (*Meyerhold reads the speech again.*)

See, this is Shakespeare, I mean this talking to himself, where the future is clearly sketched out: "Aha, no one dares remind you of the dreadful fate of that poor boy, but we will. We'll remind you. I'll remind you." And right at this moment, already, the struggle for power begins. So that the part of Pimen is not something you can simply read. It's a living image. We ought to be able to love him. He can love, talk about love, not only fight. He spent a period of his life wandering too. He's been here and there. Actually, what we have here is the biography of someone like Lope de Vega, Cervantes. Cervantes was a warrior, that's how he lost one hand. A writer has to know life. Vishnevsky gave us a beautiful film, *We're from Kronstadt*, perhaps because he'd been a warrior since he was fourteen. Do you know what happened when they showed *We're from Kronstadt* in Spain? After seeing the film some fighter drew the conclusion: "Aha, if you throw a bomb under a tank, it stops." And then in the next battle as a result of that conclusion he destroyed ten tanks.

So here's what I've done today. Spent my time developing the notion of theatrical type. The type of Tiresias, of Belisarius, of the wandering beggar in French melodrama—the man who lost a pile, was left penniless, and sings in the street. Oscar Wilde appeared in Paris after he got out of prison, dressed in a torn suit, out at the elbows and knees. His teeth had all fallen out as a result of scurvy. The handsome Oscar Wilde walking the streets of Paris in rags, deserted by everybody. The odor of death. We need all these tones. Someone as victim, or like Tiresias who comes in with his big speech to tell some visions he's had, and after that it gets sinister. It's the same as in *Hamlet*, when the ghost says: "If thou didst ever thy dear father love. . . ." Remarkable, eh? This is exactly the same. What kind of cue do we need for Pimen? The ghost of Hamlet's father? Not at all. But take the core of the ghost of Hamlet's father. The core of pitiful Oscar Wilde, toothless and in rags. I would surround myself with all these images, and hammer all of them into Pimen, so that it all resounds in him. That's the only way to explain the devastating effect when Pushkin read this scene out loud. Only by reading—now rising, now falling—can we obtain that.

Grigory's question should be almost tactless: "How old was he? The murdered tsarevich?" "Why, seven years old, and now he'd be. . . ." The scene suddenly stumbles and everything goes head over heels: seven, no, more; twelve. We have to show that. That way we get theater, otherwise we've got declamation or melodeclamation, and I hate that.

So that from the point of view of type Pimen has more energy than Grigory. It's only because he's been heated up by Pimen that Grigory is able to exclaim: "Boris, Boris! Before you all men tremble. . . ." (*Meyerhold reads*.) He's been infected by Pimen's passion, he begins getting feverish during Pimen's speech, and he carries that fever over into his own speech:

Boris, Boris! Before you all men tremble

. . . .

Nor yet escape the awful wrath of God!

The following scene also begins feverishly. And that way everything becomes clear.

Vsevolod Meyerhold
Notes at a Rehearsal of Boris Godunov

November 16, 1936
Scene five. Night. A cell in the Chudov Monastery.

We're dealing here with an old man who has the qualities of a child. And so for an old man like that, with the qualities of a child, great deliberation isn't natural. That is, he says impressive things but he says them somehow childishly.

Tiresias in *Antigone* comes in with a very important speech in terms of content, but the effect he produces is not only because of what's prophetic in what he says, but because he delivers it childishly.

Mikhail Chekhov as Caleb in *Cricket on the Hearth* strikes us first of all by the way he conveys the image of an old man.

This is a sage who when he relaxes from his sage thoughts can take a bit of hard-boiled egg out of his pocket and sprinkle it on the doorstep for the sparrows.

I once saw an old man who traveled from Penza to Moscow with frost-bitten hands. He arrived all stiff from the cold because he was carrying a canary in a cage and he had wrapped his warm scarf around the cage. At the moment the only thing that interested him was the canary. And this old man was a progressive, he had connections with a major newspaper, he was a kind of Chatsky-grown-old; but at that moment he was only paying attention to the canary.

We have to get that into Pimen as well, then the touches of the *raisonneur* will fall away from his speeches, so that through the chirping of an old man's speech we will fall in love with him, the way Mikhail Chekhov made us love him in the role of old Muromsky. Whether he was a positive or negative figure, we were already attached to that old man, in love with him.

In other words, what is the actor's goal? To build the character of Pimen with mumbling, with nervous energy and emotion, to create an old man whom we have accepted even before he begins to speak. Of course we can't not listen to *what* he's saying, but that *what* is so full of the *how* he says it that the impression we get is: "Oh, what a nice old man!"

In Pimen there ought to be some touch of eccentricity, and his conviction of the importance of the work he's engaged in. "Yet one final story. . . ." He uses his pen with pleasure, he probably cleans his inkwells every day. His tools of production are in perfect order. He probably has a rag that he uses to dust everything on the table. His papers are all arranged, and he takes great pleasure in all of that, and everything he says he says offhandedly, exactly the way old people talk to themselves.

This old man talks all the time, but it mustn't seem that he's addressing Grigory. If Grigory is asleep or not, it's all the same to him. It's one thing to speak a speech to someone, it's another thing not to address anyone, not paying attention to anything, just picking up scrolls, with a lot of nervous energy.

I once paid a visit to Leo Tolstoy. I've never told anyone in the company this before, but I've told some of my literary friends and they loved it.

Tolstoy is usually described through the prism of Repin's portrait—in a peasant shirt belted at the waist, with a beard like Stasov's. The general image is of a big powerful man, very strong and healthy. I thought of him that way too, when I went to visit him at Yasnaya Polyana.

I went with Sulerzhitsky; we arrived at Yasnaya Polyana in the morning. The breakfast table was covered with a white tablecloth, there were a lot of glasses and dishes on it. There were a lot of people in Tolstoy's household: his secretary, Doctor Makovitsky, his daughters, his daughters' husbands, etc. They asked us to wait, since Tolstoy didn't show himself that early. No matter what happened, no matter who was there, he never interrupted his schedule. We sat down. Someone told us "that's his room" and pointed. I don't know why he told us that, maybe so that we wouldn't talk too loudly. I picked out a point in the doorway where, judging by the image I had of Tolstoy, his head was bound to appear, and fixed my eyes on it, like this (*Meyerhold indicates a point high above his head*). For a long time the door never opened. Finally the doorknob began to turn. I fixed my eyes on the spot I'd picked out. At last the door opened and in came this little figure in a black overcoat and a yarmulke, a little man like this (*Meyerhold indicates*), and with teeny little steps he headed off somewhere, to go to the bathroom or someplace. Tolstoy turned out to be a dried-up, little old man. I was speechless. He stayed out of sight for the next few hours and showed up only at lunchtime.

My second impression of him was when he was eating lunch. They served him some kind of vegetarian casserole. It was turnips or carrots or something, I can't remember. But it was the sweetest thing, when he ate. And when I saw him it made me think of Muzil playing an old man. Muzil when he played an old man, let's say eating a baked apple, used to smack his lips the way children do when they eat something good. And that's the way he chewed on this apple. We could hear him chewing the apple and it made you want to smile, and you began to love him right away. That's the kind of warmth we felt when we watched Leo Tolstoy eat.

What kind of old man do you think the Tolstoy who wrote *Resurrection* was? That book talks about love the way only a young man could talk about it. You remember the famous scenes with Nekhludov, his love scenes. That's all described beautifully. It's simply the energy, the feeling of a young man. Now that's the charm of youth, but it's connected with child-ishness. He becomes very wise, but his behavior has some-thing of the child in it. That's why old people and children can talk very easily with one another, they speak a common language. You could never have that kind of conversation be-tween a child and a man of twenty-five.

When you start feeling out Pimen, then in relation to Gri-gory you have to play him so that we feel Pimen's fatherly care. . . .

I've been talking about Leo Tolstoy, and Mikhail Chek-hov, and Muzil eating his apple, so that you understand that finding a character for Pimen means really using your imag-ination. You have to be able to see all his details, every gesticulation.

When you get to Pimen's great tragic speech about how the Tsarevich Dimitry was murdered in Uglich, that speech will succeed only if you've started out by getting across a lot of the childlike in Pimen, and by putting humor into "your young blood burns, go cool yourself with fasting and with prayer"; when you play the youth of the part, then we will listen to your speech a hundred times more attentively than if you don't get that across.

When you begin reading it, try out different old men's in-tonations, even if the first few times it gives us a comic im-pression. We can correct that if it starts sounding too much the hoary sage, so that you don't give the impression of a vaudeville routine. . . .

I forgot one other person—Konstantin Stanislavsky, who did the crucial role of Doctor Stockman only because Doctor Stockman talks too intelligently. He set himself a task: I want to find in Stockman not the man who talks intelligently in public, but the crackpot. He started working. And once he found the crackpot, then he started to talk intelligently. For a long time he wouldn't come to rehearsal: only after he had found the crackpot did he begin rehearsing.

He made this gesture with two fingers (*Meyerhold demon-strates*). Then he started to talk intelligently. Stanislavsky told us all how he solved the problem he had set for himself. He resolved to get up in the morning not as Stanislavsky, but as Doctor Stockman. He held his spoon with two fingers, he picked everything up with two fingers. At the time all his friends thought he'd gone crazy. Later, after all those little quirks had become internalized, only then did he allow himself to speak a line of Ibsen's text. . . .

This is what the contemporary spectator is going to get. But this is a man of the sixteenth century. We have to give the feeling of that too. In order to comprehend Pimen, you have to take a look at the picaresque novel *Lazarillo de Tormes*. There's an old blind man in it—they get him a guide who robs him.

You absolutely must look at Breughel's paintings. He has a painting that portrays six blind men walking. It's a tragic painting, but I always smile whenever I see it.

One of Cervantes' *intermedios* is called *The Two Gossips*. You must read it. Take *The Two Gossips* and do it as an exercise—read it with a partner, and do one of them as an old man.

When you work on Grigory Otrepev in the monastery scene you have to remember that he isn't yet a man, you absolutely must preserve some features of the child in him. You remember the portrait of Pushkin, that shows him as a curly-haired child, sitting with his face propped on both hands? I think Pushkin had a similar age in mind for the pretender. Grigory Otrepev is still a child. That's important, because that way his dream will be like the kind of dreams you have at that age, when you're aware of your dream. Little children move about in their sleep when they dream. Or a dog, when it's dreaming, smacks its lips in its sleep, it feels uneasy. And a human being feels uneasy. I feel uneasy too. That's why, when Grigory tells his dream, he should have his eyes wide open. . . .

"My old dreams were unquiet still, and sinful." Now there's a revelation. That's the same thing as Leo Tolstoy at seventy-five writing about love as if he were a young man in love himself. And in Pimen too the flesh hasn't cooled off completely. You have to convey something of that. Mussorgsky's music leaves all that out. That's wrong. Without that tone, it isn't Pimen.

Remember: the first big speech—one tempo, the second faster, the third speech, faster still. Because when Grigory says:

Worthy father, for a long time, I have wanted
To ask you about the death of the Tsarevich
Dimitry; I have heard you say that you
Were then in Uglich. . . .

Pimen answers immediately, with great anxiety, and suddenly
that anxiety has turned tragic. The whole speech has become
staccato. He is transformed, and we have to believe him, because he really was in Uglich. We have to see this speech of
Pimen's as exemplifying a character type from the tradition
of Shakespeare's theater. But he also has to become like the
messenger in a Greek tragedy. Without changing the way he
talks. You have to convey the character of the messenger.
That's a type as well. That's a separate job. The messenger
comes on stage to tell the story of things that the playwright
was not allowed to show. That's why the messenger's part
was always given to the best actor in the company, someone
who was a master of gesture, who could command a white-
hot energy. This is the job Pimen does here. Pimen, I mean,
carries the function of the messenger, he tells the story of a
most important event, upon which a certain part of this tragedy is based. That's why you have to blaze up immediately.

Vsevolod Meyerhold
Notes at a Rehearsal of <u>Boris Godunov</u>

November 27, 1936
Scene five. Night. A cell in the Chudov Monastery.

It's been said that Pushkin's attitude to the themes of _Boris
Godunov_ is unclear. True, there are different kinds of evidence. Nicholas I suppressed the play. That's evidence of the
difficulties Pushkin experienced getting this play through the
censors.

Why did this piece cause him so many worries? We
mustn't forget that he was still in disgrace, banished. They
opened his mail. We have to look for the "fool's cap" he wrote
about. And we do know what he was referring to; the extent
to which he was able to veil the places that would be risky for

the censorship. Of course that's what makes it so difficult to perceive where he is specifically indicating the fool's cap.

Our literary historians have missed something in Pimen's speech: "Never regret, my son, that you have left a sinful world. . . ." Here Pushkin has very cleverly camouflaged a list of the kind of tsars who become monks. This is what we would call a kind of double entendre. On the one hand he becomes a monk, but on the other he does things that reveal him as an executioner. And that, I must in all honesty confess, isn't always obvious. Here we must allow the ironic note to sound a little, make the reader a bit doubtful of Pimen's religious fervor.

Later on, when he says all those things about God, you mustn't say them perfectly straightforwardly, making him out a totally devoted religious man; you also have to make clear the human being in Pimen.

What I think is that the complexities of Pimen's character are just one of Pushkin's sly tricks. Pushkin put these things into Pimen's mouth on purpose, things he couldn't have put into anyone else's mouth, and that's how he got them through the censorship. It worked like a kind of smokescreen.

Look at who he takes as his first example. Someone who in historical fact drenched himself in blood. After all, to be frank, what would be someone's reason for changing the "golden crown . . . for a cowl?" He might have started his list with Tsar Fyodor, whom Alexei Tolstoy portrayed as a guiltless idiot. But he begins with Ivan the Terrible and says:

> Tsar Ivan sought to soothe his conscience
> In acts of cloistered contemplation.
> His palace, full of haughty favorites,
> Turned overnight into a monastery;
> His hellish followers in robes of black
> Became a troop of penitential monks. . . .

See, he doesn't just say simply "full of favorites," but puts in "haughty"—"full of haughty favorites." Then he says "hellish followers in robes of black." He calls them "hellish."

"And the ruthless tsar himself their holy abbot." That's typical of this double entendre.

Look, it's an enormous speech, and what is it about? We never listened to it. In high school they were always giving us this speech to learn by heart, we even read it as a duet. But I mean, even our literature teachers overlooked what it was all about:

> And his son Fyodor? Upon the throne
> He sighed after tranquility, and wished
> To be a monk. He turned his royal chambers
> Into silent prayerful cells, and there
> The painful sorrows of a monarch's life
> No longer lacerated his soul.

He calls the "sorrows of a monarch's life" painful. He means that the things he had to do as tsar tormented him. He ran away from them and hid himself beneath a monk's hood.

You see what this speech is all about. So that here we must introduce some touch of irony. We cannot cover all this up, we cannot cover up all the poet's ideas, since when he wrote this scene he intended to say something with it.

That's why in _Boris Godunov_ there must be two truths: the first is historical truth, which of course must absolutely be brought across, and here no eccentricities are permitted; and the second, we must absolutely bring across the attitude of no one else but Pushkin himself to what he depicts on stage. Of course there are differences between the attitudes toward a historical moment of Pushkin, or of Ostrovsky, or Averkiev. Different attitudes. Anyone can get a director to direct a historical play, but we want to ask: what is Pushkin's attitude to that historical moment? Of course we can't pretend that the events of October 16 come after the events of December 12. But he made his choice of events, of confrontations, in a certain way, so that they would be understood in relation to the way they are presented.

What was it in this subject that so frightened Nicholas I and the censors? Because a presentation of historical events was so much more terrifying from Pushkin than it would have been from any other writer of the period, Bulgarin for instance. He would certainly have presented those same events "irreproachably." He wouldn't have had his ears sticking out of that fool's cap.

That's why this speech has to be done so that the audience understands the significance of a monk's cowl, so that the audience understands that the tsar could murder someone and then go make a thousand genuflections to God.

What's happening here? Of course, the church is discredited. Pushkin discredits it, and does so accurately. He was right to do it. Think of how calmly Pimen says to Grigory: "they change it for a cowl." And right after cowl he immediately sticks in: "Tsar Ivan sought to soothe his conscience in acts of cloistered contemplation." . . .

The pretender is an uneducated individual, but he has an inquiring mind, the kind you get when a child lives in a house with a big library, and if the child has an inquiring mind, then he educates himself: he looks at pictures, he reads a few pages here and there and so forth. That way he accumulates a store of knowledge, but superficial knowledge, and he'll be able to give the impression of being educated. But in actual fact he doesn't have an education. It's only the result of his inquiring mind. I think that Grigory has to be shown onstage in such a way that the audience immediately perceives that he has this inquiring mind. That's why it's a little risky to portray Grigory as a simple child of the people. The main thing about him is that he's curious. Look, here's the first indication of his curiosity:

> Worthy father, for a long time I have wanted
> To ask you about the death of the Tsarevich
> Dimitry; I have heard you say that you
> Were then in Uglich.

What do we see here? This is a boy inquiring about the world: what's a comet? What's in its tail? The next indication of his curiosity: "How old was he? The murdered tsarevich?" And then that's all. . . .

Even in the scene in the inn the question mark sticks out: "Where does that road lead?" He always has a question. In the scene with Pimen he doesn't even reveal pieces of his future biography. And it seems to me that our clever Pushkin borrowed the device from Shakespeare, that he reveals his hero (here there are two heroes, Boris Godunov and Grigory) carefully, economically. He introduces him, he's asleep. Pimen dominates the scene and sticks in one big speech, then another, then a third. Grigory doesn't reveal himself yet. . . .

He's like a bud that will grow into a flower. We have to mark the places where Grigory Otrepev is transformed into Dimitry the Pretender. And until we get to those places we have to proceed with great economy, so the audience won't know what will happen afterward. . . .

Vsevolod Meyerhold
Notes at a Rehearsal of <u>Boris Godunov</u>

November 28, 1936
Scene five. Night. A cell in the Chudov Monastery.

A certain strength in Pimen, his powerful part in the play, has
to be felt right off, even though he will be using an old man's
voice. Of course here the baked apple has gotten us confused,
but I said that so that we would get the feeling of a living
individual, so that we wouldn't get the impression of a little
old man in miniature. He has to be a figure on a large scale.
We have to depict him with powerful strokes, like Michaelan-
gelo's figures, like Leonardo da Vinci, Giotto, the ghost of
Hamlet's father, King Lear, etc. Why else did I mention all of
them?

Now—how shall we proceed technically in order to at-
tain that? I tell you beforehand that practicing on the text
won't work. If you want to find the right tone for the part,
then you can't do your homework on the part itself. You must
select a few speeches from *King Lear*—the biggest speeches—
and practice with those. You must take Tiresias' speech from
Antigone, the ghost's speech from *Hamlet*. You could take
other things of Pushkin's that are on the same scale as this
and practice on them.

When Pimen stands by his lamp, he is a king on his
throne. We always think of an old man with a long beard.
Maybe we won't have that. Maxim Gorky, for instance, gave
the impression of being a powerful individual, sinewy, strong,
despite the fact that his tuberculosis had shriveled him all
up. The painter Korin, when he paints Gorky or when he
paints old monks, tries to portray them powerfully. He portrays their features on an enormous scale, so to speak. He
flicks away the insignificant details. He tries to define whatever is most characteristic in the face by means of one single
feature or another, and he does it with the simplest means.
For instance, he does these eyebrows—and right away the
definitive character is made clear. Japanese actors, when
they're putting on their make-up, try to indicate the most
characteristic features with a single brushstroke. *Gemütlich-
keit*, coziness—that's where the danger for Pimen lies. He has

to have traits of greatness. You remember, I was saying that when he turns to his scrolls and starts his work, he becomes a figure of grandeur.

When I played Tiresias I made my entrance as a bent old man, but when I began to roar I straightened up. That was my mistake. I should have entered as a big old man and then gotten that internal strength by using my voice, with excitement, indignation. . . .

It's not true that an actor who plays comic roles can't play dramatic ones. That's absurd, because, for example, Lensky, Salvini, when he played the criminal Corrado in Giacometti's *La Morte Civile*, he practically delivered a comic monologue. I think that a highly qualified actor is defined by his ability to work in the tragic and the comic vein—and I think such an actor is making a mistake if he doesn't do both. Moskvin realized that at the end of his career; when we saw him in Ostrovsky's play *Burning Heart* we regretted he played only comic parts. The same with Igor Ilyinsky. They told me Igor Ilyinsky was a remarkable Tikhon in Ostrovsky's *Storm*. And in *The Dawns* he played a dramatic role for us as well.

(*To the actor rehearsing Pimen.*) While you're rehearsing you ought to start a huge number of scrolls. I don't mean we'll necessarily keep them all later. He picks up those scrolls, rearranges them, and says: "Someday another monk will come and find my work, my ardent, nameless labor. . . ." That is, if you keep arranging the scrolls, those words won't sound abstract. Because it *is* labor. You understand? The lifelike intonation—you can't just pick it up by listening to others. . . .

Your words have to be lifelike. They must flow as a result of the things you do in your life, not from your having heard others talking.

You must feel the life force in that cell, and the difficulty of Pimen's enormous labor. Then the line "Yet one final story—yet one more—and then I end"—and here a pause— "my chronicle." You mustn't throw "chronicle" away. Throughout this entire scene we have to feel the significance of this chronicle. . . .

This is the great horror of a director's work with an actor and an actor's work with a director, because just when an actor is beginning to get things right along comes the director and starts shouting: that's no good, don't sit down there, don't do it that way. I always try to use examples—that's what I want to do now.

How I hated Stanislavsky when I was playing Baron Tusenbach in *Three Sisters*! Tusenbach comes in, goes over to the piano, sits down at it, and starts talking (*Meyerhold does the speech*). But as soon as I would start Stanislavsky would tell me to go back. I was in a rage. I didn't understand then that Stanislavsky was right. But later when I had become a director myself and was acting at the same time, then I understood that if Tusenbach comes in and goes straight over to the piano, you get the impression that he isn't saying the lines, only reading them. In order for the speech to make the audience think that we're thinking what we're saying, then we have to say the lines, not read them. And what we say has got to seem the consequence of what we're thinking. I wasn't getting that then, and Stanislavsky told me to go back every time. Ten times, and nothing worked. Then he came up from the auditorium onto the stage, tossed me a little piece of paper, and said: "You cross to the piano, say your first three words, then suddenly catch sight of this piece of paper, pick it up, and while you're crossing to where you're supposed to sit, tear it up into little pieces as you continue your speech." And it helped a lot. I got what I needed for the scene.

Another time this happened: I didn't feel any anxiety, and I was looking for a way to make the words sound anxious. Nothing. Then he gave me a bottle of wine and a corkscrew and said: "Do your speech and open the bottle while you're saying it." And really, when I started doing it I suddenly found that what little anxiety I did have began to grow. And I got it from the struggle I was having trying to open the bottle of wine. I did it rather expertly—after all, I do know how to open a bottle of wine (*Meyerhold pantomimes; laughter from the company*). But I hated Stanislavsky, hated the bottle, hated myself, hated everybody—and I worked myself up into a state where obstacles arose, and then in my lines I found the intonation of truth.

I know it's stupid to tell stories about yourself—I did this or that—but when I began that speech and saw that little piece of paper, and bent over to pick it up, it was a living gesture. After all, we all live by means of our experience, we all bring our experiences onto the stage, and that gesture, when I picked up the little piece of paper, came from a conditioned reflex somewhere in my memory. (Someone should tell Pavlov this story.) And I got a living intonation.

Lensky writes about how he builds a character: first he sees a hand, a foot, then a neck, a head, and so on. Some actors never see their character. Yuzhin was that way. We used to call him the record cabinet: he had a kind of built-in record collection, which always gave him the intonation he needed. Lensky was the exact opposite: he would make himself over completely, because he saw the character visually. The ideal is the actor who both sees and hears himself. When I do Pimen I see him, but I can't hear him yet.

It's that extraordinary harmony between the external qualities, a harmony between gestures and the way you speak, that's what you have to find. It takes a lot of work. The worst part is to get it to come out together. It's an enormous task, finding a character. . . .

As we've already discovered, Pimen is no stranger to amorous adventure. Now here is a jumping-off place for that:

> My old age seems to me another life:
> The fleeting world now eddies past
> As once it pounded madly, full of action,
> Turbulent as some overpowering ocean.

Understand? It's a little like a Cervantes romance. Enchanting memories in a lyrical agitation. Here we must convey the surge of enthusiasm. Understand? (*Meyerhold repeats the quatrain.*) These lines are agitated, and then his line to Grigory makes sense: "Your young blood burns. . . ." It's a waltz. Something feverish. And then the dryness is all forgotten. These are the points where you can get the grand scale you're looking for. . . .

Remember? I suggested you read in a whisper:

> Oh frightful, unforeseen calamity!
> Our sins are punished for offending God—
> A regicide now reigns as Russia's tsar!

(*He stresses the word "regicide."*)

That's necessary, this is the quintessence. Pushkin has fired those words into the structure of his tragedy. You can't just speak that word. I think that we have to seek its significance in a whisper, so that I remember that line, and not only I but the audience; and also Grigory, and later in the play he

repeats that word "regicide." And Pimen has lodged that
word in his consciousness.

> And his visage shone as radiant as the sun.
> We shall not see a tsar like him again.

And then:

> Oh frightful, unforeseen calamity!
> Our sins are punished for offending God—
> A regicide now reigns as Russia's tsar!

Tell me what lexicon Pushkin has taken that from? From
Greek tragedy, of course. And it's no accident that the quatrain begins: "Oh frightful, unforeseen calamity!" That's a
formula from the classical theater, and here we have to make
use of the devices we borrow from classical theater. It has to
glitter.

> . . . beneath
> The axe the wicked men confessed—
> And swore it was Boris that set them on.

This is an emotional story. If you read it this way (*Meyerhold
reads the speech*) it's simply a piece of protocol. You're the
messenger. You describe the very words, the very spot, where
these horrors took place. I would say that this is the young
Pimen talking, and of course he's in a powerful trance, it's
almost as if he's lost his mind. And when Grigory asks him,
calculatingly as a mathematician: "How old was he? The
murdered tsarevich?" then he catches you in a trance-like
state (*Meyerhold demonstrates*):

> Why seven years old, and now he'd be—
> (It's ten years now since then—no, more;
> Twelve years). He would have been your age
> And would have ruled. But God willed otherwise.

You understand? The man is in a state of transport and you
get a terribly slowed tempo, which gives Grigory time to
imagine everything. "He would have been your age." That's
the spark that fires Grigory's mind. Those are the forces that
feed Grigory's imagination. You have planted in Grigory the
seed he was waiting for. At this moment the knot is tied, with
the fact that they are the same age. This is the first impulse

toward the theory that he is Dimitry. That's why your story and afterward in the trance the final words ought to be spoken with the voice of a prophet. You must give the impression of a man transported. Then he turns back to his manuscript and there he finds peace. But that's afterward.

Let's go on: "This mournful story . . ." This speech should arouse our pity. It's a dying speech, and that will be an easy matter for you. You say:

> This mournful story ends my chronicle;
> My work is done. I have spent little time since
> In the world's affairs. My son, Grigory—
> I have taught you how to read and write.
> I pass along my task to you.

He says that impromptu. It just that minute entered his head to make Grigory heir to his throne, as it were. It's as if he were dying. He embraces him, strokes his head, as if he were his son. Here you can't perform the business coldly. Of course, I was mistaken when I said that he finds peace when he turns to his manuscript—his agitation must stay with him. That prepares the audience. We have already fallen in love with him, and when he takes his crutch he goes off into oblivion. The audience never sees you again, but they have to get the feeling that you're not going off just to pray, there has to be a feeling that the audience is saying goodbye to you.

That's why the decisive factor here is that you are embracing Grigory, turning over your labor to him, otherwise the knot remains untied. And here again there's a conflict: you embrace Grigory and intend him as your successor, to continue writing your chronicle—and he's thinking about how he can take the place of the murdered tsarevich. Here's the conflict. We have to play out the whole of these conflicts. And the actor must feel that, otherwise we get an epic story. And that doesn't interest me. What interests me is a story based on strong emotion.

Mejerxol'd: Stat'i, pis'ma, reči, besedy, II (Moscow, 1968), pp. 373–374; 377–391; 394–402.

Meyerhold to Sergei Prokofiev

August/September 1936

Dear Sergei Sergeyevich:

This letter will note exactly all the musical sections we need for *Boris Godunov*, scene by scene. Essentially it's a record of our conversations, only in more concrete detail.

Besides all the musical sections indicated below, I would very much like to have 4–5 extra songs that I could use at various places throughout the production, repeating them whenever necessary. One or two of them should have an Oriental flavor, two or three should be Russian. The basic theme of all these songs is sorrow, the sadness of someone alone and wandering, lost on the roads or in vast fields and forests.

Now for the music for each individual scene.

I very much want the first three scenes of the play unified by crowd noises. Nevertheless these sound passages, as the action progresses through the first three scenes, must exhibit different natures and different tensions. These sound passages, as we've already discussed, should be based on a chorus plus braying instruments like the double bass, bass notes on the cello, etc. It seems to me a harmonium (using these or other registers) would do very well to sustain and unite the heterogeneous sound passages with the roar of the crowd. We can even make use of sound effects—rustling noises, low rumbling, etc.

In scenes I and II men's voices predominate, while in the monastery scene (III) a mixed chorus with women's voices.

Scene I. The Kremlin

The crowd begins at Vorotynsky's line "We cannot easily cross swords with Godunov." The sound here is fairly sluggish, lacking in energy. This is how Pushkin describes it: "The people retreat, in scattered groups . . ." "The people keep on wailing, and weeping . . ."

In this musical section (beginning with Vorotynsky's and Shuisky's lines, through the end of the scene) we would like to have two waves of sound from the crowd—a flow and an ebb, as if the crowd were approaching and then retreating.

Length of this first musical section: 30 sec.

Then comes the scene change for scene II. We are doing everything we can to keep the changes short, especially between these first three scenes. So we estimate the length of the second musical section, which will accompany the scene change, as no more than 15 sec.

This part is also the roar of the crowd, of the same restrained nature as the first part (for Vorotynsky's and Shuisky's scene).

Scene II. Red Square

Starting with the beginning of the scene, three music sections. Also crowd noises, but more aroused. It breaks off when Shchekalov starts to speak.

Length of this section: 15–20 sec.

When Shchekalov speaks, the noise only quiets down partially; the groups nearest him quiet down, but the groups farther off keep on; this sound (musical section #4) continues through Shchekalov's entire speech, approximately 50 sec.

The end of Shchekalov's speech is the end of the scene, and during the change we hear the crowd moving off (the ebb).

This ebbing section: 10–15 sec.

Scene III. In front of Novodevichy Monastery

We jump in immediately with a very excited noise (. . . people milling about on the square . . . sounds of the crowd, and furious howling).

This section lasts 37 sec.

Then immediately out of this section we change in 3–4 seconds to an even stronger roar from the crowd. This is "struggle, battle"—weeping, sobbing, etc. Always at moments like this the image of the sea is clearly in Pushkin's mind: "The people fall to howling; they fall like waves, one upon the other . . . yet again . . ."

Length of this weeping section: 52 sec.

However, remember that after the line "I'll wipe my eyes with spit," new sounds arise out of the general howl—from the distance rolls a wave of shouting: "Long live Boris!"

All of the scene IV (An apartment in the Kremlin)—following these three scenes full of crowd noise—I intend to stage in silence, without any reference to the people, in quiet rooms inside the Kremlin.

For the rest of this letter, whenever a scene won't have any music, I'll just leave it out without comment.

Scene VII. The Tsar's apartments

This scene will be staged in accordance with Pushkin's own stage direction (in one of his earlier drafts of the play): Boris and the Sorcerers.

From beginning to end of the scene, a constant chorus from the male and female sorcerers who surround Boris in a stuffy, overcrowded space, telling his fortune. This peculiar ensemble can include a whole group of sorcerers, diviners, and fortune-tellers.

One of them is a shaman (with a bell and rattles).

2nd—pours dried beans back and forth

3rd—pours hot wax onto water

4th—makes a chicken peck at grain

5th—plunges hot metal into water

6th—whispers incantations

7th—recites charms in a singsong voice

8th—beats an Eastern (Mongolian) drum

9th—plays a pipe (as if charming a snake)

10th—a Kalmyck of some kind (or a Bashkir) who sings a lyrical, mournful song. This too is sorcery or an incantation of some kind. What I would like is to have this singing express Boris' inner state while he is speaking his monologue.

The music is divided into two parts:

1. From the opening of the scene to the first pause (which I've marked in the text for you) lasts 20 sec.

2. After this pause the entire monologue is spoken against the background of the same ensemble. The length here is about 2 min. 10 sec. to 2 min. 25 sec.

This letter will include a list of those percussion instruments we already have, but please don't feel yourself restricted by it; we will try to get anything you feel you'll need.

VIII. An inn on the Lithuanian border.

For this scene we need the following:

1. The monks first make their appearance singing the sort of thing blind beggars always sing while begging alms. This singing is of a religious nature. Then we hear a very sharp contrast, the debauched drinking songs of Varlaam and Misail, of a "secular" nature . . .

The blind beggar singing is very short (one verse).

2. Varlaam and Misail's songs.

Here's a note on them (from the Prosveshchenie ed.): Pushkin changed the monks' songs several times. In the second draft Misail sings: "Oh love, love, my love," and Varlaam continues: "Oh love, come look at me." Then in the third draft the first sings: "You walk past my cell, little darling . . ." and the second continues: "When they made an unwilling monk out of me." But by the 1831 edition they are already discordant; Misail starts out "Once upon a time in the city of Kazan," and Varlaam sings "There was a young monk . . ."

In this connection, see the very interesting collection of Ivan Pratch (1792), which includes the song "Once upon a time in the city of Kazan."

In addition see the following articles:

Chernyshev, V. I. "Varlaam's Song" (*Pushkin and His Contemporaries*, vol. V, pp. 127–129).

Vinogradov, N. N. "More on Varlaam's Song" (*Pushkin and His Contemporaries*, vol. VII, pp. 65–67).

3. At the end of the scene, when everyone rushes off and the hostess is left alone—this is where I would like to use one of those extra songs I mentioned earlier. It's the song of a solitary wanderer, a homeless beggar. It must be full of enormous sadness. The song of a man wandering alone on the open road, through vast fields, huge forests and rivers. The spectator will involuntarily connect this sadness with Grigory's fate.

Scene IX. Moscow. Shuisky's house.

From the very opening words we want to hear the guests singing. A chorus of drunken voices. An Asiatic feast. Food in abundance, rivers of wine, like a Rubens.

The guests sing loud and off-key.

The singing shouldn't last long at all, perhaps only one verse, over which Shuisky begins his speech "More wine! . . ."

Scene X. The Tsar's apartments

Ksenia sings a song (accompanied by a string trio). This edition doesn't have this song. It's in the others, at the beginning of the scene. Here's the text:

Why do your lips no longer speak,
Nor your bright eyes look about?
For your lips are sealed,
Your bright eyes are shut . . .

After this the dialogue begins. In connection with Ksenia's song there's an interesting book: Simoni, *Great Russian Songs Collected in 1619–1620 by Richard James in the Northern Parts of Muscovy*. See the Collected Papers of the Department of Russian Language and Literature of the Academy of Sciences, vol. 1, XXXII, St. Petersburg, 1907.

Scene XIII. The Castle of Mnishek at Sambor.
For this scene we need the following musical sections:
1. Entrance music—some kind of Polish *Reverie*—lasts 37 sec. (starting with the first speech and ending on the line ". . . She has enmeshed him").
2. Polish music, where the author has it. 48 sec.
3. After the pause music plays. Approximately 55 sec. Very short, in proportion to the shortness of the scene.

Scene XIV. Night. The garden. A fountain.
For this scene we'd like three musical numbers in different moods:
1. Something bravura (a reprise?)
2. Scherzo
3. Amoroso
This should have the music sound as if it came from a distance, from within the castle, where the celebration continues. Seeing that we've already used the polonaise and mazurka in the previous scene, it would be best to use something here with a Hungarian flavor, a polka-mazurka or something.

The length as well as the sequencing of these musical sections is hard to estimate at this point. The best thing would be to have brief musical sections that could be repeated where necessary.

Scene XV. The Lithuanian border.
This scene we intend to stage without music.
Night. Silence. A nightbird calling in the distance. The Pretender and Kurbsky ride quietly, stealthily.
At the end of the scene all we hear is the receding sound of hoofbeats.

Scene XVII. A plain near Novgorod-Seversk
For this scene we need a sound passage as if from two ensembles:

1. Asiatic, warlike, stupefying, and
2. A more controlled, harmonious, civilized, Western European sound, but also warlike.

No. 1. The scene begins with the opposition of the Asiatic and the Western European ensembles. We hear the clash of swords and of two alternating ensembles before we hear any words. When the Western European music finally gains the upper hand, we hear the words of the text.

No. 2. The entrance of the Germans should be funny. For that reason we want a moment of very funny music, something that sounds specifically German, with a comic orchestration (for instance, piccolo and drum).

No. 3. Then there's a reprise of the first musical clash (that is, No. 1 again).

No. 4. Dmitry appears to the sound of a drum.

No. 5. After the Pretender's line "Sound the retreat!" we should have a trumpet, and in what follows we want not just the drum but also a march, something that might be described as a "victory celebration."

All the musical sections I've indicated can be very short. Where the length is concerned we rely entirely on your sense of time.

Scene XVIII. Moscow. A square before the Cathedral.
All we need is the Fool's song. We don't hear the church choir: we intend to stage the scene as if it takes place at a comparative distance from the cathedral porch.

Scene XXI. Moscow. The Tsar's apartments
Here at the end of the scene we must have music for the reception of the tonsure. Nevertheless Boris' death is unexpected. Agitation, confusion everywhere. The preparation for the rite is hurried, confused. Perhaps instead of a choir we hear only the voice of a protodeacon. The whole effect is one of disharmony.

We see this moment as the *preparation* for the reception of the tonsure, not the rite itself. For that reason it would be better if instead of the usual choral harmonies we hear some sort of single bass voice, a protodeacon, now loud, then soft, constantly breaking from agitation.

Perhaps also the sound of church bells.

XXII. Military headquarters

Here we need only trumpet signals (the "rally" that sounds at the end of the scene).

XXIII. Red Square. The Place of Execution

We need a musical chorus effect: moaning from the crowd, yelling, noise. Preferably a coloring different from that of the opening scenes. In these voices we should hear a tragic note we don't hear in the first scenes. In this scene the crowd noise is divided into two parts:

1. From the opening of the scene through the end of Pushkin's speech, this part is only incitement, galvanizing.

2. After Pushkin's speech comes the outbreak of violence, the roar of an avalanche that sweeps away everything in its path.

Scene XXIV. The Kremlin. Boris' house.

We need a musical chorus effect: the roar of the crowd, anxious, threatening, like the roar of the sea. We ought to feel that sooner or later this undisciplined crowd will solidify, consolidate itself, and fight against its oppressors, whoever they may be.

The roar is not lengthy; it corresponds to the length of the scene.

The people fall silent at Mosalsky's words: "People! Maria Godunov and her son Fyodor have taken poison . . ." etc.

quoted by Victor Gromov, in *Tvorčeskoe Nasledie V. E. Mejerxol'da* (Moscow, 1978), pp. 392–399.

V.

■ Meyerhold and Music

On March 25, 1928, in Moscow, the poet Boris Pasternak went to see Meyerhold's production of Griboyedov's play <u>Woe from Wit</u>, with Meyerhold's wife Zinaida Raikh in the role of Sophie. Pasternak went backstage at intermission to see the Meyerholds, and found himself at a loss for words.

The words came later that night, and they produced two extraordinary documents—a letter and a poem. The letter was addressed to Meyerhold, the poem to both him and Raikh. The author of both is Pasternak the poet, Pasternak the pianist, the pupil of Scriabin, the admirer of Chopin. And the subject that called forth his letter and his poem was a production of a famous play where music was used in a way entirely unheard-of in the theater. No longer accompaniment, no longer simply mood music, melodramatic background, music became an integral part of the drama, making it into an opera—a dramatic spectacle where emotion and action are both expressed by music.

The greatest casualty to the passage of time, where theater is concerned—the least recoverable memory, the unrecallable image—is rhythm. We have descriptions of performances, we have photographs and drawings, and we can resee what must have been. But not before sound recording and television—and, strangely, rarely since—did we have anything to help us rehear what occurred on a given evening in the theater. Because photographs exist, and drawings have survived, much has been made of Meyerhold as a Constructivist. But Constructivism is as much concerned with time as with space. What of Meyerhold as musician, the intimate of musicians, the successor, in intention, to Wagner?

The texts that follow reveal some of Meyerhold's most fundamental principles as a stage director: Pasternak's letter; a letter from Boris Asafyev, who arranged the music for <u>Woe from Wit</u>; Erast Garin's description of some of the musical devices used in <u>Bubus the Teacher</u>; and, finally, some of Meyerhold's own remarks on the matter of music. And we shall see in the next chapter of this book Meyerhold's very specific application of these principles in his production of <u>Camille</u>.

Boris Pasternak to Meyerhold

Moscow
March 26, 1928

Dear Vsevolod Emilievich,

I regret stopping by to see you at the entr'acte last night. Nothing I said to you made any sense—but if it had, it would have been false anyway. And now today I have been practically obsessed all day long, unable to get anything started. And it's because I have been longing for last night. Now that's a different matter. That's clear proof; that I understand.

The Inspector General was an extraordinary production and I don't intend analyzing it in detail. Not that everything in it was of equal stature, but that's the way any creative organism exists: nucleus here, protoplasm there.

It may be possible that in *Woe to Wit* the very same virtues are arranged less systematically, it may be that they are distributed less lavishly there, but those same virtues and subtleties in this production, in contrast to *The Inspector General*, have become much more profound. If the two productions are viewed sequentially this profundity is absolutely obvious and there's no point in wasting words to prove it.

It would have been much pleasanter for me to live with my silent awareness of this than to be telling you about it now, and if it weren't for the nonsense that I know you have had to listen to and read about your production, you would never know of my delight.

I don't know much about theater and I am not much attracted to it. Suffice it to say that I have lived all my life in Moscow and I have never been to the Maly nor to the Chamber Theater. I read once in Swinburne's book on Shakespeare that Shakespeare had intended his best works to be read and not to be staged, and this view, even applied to such a name, did not surprise me. It is clear that Shakespeare more than anybody else was addressing the human imagination, not just companies of actors. But let us suppose (we want so much to believe it, and perhaps it really was so) that Blackfriars was a *true* theater. That means of course that it was a *realistic* theater. In which case it was patterned and modeled after *nature*. What then could be the *model* for such a theater? Human types, behaviors, habits, temperaments? No, all that is still not enough, all those living particularities demand to be imitated, and certainly they are, but they can serve as models only for the actor, that living and fundamental element of theater, not for theater as a whole. True, even a talented actor is so rare that sometimes a culture must be satisfied with him alone, but nonetheless, given even those rare cases, a culture is entitled to want more and to yearn for a totality, i.e., for theater.

It seems to me that the only possible model for the composition of a theater can be the *imagination*, the imagination as a whole, as a system, as an inimitable unity, a pounding musculature, total in its singularity. To put it more simply, by virtue of the imagination all arts tend toward an ideal theater, and sometimes, very rarely, they manage to find it.

I remember several of Stanislavsky's productions; when I was thirteen and visiting Petersburg for a few days, I would go every evening to watch Kommissarzhevskaya; I've seen Mikhail Chekhov—and I am very much indebted to them to the same degree and in the same sense as I am to you. But one thing is incomparable: when I saw your work I experienced *theater* for the first and only time in my life. I realized what it meant, and began to believe that as an art it was indeed conceivable.

When the spirit of genuine talent touches me it turns me into nothing more than a naive child, I become utterly devoted to the work of art and quail before its author as if I had no experience of life and it was all new to me, and I reach for my handkerchief much too often. After this immediate wave of emotion subsides and I begin to understand what has taken place, then, interestingly, what invariably affects me are the common generic forms that express themselves through the work of art, the laws that determine it, the most general secrets of human nature to which the work of art owes its attraction. It's strange to me, but clear to me, that I can give my attention only to something not worthy of it. Because everything worthy of my attention makes me inattentive—doubly so: first, because it stuns me, and second because it gives rise to reflections that distract me from observing it in detail. But I am happy with this trait of mine, and would not want to live otherwise.

What then is the lesson you so casually offer; what is it you make us remember? The main thing I have already said: that rare and barely conceivable enterprise to which Shakespeare, according to Swinburne, addressed himself, has been realized by you. On Triumphal Square. I have been to your theater three times now and—don't be angry, and please don't laugh—three times is a lot for me. In your production of *Cuckold* two things astonished me: your attitude to virtuosity and your attitude to the material. I saw the way you were accumulating virtuosity, hoarding it, or to put it more precisely, what forms of it you were cultivating. You have allotted to it just the role it deserves to play in a great and fascinating art. It occupies in your work the place of a fire extinguisher or an emergency brake in a train—both devices developed to perfection, both always close at hand, and both inconspicuous when not in use.

You have realized better than anyone that art as a whole is a tragedy—a tragedy which can afford no tragedies and which must be allowed to run its entire course smoothly, guarded against catastrophe. And so you have avoided the error of certain talents that soon burn themselves out: you have not lapsed into the common error typical of misunderstood mastery. You have not become the slave of a degenerate virtuosity, you have not furnished your home exclusively with fire extinguishers, as evidently happened with Briusov and is happening now (strange as it may seem, given Mayakovsky's temperament) with the *LEF* people. Your train is genuinely gathering speed and moving off, not standing with brakes frozen by petrified formal habits.

Also, as I said, I was astonished by your attitude to the material. Once, around the time of Shakespeare's three-hundredth anniversary, I spent a great many hours thinking about his use of metaphors, his poetic richness. I came to the conclusion that it was only Mirandola alive who did not resemble Mirandola dead in Shakespeare; everything else, everything alive was connected in a flood of circular, whirling similitude. I discovered, behind his imagery, all those things constantly resembling one another, that sense of universal inter-relatedness which grips a great poet at moments of impetuous creativity, that most dynamic of all dynamics. Georg said of Dante: "He took a handful of ashes from the stove, blew on it, and thus created Inferno"—and his words express exactly what I mean just now. When I saw Ilyinsky and Zaichikov smash to pieces that theatrical intonation we are so used to, and then take the fragments—which ought to have made us laugh, they were so formless—and press them and carve them into fleeting forms of expression, forms which began to astonish the spectator and which became the special language of the work of art—it was then I was reminded of the rare and fulgurant summit of art where one can speak of the absolute *indistinguishability of the material.*

I have found that in Aeschylus, in Dante, in Shakespeare—I know it's stupid to make a list, no great poet is conceivable without it. But I never imagined a metaphor could be realized in the theater.

And then to find, suddenly, after this initial moment of insatiable energy with which every great creative enterprise ought to begin, but which in most cases either ends in catastrophe or degenerates into a futile pointlessness, suddenly and delightfully to find that you are also an inexhaustible master of plastic composition, a dramaturge no less than a director, an astonishing historian, and, most importantly, a vital and strong-willed historian, that is, a historian who cannot fail to love his homeland and its past because he performs an act of love for its future in his daily work. And this is the only kind of futurism I can accept: futurism with a genealogy. I can't tell you how much I have been granted by your *Inspector General* and *Woe.* It was easy to recall what was essential in *Cuckold*; two things in it astonished me, I was able to say, because the production made its principles clear, and principles always astonish me, if they can be named and counted. The vital virtues of your recent organisms are incalculable, though—precisely because they are indeed organisms.

If I had gone backstage after *The Inspector General* I would not have been so confused at meeting Zinaida Nikolaevna. The reason I was confused this time is not only that she is so brilliant as Sophie in *Woe to Wit* (the role is generally less grateful in performance, and in Griboyedov's text as well), but the incredibly absurd reaction she has gotten from the rabble. I was horribly embarrassed by that, and I felt that no matter what I said she wouldn't take my words at their face value, that whatever praises I might have uttered, she would invariably connect them with the fact of her mortification. And all that is only a specter of the worst sort of emptiness, I pay no attention to it. I admire both of you and I write this to both of you, and I envy both of you the happiness of working with the person you love.

Entirely yours,
B. Pasternak

Boris Pasternak

TO THE MEYERHOLDS

All the corridor-gutters have emptied.
The chatter subsides, dies away.
At the window, late for the performance,
The storm knits a stocking of snow.

You hole up backstage in the darkness
While out here in front I turn pale.
Like a fool, I stop by at the entr'acte,
Get confused and don't know what to say.

I catch sight of treetops and rooftops,
And a whirlwind of flies in the dark.
I will learn from this raggle-tag winter
How to play cat and mouse just like you.

I will say that below, those grimaces
Have taken my breath away.
That my present got wet and unraveled,
But I'll bring you another someday.

That on earth you can't help people's feelings,
That I carry applause from the hall,
That these tokens I bear are intended
For you both—but for her most of all.

I adore your awkward way of walking,
That lock of hair, eagerly gray.
Even if it's a part you are playing
To the hilt—go ahead: one must play.

Just as one rather gifted director
Played a part in a very young world—
A spirit adrift on the waters
With a rib-bone he thought he could mold.

He entered from behind an arrangement
Of stars, and a planet or two,
By a trembling hand leading an actress
Onstage for her fatal debut.

And inspired by that unique performance
As if by the odor of kohl,
You efface yourself, leaving your make-up.
That make-up which we call your soul.

Boris Pasternak, *Stixi i poemy* (Ann Arbor, 1961), pp. 226–227.

Boris Asafyev to Meyerhold

Detskoe Selo
March 27, 1928

Dear Vsevolod Emilievich,

I've been intending to write for quite a while, but haven't been able to. I have an intermittent grippe with its attendant complications. All I have to do is stick my nose out of Detskoe toward town, and it starts all over again. I can't even think of going to Moscow until my temperature returns to normal. But I can't keep from letting you know how upset I am over everything that's going on because of *Woe from Wit*—to which you've given back its real name of *Woe to Wit*. I've read all the reviews, including Gvozdev's, and I'm horrified. What happened? Is such cultural stupidity possible, such a bloody squabble, and no way around it nor a ray of hope? For a long time I couldn't understand a thing. I finally had a chance to talk to someone who'd seen it, to Gvozdev, and tried to get the facts out of him. I did eventually manage to understand a bit of it—at least I understood what it was they didn't understand. The decadence is all in Beethoven's music, in the _sound_ of it? What kind of nonsense is that? How can _Beethoven_ sound decadent? Then I began probing Gvozdev—as someone who had a grasp of the essentials—and I finally figured out the whole mess. According to what he said, wherever the orchestra played, whenever the music accompanied the ensemble generally, everything was fine. As soon as the music accompanied Chatsky alone, then it seemed decadent. Gvozdev explained it by saying that Chatsky is a Decembrist, and doomed. But I remembered how healthy the dialogues between Chatsky and Famusov sounded in Leningrad, and I kept Gvozdev talking and got another explanation out of him, this: the chamber-music principle and the orchestral principle were confused. So, evidently, in tiny rooms a Beethoven sonata cracks the walls, while on a huge bare stage it destroys itself and destroys the dialogue. (I'm summarizing all of this in my own words.)

Well, if that's in fact what's happening, if that's the reason, then of course it's my fault, since I never even _imagined_ such a possibility. So take my name off the program, get another musician, and he can find something more suitable for Chatsky-as-tribune and get rid of the decadent chamber-music atmosphere. Since, as far as I understand, the show is still being worked on. That's why I wanted to write you immediately after I talked with Gvozdev. But one of his remarks hit me like a cold wind, and I realized the problem had nothing to do with Beethoven, that the problem has to do with the current tragedy of music and the tragedy of my own position as a musician and intellectual.

I'll try to explain exactly what I mean. Gvozdev said: "In _Bubus the Teacher_ the music was constant throughout and it worked, but in this it keeps on breaking off, and it's all wrong." That's when I understood what the problem is. For most people, even really cultured ones, the idea of melodeclamation, or rather the melodramatic principle (Rousseau's idea), music included as part of the dramatic spectacle, is easier to understand than what you had in mind, as I understand it, when you thought up the idea of Chatsky as a musician. I would use the word _symphonic_ to describe the principle by which you were using music, even in the first version of "Chatsky's score," music as part of the dialogue—not as background or accompaniment, but as expressing the interior life of the character, as his psychological state. People don't want to understand the simple fact that the hero is not always a mere orator, and that even the most abstract philosopher possesses this interior life with its temperatures of feeling, and that he also can love, and weep, and dream, and doubt, and suffer, etc. And I do not believe that music is incapable of continuing Chatsky's dialogue. Your principle was correct, and of course there's no music that could better reveal the soul of such an "intellectual" than Beethoven and the other classics.

So far so good. But here's where the trouble starts. Musicians understand music only as music, a piece of craftsmanship, and the public understands music as pleasant entertainment, something that soothes or shakes up the nerves. In the theater music, as far as the public is concerned, is only a lulling background or any annoying accompaniment that gets in the way of "what the words mean." And that's the whole problem. Music as a living impulse, music included in a dramatic production as an integral element in the dialogue—that, alas, no one understands. So the reaction you get is: there's an orchestra playing during dinner and everything's fine, and all of a sudden some nut comes in and starts making scenes and pounding the piano. I'm summing up the man in the street's opinion, but the opinion of the cultured spectator isn't far removed from it.

So. Our society rejects the notion of music as an organic part of the performance, as an element of the dialogue, as a symphonic moment. As usual, you have gone far beyond the era and the age. But what's to be done now? How can we proceed in order to make the notion understandable? Of course it could be made totally understandable only in a situation where the actor was also a real musician/improvisor and actually found the stimulus and the support for his lines in the music. It's possible. Only one thing: shouldn't "Chatsky's music" then be compressed to the utmost, to the most concise formulations; and Bach, Mozart, and Schubert be totally abandoned; and everything be loaded with Beethoven alone, and only with Beethoven's most explosive formulations?

And most clearly the idiots don't understand Chatsky's big solo and think of it as a concert musical number. It's clear to me here that your idea has come up against impenetrable vulgarity—of every kind: philistine, scholarly-researcher, quasi-socialist, etc., etc. It's a many-mouthed monster.

I feel miserable and I don't know what I can do to help. With my nerves, unfortunately, I'm no orator and I'm no good at debates.

If the observations I've made in this letter can be of any use to you, I'd be very glad, and in turn let me ask you to send the letter back so I can make a copy in case I need it. But I doubt I will.

Did I hear that Oborin is playing for you? Should I perhaps write him about "compression" and "explosiveness"? He's a bright boy and a sensitive musician, and very open-minded. We could work something out.

In a word, I'm ready to do whatever is necessary to get your ideas straight. But I'm afraid there are a lot of asses' ears involved! . . .

My very best regards to you and your wife. I've recently gone through something similar to what's been happening in Moscow with *Woe to Wit*—here it was *Boris Godunov* and trying to defend Mussorgsky's original score. The whole thing has gone as far as anonymous threats in the mail. What a wicked irony: to be forced to defend the rights of a composer of genius from the stupidity of music historians in his own country. One horror after another. And there's no support anywhere. Nothing but gloating and silence.

I was just about to send off this letter when someone sent me the piece about *Woe to Wit* from *Komsomolskaya Pravda*. At last a serious review! I don't know who sent the clipping. Just an envelope postmarked Leningrad; there was nothing in it but the article. I read it with pleasure and it calmed me down a little.

I know how busy you are and that I shouldn't count on an answer. I'm sending this letter because I can't not send it. But I'd appreciate a few words. Things are going badly with *The Gambler*. My piano lies motionless and still.

Yours,
B. Asafyev

Telegram from Meyerhold to Boris Asafyev

Moscow
March 29, 1928

Your work on *Woe* totally understood by the ordinary spectator. No changes, no compression contemplated. Gvozdev was telling you stories. The drama historians only wanted to show off by using quotations. The Schubert concert piece is received daily with long-lasting applause. *Woe to Wit* is enormously successful with the public, even more than *The Inspector General*.

Meyerhold

Erast Garin

In Faiko's play *Bubus the Teacher*, two new tasks were added to the principles that had been worked out in *The Magnanimous Cuckold*: pre-acting, and acting to music.

The actor turned the verbal material into an original recitative. The music that accompanied the scene would sometimes illustrate it and, sometimes, as in the Chinese classical theater, would serve as a stimulus to the spectator, enforcing his strict attention.

"Acting to music is not at all like melodeclamation," Meyerhold's notes remark. "The music of Liszt and Chopin, standard fare in bourgeois salons, fits organically into that group of devices which serve to reveal the world of the characters of the play: its contradictions, its over-refinement and decadence."

The "actor tribune" does not play the situation itself, but what is hidden behind it, whatever the situation makes clear in terms of a definite goal, of tendentious purpose.

The solutions to the acting tasks in *Bubus the Teacher* were very interesting and very complicated. The tasks set for the actors (pre-acting and acting to music) were realized onstage as follows: the backstage space was hidden from the spectators' view by a curtain of bamboo poles hung on brass rings. At the back of the stage was a raised platform-shell, with a grand piano on it. In the center of the stage during the first act was a fountain encircled by a garden bench. The stage area was covered with carpet.

The performance began with the arresting opening bars of Chopin's twelfth étude. From the street outside came shouts and crowd noises. Trained footmen ran about in agitation; the feeling of unrest was conveyed to the spectator. The precipitous entrance of each of the characters through the bamboo curtain was accompanied by the clack of the bamboo poles striking one another.

On the penultimate chord of the étude appeared Valentine (played by Kirillov), the major-domo of van Kamperdapf's household.

Chopin's fifth étude accompanied the entrance of Baron Feuerwary (Vladimir Yakhontov). He brought with him the ironic composure of an over-refined hanger-on. Top hat, gloves, a cape, and a walking stick.

"What's going on out there?" he asks, in a high tenor, with a declamatory superciliousness.

"A demonstration of jobless workers, Herr Baron." Valentine's replies are precise, respectful, and subtly ironic. His movements are dynamic—a twentieth-century Figaro.

The rhythm of the Chopin étude provides each character with possibilities for a completely different free arrangement of movement and speech.

The baron slowly removes his gloves.

"Jobless. They are the people who can't work—or who won't?" He throws his words negligently over his shoulder to the servant, followed by his gloves.

"Neither, with your permission, Herr Baron. They are the people who *want* work."

Finally the Baron takes his cape and hat. Bright Oscar Wilde-ish hair lies negligently on the well-groomed head.

In terms of the traditional *type* of drawing room comedy the baron is the "fop/lover." Meyerhold enriched the traditional type with graphically effective pantomime, based on the free rhythm of the études of Chopin and Liszt. If you exaggerated these directorial devices, the effect would be like dancing. The baron might have danced his part; he might also have sung it, if we were to carry to the limit the free recitative of the actor's vocal score. Spectators in those days were accustomed to silent films accompanied by a piano or a salon ensemble, and this made it easier for them to accept the theatrical device of musical accompaniment to the performance.

The master of the house, van Kamperdapf (played by Boris Zakhava) made an especially clear and impressive use of the device of pre-acting. Van Kamperdapf doesn't see Bubus, who is hiding. Thinking he is alone, he acts out a scene in which he imagines himself as a soldier. He has a walking stick in his hand:

Soldiers marching, tra la la. . . .

He begins playing with his stick as if it were a rifle:

Rifles firing, bang bang bang. . . .

But the rhythms of a cabaret song that he has evidently heard only recently begin to overlay the military march with an air of frivolousness:

The drum bangs on,
Rataplan, rataplan, rataplan. . . .

Bubus understands this cheap march as a hint that they may shoot him!

Getting into the spirit of the act, van Kamperdapf even begins to twirl his behind:

What a sight, Babette,
Oh what a sight,
What a strange sight, gentlemen!

And having indissolubly combined the frivolous cabaret song and the military march, he speaks aloud his basic thought: "No, I cannot pardon them."

Here the terrified Bubus reveals himself, and the scene of reciprocal fright begins.

This scene of lyric/satiric self-exposure afforded the spectator such "biographical particulars" that all the pseudo-aristocratic speeches, poses, and maneuvers of Commercial Councilor van Kamperdapf are perceived as the disclosures of a pharisaical bourgeois.

Erast Garin, "O Mandate i o drugom," *Vstreči s Mejerxol'dom* (Moscow, 1967), pp. 319–321.

Vsevolod Meyerhold

I have read all of Wagner, in German. We know him as a composer and author of the texts of his own operas, but he also wrote ten volumes of extremely interesting essays. I have studied them thoroughly. If you go to those volumes and look at the pages I have covered with my own notes, you will understand at once what has interested me.

Wagner introduced two new factors, unknown before his time: the leitmotif, and the "endless" melodic line. He marked off in the orchestra those emotional states which had to be taken into account in the spectator, and expressed them not only in words—words spoken in dialogues written by Wagner himself—but, in order to gain time at that moment when a character says something, he has the orchestra play certain melodies, he arranges certain harmonies, by which he causes certain ideas to arise in the spectator's brain; that is, the spectator experiences certain associations.

In Wagner you often stop listening to the singer, because he isn't singing; at moments of a concentrated emotional staccato, at certain points of structural importance to the text, he is only speaking in harmony at a fast tempo. But you *do* hear the orchestra—it makes itself heard—and you follow what is going on in the orchestra. The orchestra is thus used as a new element in theatrical activity.

Before being staged, music was able to create an image in the mind only in time; through staging, music conquered space. The mental image becomes real through the mime and movement of the actor, subordinated to the musical design; what had unraveled itself only in time was now made manifest in space as well.

Acting is melody, directing is harmony. . . . I discovered that not long ago, and I astonished myself, the definition was so exact. Don't you think so? . . . Musical terminology helps us a great deal. I love it because it possesses an almost mathematical exactness. . . . I understood what the art of the stage director was when I learned to harmonize in my staging the melodic line of the performance, which is what the acting is. That's very important. . . .

And in *Bubus the Teacher*, when Stefka says: "Why? Well, because. . . ." and then falls silent, the music speaks for her. Music reveals the inner essence; it spares us, comrades, from what? From the need for authentic emotions. Why must I have an authentic emotion when such a marvellous means of expression exists?

Have you ever considered why there is always music during the acrobatic numbers at the circus? You may say: "oh, to create a mood, for the sake of festivity," but that would be a superficial answer. Circus people need music as a rhythmic support, as an aid in keeping time. Their work is based on an extremely exact time-count, the least deviation from which could lead to breakup and catastrophe. With familiar music as a background, counting time is usually faultless. Without music it is more difficult, but still possible. But if the orchestra were suddenly to play music different from what the acrobat was accustomed to, it could lead to disaster. In a certain measure this is also true in the theater. Supported by the rhythmic background of music, acting gains precision.

Once in Constantinople I visited a Moslem school during a lesson, and I was struck by the fact that the student, learning the Koran by heart, held the teacher's hand, and both of them rocked rhythmically back and forth. And then I understood that a strong rhythm helps the student concentrate, and provides for easier recall. Rhythm is a great help!

A director must be able to feel the time without looking at his watch. A performance of a play is an alternation of dynamic and static moments, as well as dynamic moments of different kinds. That is why the gift of rhythm seems to me one of the most important a director can have.

Dragging out or speeding up an act can completely change the character of a performance. Play Maeterlinck fast, and you get music-hall routines. Play music-hall routines slow— and you begin to think it's Leonid Andreyev.

It is precisely in the possibility for the actor to improvise that drama is distinct from opera. In opera the conductor does not permit the extension of any temporal sections, and only the tempi can be extended. . . . I will never renounce the right to stimulate an actor to improvise. The only important thing in improvisation is that secondary concerns do not overwhelm the main thing, which is the matter of timing, and of the interdependence of temporal sections on stage.

Pauses are attractive to a good actor, one who has mastered his craft, but in an actor who has no feeling for time they can be insupportable. That's why an intelligent sense of self-restraint is so necessary. In the directorial scores for my productions I have attempted to discover various devices for self-restraint. In *Bubus the Teacher* the musical accompaniment helped the actors to restrict themselves in time. In *The Inspector General* the little moving platforms were intended to restrict the actors in space.

Directing is not a matter of static groupings, it is a process— the influence of time upon space. Beyond the spatial idea it includes the temporal idea, which is rhythmic and musical. When you look at a bridge you see what might be a leap frozen in metal. Movement, that is, not something static. The tension in the bridge is the main thing, not the decoration of the guardrail. It's the same with directing.

Mejerxol'd: Stat'i, pis'ma, reči, besedy, vol. I, p. 149; ibid., vol. II, pp. 66, 83, 71; Aleksandr Gladkov, "Mejerxol'd govorit," *Novyj Mir* 8 (1961), pp. 214, 216, 217, 218, 229, 232; Aleksandr Gladkov, "Iz vospominanij o Mejerxol'de," *Moskva Teatral'naja* (Moscow, 1960), p. 369.

VI.

■ Zinaida Raikh and <u>Camille</u>

The most popular production of the last years of the Meyerhold
Theater was Alexandre Dumas fils' <u>Camille</u>. It opened on March 19,
1934, and played 725 performances in repertory. It played for the
last time on the evening of January 7, 1938, the day the decree was
passed that liquidated the theater. It was a triumph for Meyerhold's
wife Zinaida Raikh in the part of Marguerite Gautier.

The wellspring of art is often obscure, but we find one of its
most interesting manifestations in theater, in the erotic relation between impresario and star. Was Diaghilev's passion for Nijinsky
erotic, or esthetic? Or is there a point where we can no longer make
that distinction?

Even outside theater there are monumental displays of eroti-
cism where the beloved is fetishized as an object—but celebrated
always in public, monumentalized, and thereby celebrated in some
sense theatrically. In these loves, surely, the true consummation of
the affair is the public monument it engenders. And here the basic
impulse is the power of absence and the triumph of the imagination
over fact, for the greatest of such monuments are those called up by
absence:

A beloved had and lost is transformed, made present, in the Taj
Mahal, and in all those marble faces of Antinous.

A beloved never had is transformed, possessed, in Dante's <u>Para-
diso</u> and Shakespeare's sonnets.

It is the presence, though, the <u>having</u> of a beloved, that is usually celebrated onstage: the possession of what the lover has a right
to possess, since he has in some sense created it. Pygmalion's story is
the blissful prototype, Svengali's the anguished corruption of it. Between these polarized fantasies the facts of such cases are always
suspended: Diaghilev's love for Nijinsky, Meyerhold's love for Zinaida Raikh.

In the abrupt manner that marked so much of his personal life,
the poet Sergei Esenin writes: "In 1917 I got married for the first
time, to Zinaida Nikolaevna Raikh. In 1918 we separated."

She was twenty-three when she married Esenin; he was twenty-
two. They were both beautiful. Their daughter Tatyana was born in
1918, a son Konstantin the following year.

In 1921 Zinaida Raikh enrolled in Meyerhold's directing classes; within a year he married her, and later adopted her children, and she began to act in his company.

Meyerhold's love for Raikh was inseparable from his image of her onstage, his vision of her as an actress. How much of his repertory, how much of his work on a play, did he let her image dominate? She was a beautiful woman and a fine actress. Not a great one, some critics commented; merely a mediocre one, sourer critics claimed—and Meyerhold's mises en scène were designed to show her off to her best advantage, they added, as if this somehow vitiated the enterprise. Yet what better spur for creation than love?

No one realized this more clearly than Pasternak. One could desire no more in life, surely, than the last line of his letter: "I envy both of you the happiness of working with the person you love." It was a love that transformed Zinaida Raikh. Her daughter Tatyana, in a sketchy account torn between images of her actress mother and her poet father, gives us a few glimpses of that transformation—and of a domestic Meyerhold too, transformed in turn by his wife.

Meyerhold worked on Camille for well over a year; Leonid Varpakhovsky was at the time secretary of the Meyerhold Theater, and took copious notes at rehearsals. Lev Snezhnitsky and Mikhail Sadovsky were young actors brought into the company to play, eventually, Marguerite's lover Armand. We can trace in their accounts the loving work that Meyerhold devoted to this production.

Tatyana Esenina

In the fall of 1921 mother began to study at the Advanced Theater Workshops, not acting but directing, together with Sergei Eisenstein and Sergei Yutkevich. She had met the director of the workshops, Meyerhold, while she was working at the Peoples' Commissariat of Education. In those days he was referred to in the newspapers as the leader of the "October Revolution in the Theater." A former director of the Imperial theaters in St. Petersburg, a Communist, he too was experiencing a kind of rebirth. Not long before this he had been imprisoned by the White Guards in Novorossisk and condemned to be shot, and had spent a month in prison waiting to be executed. In the summer of 1922, two totally unknown individuals—a mother and a stepfather—came to Orel and took my brother and me from my grandparents' house.

Many people in the theater were afraid of Meyerhold. But at home he would often go into ecstasies over little things—something funny one of us children had said, something good to eat for dinner. He was the family doctor for us all—he would fix compresses, remove splinters, prescribe medicine, put on bandages, and even give injections, and he constantly bragged about his ability and loved to call himself "Dr. Meyerhold."

From Orel, where the world was quiet and grownups talked about things a child of four could understand, my brother and I now moved into a different world, one full of mysterious excitement. I belonged to that vast horde of little girls who were constantly hopping about dreaming of becoming ballet dancers. But even though I was scatterbrained, I missed Orel, and never stopped being amazed at people who could sit for hours talking about things I couldn't understand. Mother was one of them. I still wasn't used to her and couldn't confide in her. But I was at the age when children ask questions, and since I didn't want to be asking "why" every other second I tried on my own to find out what Meyerhold was always talking about with his assistants all the time. I fixed up a little chair for myself beforehand, determined to sit quietly and try to catch the conversation when it first began—I somehow had the idea this would be all I needed to untangle those complicated matters. Alas, at the crucial moment something intervened; the experiment never took place.

An interior staircase led from our room to the floor below, the students' area where the theater classes took place. We could go downstairs and watch classes in biomechanics. Sometimes our entire apartment would be crowded with people, when there would be a play reading or a rehearsal. At mealtimes mother would sometimes go into gales of laughter talking about some line or other in the play. She was always elated, on her feet from morning til night, constantly busy with something. After a while some relatives from Orel moved in with us; there was always someone visiting for an extended stay, and mother managed to take care of a house full of people and get a routine established. The apartment, which at first lacked even the basic necessities, soon began to feel inhabited. Mother even used to make up a special children's menu and would hang it up in our room. Since I knew how to read early on and always suffered from lack of appetite, I would read the menu reluctantly and whenever I read something on the order of "8 o'clock: tea and cookies" I would announce, well before the hour: "I don't want any cookies." We got spoiled very fast in Moscow. Finally they got tutors for us and began to teach us how to behave. But up til then we would spend most of our day out walking on the boulevard with our nurse.

The place we lived was still, through force of habit, referred to as "32 Novinsky Boulevard, the former Plevako house." Our house and a few of the adjoining buildings had previously belonged to the famous lawyer. In 1927 we had a fire which was written up in the newspaper, and from its account we learned that our house had been built before the Napoleonic invasion and was one of the few that had escaped the great fire of 1812. The entrance staircase was made of wood and curved in a spiral, and all the rooms were at different levels—there were always one or more steps leading from room to room. They had a complicated way of keeping the little windows from frosting over in winter: between the inside and the storm windows they put a sinister-looking glass of sulphuric acid, while below the windowsill hung a bottle, and into that they stuck the end of a strip of bandage that absorbed the moisture dripping from the windowpanes.

Across the street on the opposite side of the boulevard was a similar house with a memorial plaque—Griboyedov once lived there. He and his contemporaries must once have wandered about our house—but somehow, in the twenties, nobody spent much time thinking about things like that.

Novinsky Boulevard was a lively spot—Smolensk marketplace was not far away, it was noisy and had a huge flea market where old ladies with veils on their hats went to sell fans, cardcases, and vases. Gypsies with bears and itinerant acrobats used to go up and down the boulevard. Peasants in from the country wore bast shoes and homespun cloth coats, carried packs on their backs, and scurried with frightened faces across the trolley tracks.

It was on the boulevard that we unexpectedly and unwittingly made the acquaintance of our own stepbrother, Yura Esenin. He was four years older than I was. One time he was taken out to play on the boulevard like us, and since he couldn't find anyone else to play with he took us for a ride on his sled. His mother, Anna Romanovna Izryadovna, started talking with our nurse at the newsstand, asked whose children we were, and exclaimed: "They're brother and sister." She immediately wanted to meet our mother. From then on Yura used to come play at our house and we played at his. . . .

She and mother got along together. Over the years she became very close to our family. At the end of the thirties she said good-bye to her son, and never heard what happened to him. For ten years, until the day she died, she kept expecting him home.

Esenin hadn't forgotten his first-born; he sometimes came to see him. In the fall of 1923 he started coming to see us too.

With children it is not the everyday occurrences that leave their mark, but the out-of-the-ordinary ones. For example, the day my life really began, I was a year and a half and caught my finger in the door. Pain, screams, crying; everything opened up and began to move—I really existed.

Whenever Esenin was coming the grownups all acted different. One person didn't feel quite herself, someone else was dying of curiosity. We children were aware of all this.

In my memory his first visits have no words attached, like a silent movie.

I was five. I was jumping around the way I usually did when, all of a sudden, one of the servants grabbed me. First they held me up to the window and pointed out a man dressed in gray coming into the courtyard. Then they changed me into my best clothing as fast as they could. From that at least I knew mother wasn't home—she would never have changed my clothes.

I remember the amazed look on the face of our cook Marfa Afanasievna when she saw the visitor. Marfa Afanasievna was a major presence in our house. She was somewhat deaf and she talked to herself loudly and constantly, never suspecting anyone could hear her.

"You've overcooked the cutlets," my mother would say to her, speaking close to her ear.

"Overcooked! You overcooked them yourself! Who cares? They'll eat 'em. Actors'll eat anything."

The old woman evidently knew that the children of the family had a real father, but she hadn't suspected he was so young and good-looking.

Esenin had just returned from America. He was perfectly dressed from head to toe. Young people in those days were rarely well-dressed—some because of poverty, others out of principle.

His eyes were happy and sad at the same time. He kept looking me over without smiling, while listening to someone or other. But I felt good because he was looking at me, and because of how good he looked.

The next time he came we didn't stare at him out the windows. Mother was home and she went to the door herself. It had been several years since they separated, although they had seen each other comparatively recently. Esenin and Isadora Duncan had been in Paris a number of times and once— probably early that same year, 1923—Meyerhold and mother had been there at the same time. They hadn't tried to avoid each other; mother had met Isadora, and told Esenin all about us children.

But the poet was now on the verge of illness. Mother met him with a welcoming smile; she was animated and caught up in her present life. It was the period she was rehearsing her first big role.

He swerved sharply at the entrance door and went into the room of his former mother-in-law.

I saw the entire scene.

Somebody went into grandmother's room and then came out and said "both of them are crying." Then mother took me up to my room and then went off somewhere. There was a man in my room, but he didn't say anything. All I could do was to burst out crying, which I did, despairingly, at the top of my lungs.

Father left without saying anything.

And immediately following there was another scene, in an entirely different mood. Three people were sitting on the sofa. Meyerhold on the left was smoking a cigarette, mother in the middle was leaning back on a cushion, father was on the right, clasping one leg, eyes cast down but looking to one side, in his typical way. They were talking about something or other, one of those things that I had long since despaired of understanding.

Tat'jana Esenina, in *Esenin i sovremennost'* (Moscow: Sovremennik, 1975), pp. 364–368.

Leonid Varpakhovsky

I was still tormented by the dream of becoming a theater director. I knew that it was only from Meyerhold that one could learn the art of modern directing. But how to find a way to Meyerhold? I turned to my old friend, the pianist Lev Oborin, hoping for his assistance. I knew he was very close to Meyerhold, who had even dedicated to him the first version of his production of Griboyedov's *Woe from Wit*, and I counted very much on Oborin's recommendation. I was not mistaken. Very shortly he arranged for me to meet Meyerhold and my hopes came true with improbable ease.

My meeting with Meyerhold took place in the summer of 1933, in the building on Gorky Street that used to house the Tverskoy Passage and is now occupied by the Ermolova Theater.

Meyerhold received me in a small room without windows that could be reached only by way of the stage. He asked me several trifling questions and then immediately made the stupefying statement that I was to be given the position of academic secretary to the theater. Later, after some years had passed, I asked Vsevolod Emilievich why he gave me the position in his theater so easily. He answered that before we met he had asked around about me, read my work on Vishnevsky in *Znamya* magazine and—the decisive factor—learned of my sharply negative attitude toward Tairov's Chamber Theater.

It was in March 1933 that the period of my close cooperation with Vsevolod Emilievich began, a period that lasted almost three years. It was the period of Dumas' *Camille*, Chekhov's vaudevilles, Tschaikovsky's opera *The Queen of Spades* at the Maly Opera Theater in Leningrad, and the creation of the second version of Griboyedov's *Woe from Wit*. During this period I would meet Meyerhold almost daily, not only at the rehearsals at the theater but also at his home, where all the preparatory work was done in the evening and sometimes late into the night as well. Those who visited Brusov Street during this period remember well the yellow dining room with a round table in the middle, a grand piano in the corner, and a painting in Constructivist style above the telephone table. This painting was done and presented to Meyerhold by his passionate admirer Fernand Léger.

When I joined the theater, work on _Camille_ was already in full swing there. During the day the play was being read at the theater "at the table," and in the evening Meyerhold worked out his blocking diagrams, made notes concerning the costumes, furnishings, and props, and from time to time would go see designer Ivan Leistikov, who was working on the scale model at his home on Bolshoi Karetny Lane. At night Vsevolod Emilievich studied the enormous heap of iconographical material brought to his home from the libraries and museums of Moscow. Meyerhold included me in his headquarters staff (he had a general liking for military terms like "production headquarters," "the director's post," "commandant of the performance"), and I performed my duties with enthusiasm. Meyerhold told us that he saw Dumas' play through the eyes of Manet and Renoir. On his instructions we were going through a great number of reproductions and illustrations, searching for elements of the style and the theme he had set. Then we would show Meyerhold the results of our exhaustive work. He would put on his glasses and study what we showed to him for a long time and with much attention. He would put check marks in some places and insert notes: "staging," "the square décolletage," "Prudence's entrance," "ladies of the demimonde," etc. The Central Archive of Literature and Art has several albums with my photographs of materials marked by Meyerhold. With their help one can trace step by step the materials Meyerhold selected in the process of preparing the production, and the way the selected materials turned up in performance. These materials would be a useful source of information for all directors—especially for those directors who rely only on their experience and intuition, who do not make preparations for rehearsal, and who seem, moreover, to make a working principle of their unpreparedness.

Meyerhold possessed experience and intuition enough to suffice for a dozen first-rate directors, yet during the period of staging _Camille_ he worked round the clock, paying attention to everything—from the music of Lecocq and Offenbach, to nuances of how the part of Marguerite Gautier had been played by great actresses of the past. We collected all the information available about how the role was played by Eleonora Duse and Sarah Bernhardt—and how different were the approaches of these two brilliant actresses to one and the

same episodes of the part! Meyerhold almost always preferred the interpretation of Duse and used some of her devices openly in his performance. For instance, during the
reading of Armand's letter just before her death, Duse gradually lowered the letter while continuing to read it from memory. That was precisely the way this episode was directed by
Meyerhold and acted at the performance.

Over the course of his thirty-five years of directing Meyerhold's methodological approaches changed, which was natural. His directing copies of plays have been preserved; some
of them are filled with drawings, remarks, and notes on staging, while others are almost blank and bear no traces of the
work. As examples of blank copies one could cite his texts of
Camille and the Chekhov vaudevilles, _Thirty-Three Fainting
Fits_. But in any case Meyerhold would have accomplished a
great amount of the preparatory work before the rehearsals
began, irrespective of whether it had been written down.

I have watched Meyerhold's genial improvisations at rehearsal many, many times. These improvisations were born
before our eyes as a part of the process of creative communication between director and actors, but these improvisations
would have been unthinkable without great inner preparedness. Only some extraordinary circumstance would prevent
Meyerhold from coming to rehearsal without thinking over
its plan first and preparing in advance several variants of key
moments in the episode. Everyone who has ever worked with
him remembers well seeing his stooping figure on the
darkened stage long before the initial blocking rehearsals. On
the first of December 1933 the second scene of _Camille_ was
brought to the stage for the first time. Vsevolod Emilievich
came to the theater almost an hour in advance. After comparing the stage layout as prepared by stage mechanic Lutsiko-
vich with his own plan of it, Meyerhold requested that
carpets, shawls, candles, crystal, fruit be brought to the stage.
He meticulously distributed everything on the stage, scattered pillows on the floor, and then spent a long time arranging separate objects on a small table as if preparing a still
life. Everything seemed in its place but Meyerhold, after
glancing at the stage, came to the table on which there was a
lighted candelabrum and moved it to the left. My supposition
is that he wanted to present a more open view of the armchair
that was evidently necessary for the scene he had in mind.

All the actors were already present, waiting for the rehearsal to start. Vsevolod Emilievich apologized, saying that it was impossible to create the atmosphere needed for the scene without setting the correct lighting for it first. Then he busied himself for a long time with the lighting men and put a dazzling white light in the background and a warm, yellow, much less concentrated light in the foreground.

No one could doubt that Meyerhold had played all of the scene in his head before the start of the rehearsal. He knew not only its precise atmosphere but also which pillow on the floor would be occupied by what guest when the couplets of Béranger were performed.

And on the thirteenth of February 1934, when he was preparing the death scene in the same painstaking way and I was helping to arrange the furniture and properties he said: "One thing is particularly clear; in this scene the furnishing and the things on stage are accessories for acting. Nothing is superfluous. Everything is arranged and lighted in such a way that one could predict the action to come: on the grand piano there is a clock—we will direct a narrow stream of yellow light on it—which Gaston looks at. The books we'll arrange in such a way that they block the source of light on Marguerite's face when she sits down in the armchair, and the two lighted candles will justify the hidden source of light perfectly. Behind the armchair, camelias in a vase. That's where our lady will die. And here the moneybox will be placed. On the grand piano we'll put Gaston's cane and top hat. He has fallen asleep in this armchair. I like the idea of this large half-lit room with only Gaston asleep at the beginning of the act. When he leaves he will take his cane and top hat directly from the grand piano. Gaston doesn't even suspect the approach of death—because he is young and healthy. After Marguerite has died and everyone realizes that she is dead—only then will Gaston take out his handkerchief." In this way Meyerhold fantasized before the beginning of the rehearsal. After furnishing and props were arranged Meyerhold again spent a long time fixing the correct light. And all this took place long before the first blocking rehearsal. How often I remember that now, when it's only at the final rehearsals that I manage to obtain the correct light. And light is such a great help in achieving the right creative mood for the actors in that especially crucial period of rehearsal, the period of transition

from textual analysis to staging. It is precisely at this time
that the fate of the eventual performance is being decided.

Meyerhold's work on a production never stopped for even
a minute until the opening night. He would read a vast number of books. He would work at the theater, at home, on the
street, sometimes even at a concert, sometimes during dinner,
when he would answer questions absent-mindedly. He
worked all day, all evening, and all night. This is the way
those scenes were created, painstakingly thought out; this is
the way the brilliant Meyerholdian improvisations were
born. Meyerhold came to every rehearsal with new ideas that
had come into his head since the previous rehearsal. And he
liked very much to flaunt the unexpectedness of what he had
made up. At one of the rehearsals of Chekhov's _Jubilee_ the finale, the solemn entrance of the delegation of employees of
the bank, was to be staged and it was a matter of coming up
with the most vulgar gift possible for Shipuchin. Meyerhold
suggested that everyone taking part in the rehearsal submit
suggestions. The gift, Meyerhold specified, had to be something stupid and pompous, something incongruous in the
context of the scandal with Merchutkina which had ended
just a short while ago, and at the same time the gift was to be
a link, as it were, to the second vaudeville to be presented
that night, _The Bear_. Meyerhold took twenty-five rubles from
his pocket, put the money on a small table in front of him,
and promised it as a prize to the one who could think up an
appropriate gift. All the actors except those in the delegation
of bank employees, who were backstage preparing their entrance, surrounded Meyerhold and vied with each other in
suggesting ideas. The situation resembled Chekhov's story "A
Horsey Name." "Flowers," "a bicycle," "a dinner set," "a
harmonium"—suggestions were coming from all sides.
Vsevolod Emilievich wore a triumphant smile and kept shaking his head negatively, absolutely sure that his twenty-five–
ruble note would remain untouched. And then one of the students from the theater school suggested timidly: "A bear?"
. . . "Touché!" cried Meyerhold, and he handed the money to
the astounded young man. The orchestra began to play, and
onstage appeared the delegation of bank employees headed
by actor Nikolai Poplavsky—carrying a huge stuffed restaurant bear. And, indeed, what could have been more vulgar
and grotesque, and at the same time what a better way to

announce the title of the next vaudeville? It was obvious to me though that Meyerhold was hurt, childishly so, by the fact that someone else came up so easily and off-handedly with something that had taken him so much time to invent. The effect of the whole thing was half-destroyed for him.

On the fifteenth of January, 1935 we were working in the building of what was formerly the Ukrainian Club on Gorky Street and began rehearsals for one of the most difficult scenes in *Camille*, the finale of act four. Those who have seen the production remember the episode of the meeting between Marguerite Gautier and Armand Duval in the empty hall near the staircase. Flickering candles, soft music from the orchestra, and two figures in black clothes that showed off in relief the excited pallor of their faces.

In the hall—which, by the way, was extremely unsuitable for rehearsing—there was the outline of a staircase done with Viennese chairs put sideways upon the floor. After the scene in which Marguerite Gautier (Zinaida Raikh), on her knees, implores Armand (Mikhail Tsarev) to leave Paris, and he agrees on the condition that she go with him, Armand hears: "Never." This "never" triggers off the new scene, Armand's long monologue beginning with the words: "Marguerite, I'm insane, I'm delirious, my brain is on fire . . . ," etc. Armand dashes up the staircase to leave Olympe's house and perhaps Paris itself as soon as he can. But he does not have the strength to leave. He slows his pace, turns slowly to Marguerite, and begins his monologue.

Following Meyerhold's instructions, Tsarev went to stand between the chairs, at approximately the place where the top of the staircase was to be, and began his monologue: "Marguerite, I'm insane, I'm delirious, my brain is on fire. I've reached the state where a man is capable of anything, of any base action. . . ."

At this place came the voice of Meyerhold, that voice so familiar to any who had a chance to be present at his rehearsals: "Step!" Tsarev made a move in Marguerite's direction, as if descending a step or two on a staircase, and went on: "Marguerite, for a brief moment it seemed to me it was the unknown that captivated me in you. But it was love, irresistible love, love that borders on hate, love, tormented by pangs of conscience, of contempt and shame."

And here again came the calm and steady voice of the

director: "Step!" and Tsarev made another move, coming closer to Marguerite. "After what has taken place," Tsarev continued, "I despise myself for still loving you, Marguerite."

And again Meyerhold made the actor repeat the move. "Just say one word of repentance, put the blame on chance, on fate, on your weakness—and I will forget everything! This man does not concern me in the least. But I hate him because of your love for him! . . ."

Meyerhold sat listening intently to the monologue. His copy of *Camille*, bound in black leather, lay in front of him. In my copy of the text I underlined all those places where Meyerhold asked Tsarev to make a move, and also noted that when this scene was repeated during the same rehearsal Meyerhold was insistent that it be repeated exactly the same way.

Three months of hard work at rehearsal went by. Now the rehearsals were transferred to the stage. The same final episode of act four was now played on a real staircase made of light metal. There onstage were Zinaida Raikh and Mikhail Tsarev again. The rehearsal went very energetically. The continuous action and the introduction of new elements (orchestra, light, the set) created a festive mood. By the beginning of Armand's monologue the actors were separated by a large distance: Raikh was near the proscenium stage right sitting in an armchair with her head bowed, while Tsarev was on top of the staircase upstage left. His face was lit by a narrow shaft of bright light.

"Marguerite, I'm insane, I'm delirious. . . ."—the passionate words of the by-now familiar monologue. And then that other voice burst in. "Step" called Meyerhold loudly and insistently from the auditorium.

On that day Meyerhold's voice was heard four times during the monologue. I consulted my notes, made on the fifteenth of January, and saw that Meyerhold called for the actor's move precisely at all the places of the monologue he set at the first blocking rehearsal. The auditorium was dark. Meyerhold was sitting in one of the last rows of the orchestra, his copy of the play, closed, in front of him on the director's table. What had happened?

The actors, not yet having mastered completely the outline of the scene, the scheme of the role, had lost some of its details working under conditions new to them; it is something that always happens in theater when work moves from one level of rehearsal to another. Tsarev had begun his monologue while slowly descending the staircase. This was the correct scenic action, and expressed the established motives quite correctly. But during this rehearsal he got somewhat confused and lost the shape of the action: its musical phrasing, which was composed of two different elements of theater—words and movement. Only in an exact compositional interaction can they create the genuine music of theater. The highest form of theater cannot obtain where only the word is compositionally correct and movement is merely incidental.

Studying Meyerhold's archives I was interested to come across his directing copy of *Camille* and find there the page with Armand's monologue. There were no notes in Meyerhold's copy. . . .

The most prominent trait of Meyerhold's talent was his gift for scenic composition. It was in this that his directorial genius was primarily expressed. Evidently Meyerhold himself clearly realized this, and when speaking about himself liked to replace the conventional term "director" with the French phrase *metteur en scène*, which may be translated as "one who transposes onto the stage." That was his enterprise exactly, transposing a literary work into the language of the theater, unfolding it in time and space.

A striving for monumentality, for broad generalizations, for hyperbole, could in all fairness be called the most characteristic trait of Meyerhold's directing style. It was with a special pleasure that Meyerhold, when staging *The Bathhouse*, put up in the theater Mayakovsky's well-known slogan: "Theater is not a mirror but a magnifying glass."

Everything that takes place onstage is invariably significant, weighty, expressive, and visible. The stage direction to Chekhov's vaudeville *The Bear* says that the heroine is in deep mourning and can't take her eyes off the photograph of her deceased husband; in Meyerhold's production an enormous life-size oil portrait of the late Nikolai was hung on the wall. Meyerhold, by "staging" the stage direction, not only made visible to the spectators the object of the widow's suffering but also considerably increased and heightened the comic effect of the vaudeville by making the late Nikolai the silent witness to his wife's betrayal. The mayor in Gogol's *Inspector General*, stunned by his unexpected luck, ecstatically ex-

claims: "Holler it to everybody, ring the bells, goddammit!"—
and Meyerhold had those bells actually ringing, and their
chiming merged grotesquely with the melodies of a group of
wandering Jewish musicians, the kind that used to play at
weddings in provincial Russia. It was not only the physical
realization of a metaphor, but an entire scene "rampant," one
of Meyerhold's favorite expressions, the atmosphere of an
ordinary wedding engagement enlarged to the dimensions of
a supernatural occurrence. In the same _Inspector General_ the
characters "suddenly change their positions and remain petrified" at the appearance of the gendarme; in Meyerhold's
performance there was the unforgettable dumb scene in
which all the actors were miraculously replaced by their wax
effigies. Meyerhold had raised the dumb scene to its highest
expression. Every scene in Meyerhold's handling acquired the
broadest significance, every role became typified, every play
became a social generalization.

Those who visited Meyerhold's rehearsals often heard
two enigmatic words: "retard" and "reject." Meyerhold often
used these words when speaking about the directorial concept for a certain episode or to explain their objectives to the
actors. Often he would simply shout these words from the
darkness of the auditorium, causing astonishment among the
uninitiated. But the actors knew at once what Meyerhold
meant and immediately made whatever corrections were
needed in the staging and in their actions.

"Retard" and "reject"—these two elements of the tech-
nology of directing determined the style of Meyerhold's theater to a very large extent.

Meyerhold used the first term, "retard," to refer to any
hindrance, any slow-down and stop that arose in the path of
the determined movement. Just as in music (the middle
movement of a sonata), in theater, or in a work of literature,
this retard may occupy large periods or small episodes.

In his poem "Count Nulin" Pushkin describes the state of
boredom that overcame the heroine after her husband had
left on his hunting trip. She sits by the window, tries to read a
book but cannot concentrate on it:

> Beneath the lady's window then
> With mournful clucks the turkey hen
> Plods after a bedraggled cock;

> Three ducks are paddling in a pond.
> Across the dirty yard the cook
> Hangs up the laundry on the fence;
> The weather's gotten somewhat worse:
> It looks like it might snow as well. . . .
> Then suddenly—a distant bell.

The last line here is crucial. It anticipates a number of things, and the reader is ready to dash off together with the heroine in the direction of what is about to come. It would seem then that what should follow is:

> Natalya Pavlovna to her balcony
> Runs, delighted at the sound,
> Looks, and sees a carriage coming,
> Beyond the river, near the mill. . . .

But that's precisely not what happens! Pushkin does it differently.

So that the scene of the count's arrival can gain in expressiveness or, as Meyerhold would have put it, acquire a broadened significance, Pushkin inserts the well-known ten-line stanza between the line, "Then suddenly—a distant bell," and the line, "Natalya Pavlovna to her balcony." This stanza stops the action, thus creating and strengthening the tension of anticipation. Here is the stanza:

> Spend a year in the dreary country,
> Friends, and you yourselves will know
> How strongly a distant carriage bell
> At times can move your soul.
> Is it perhaps some long-lost friend,
> Companion of dear days gone by?
> Is it perhaps even *she*? Dear God!
> Closer, closer all the time. Your heart throbs. . . .
> But it passes on. The sound of the bell
> Grows faint, and dies beyond the hill.

This stanza is astonishing not only for its poetic profundity, but also as an example of retardation of the rapidly approaching event.

Not only in Pushkin but in practically any work of literature we can find countless instances of such retards, be it in character biographies, lyric digressions, or descriptions of nature.

Meyerhold used to say that the second scene of Pushkin's play *The Covetous Knight* (the baron's monologue), significant as it is by itself, corresponds to the second movement of a sonata. It is a typical and highly expressive *andante* which contrasts with the first and the third parts of the tragedy; by slowing down the unfolding of events it increases the strength of their impressions.

In front of me is the production score for *Camille*, Meyerhold's opus 118, from the year 1934. In the score, as in the original text, the play is divided into five acts. But in the score each act is in its turn divided into a number of parts and episodes, and these were viewed by Meyerhold as independent compositions, structural parts of the whole. Each episode is marked with a musical notation determining its tempo and character, so that the scenic score is very close to a musical score.

Let me analyze the second part of act one as an example. We see that between the lively first episode (*capricioso*) and the exciting and playful third episode (*scherzando*) there is a middle part, a slow one (*lento*), just as in the case of a regular composition in sonata form.

How did the scenic action correspond to these three episodes of the second part of act one?

In the middle of act one the action continues in the home of Marguerite Gautier. Supper is at an end, and the guests have adjourned to the drawing room. This is, as the program described it, "one of those nights."

The wine drunk at supper has caused a general liveliness. As always happens after supper, the guests have broken up into several groups. At one side of the room the elderly *bon vivant* St. Gaudens is talking to Armand about his relatives, while at the other Marguerite Gautier is speaking to Gaston, who is telling the lady of the camelias how much Armand loves her. The guests have dispersed all over the drawing room, laughter is heard, somebody strums a waltz on the grand piano. The composition of the scene is complex, polyphonic. Finally some of the young men persuade the old profligate Prudence to sing an off-color song. . . . The noise subsides. A bravura introduction on the grand piano, and Prudence emerges in the center of the room. I remember how long it took us to find the text for her song. We looked through a heap of texts until we came across some verses in

Béranger which were equally graceful and scandalous. Shebalin composed a lovely melody for them, and the performance of this song became the center of the first episode.

The song began like this:

> Young and fresh and beautiful,
> Open to all new delights,
> Every feature quite divine. . . .

The guests applaud; there is laughter, joking, music, but beneath it all the main theme can be discerned—the first meeting of the pair of lovers. During this entire scene they listen to their interlocutors absent-mindedly because their thoughts are directed only at each other. Finally they find themselves standing side by side and are ready to start a conversation. The dramatic plot of the play seems about to begin but Meyerhold, true to his principles of composition, shifts from a rapid tempo to a slow one (*lento*), and delays the beginning of the declaration of feelings with the appearance of Marguerite's friend Adèle in a mask. She imitates an actress from the Théâtre St.-Germain and begins to recite, in French, a monologue from Molière's *Amphytrion*, which she does in the old-fashioned way, with a melodramatic intonation.

"Ma peur à chaque pas s'accroît"—we hear Adèle's voice in the lowest possible register, accompanied by the sound of the grand piano. The light is subdued, everything is quiet, the guests are all over the stage, motionless. As the piano interlude continues we hear several brief lines from the protagonists:

> "Monsieur Duval!"
> "Madame?"
> "Is it true that you came every day to inquire after my
>   health when I was sick?"
> "Yes, Madame!"
> "I can't find words to express how much I am obliged to
>   you."

But now Adèle has finished her monologue, the lights brighten, there is laughter and applause and "Sarah Bernhardt" is triumphantly carried out in uplifted arms. The love scene is interrupted, the slow middle part gives way to a rapid one (*scherzando*) again.

Meyerhold realized perfectly the necessity of alternating

rapid and slow scenes. I still have the notes I used to make during rehearsals of *Camille*, and in these notes I often come across an observation that is typical of Meyerhold: "This episode must be light and in a rapid tempo because the next scene will be ponderous and slow."

On the fifteenth of November, 1933, when Meyerhold was working on the scene of the decisive conversation between Marguerite and Armand discussed above, his attention was concentrated on staging the beginning of the scene "with as much retard as possible" he said. Only that way would we achieve a really explosive effect at the high point of the play, where Armand publicly insults Marguerite by throwing money in her face. Trying to find a way to create for this scene a slowed-down, tense feeling, Meyerhold began to block it to musical accompaniment. After he tried a number of musical themes he found one that was close to the mood he wanted and began to work with the actors. This temporary rehearsal music was usually either discarded later after the scene had been staged or replaced by specially composed music. But in this instance nothing turned out the way he wanted. The actress started objecting very sharply to the music, saying that today the music was preventing her from finding her way toward the shape of the role. Meyerhold stopped the pianist and went on blocking the scene. That day I was witness to how inspiration dries up: creative energy, sparkling imagination, and excitement were replaced by indifference. In ten or fifteen minutes Meyerhold came up to us, who were his juniors and disciples, and complained softly in a conspiratorial tone: "I can't stage this scene without music. I have to find some way to slow it down enormously, so that later I can bring it up rampant, and you just can't do it in this dried-up way."

Although he realized perfectly the importance of alternating quick and slow tempi, in practice Meyerhold often tended to make the tempo of a whole act and sometimes even an entire performance predominantly slow. He was aware of his partiality for a slow tempo, and often complained about this failing of his and tried to overcome it. I think this partiality was the result of Meyerhold's attitude toward the scenic action. Everything that took place onstage Meyerhold regarded as significant, equally important, and for this reason he would lavishly pour out his talent even on minor episodes.

When asked once what he meant by "reject," Meyerhold answered laconically: "In order to shoot a bow you must first draw the bowstring." Then, after a short deliberation, he started talking animatedly about how the last scene in *Othello* ought to be played. Before strangling Desdemona, the actor must perform a scene of unbounded love for her. Only in this way could the dénouement reach genuine tragic heights.

I remember Meyerhold speaking once about Delacroix's painting "The Death of Don Juan." A storm is threatening to overturn a boat. One person needs to be sacrificed to save the others. They decide to draw lots. In the painting displayed in the Louvre we can see this boat, full of people, about to be swallowed by the waves. In the center of the composition is the hat from which someone is destined to draw the fatal lot. Almost all the figures in the painting are turned in the direction of the hat, their gaze fixed on this foreboding object. Only a few figures are turned in the opposite direction: in the foreground we see a nude male back leaning practically overboard, and to the right and left are female figures turned in the opposite direction. All these figures countervailing the main direction of movement are, to use Meyerhold's terminology, in a state of "reject" in respect to the focal point of the spatial and semantic construction of the painting. Not only do they individualize the varying psycho-physiological states of the survivors of a shipwreck, they also accentuate the dominant theme of the painting—fear of death.

We recall, by analogy, Meyerholdian études from his biomechanics classes: "Shooting the Bow," "The Stone," "The Dagger Attack," and others. Each of them had its element of "reject" carefully thought out: stepping back before moving forward, lifting a hand before hitting, squatting before rising to one's feet, etc. I think the amazing expressiveness of all the biomechanical études was to a considerable extent the result of a thorough elaboration of the notion of "reject" and its expert application.

At any of Meyerhold's rehearsals one could see in practice the wide application of "reject"; it was used in the most varied circumstances, sometimes in a psychological sense and sometimes in terms of spatial composition. But each time it was used by Meyerhold to enhance and accentuate the scenic action.

One of the most powerful scenes in *Camille*, the death scene, was based on "reject." The notion was applied there by Meyerhold in very different areas: in the text itself, in establishing the mood, and in the staging.

Meyerhold used "reject" in the following way for Marguerite's final speech: "I am not suffering! I feel that life is returning to me. . . . I have never felt so relieved. . . . Doesn't that mean that I'll stay alive? . . . You see yourself, I'm smiling, I'm strong. . . . Life is coming! It is life that makes me tremble!"

During this speech Marguerite unexpectedly rose from her armchair, straightened up, clutched the window curtains in both hands, and threw them open. Bright sunlight burst into the half-dark room, illuminating all the stage. Then Marguerite, letting the curtains run through her hands, sank down into the armchair with her back half-turned toward the spectators. A benumbed stillness on the part of the other characters. After a pause there was only one movement: Marguerite's left hand slipped from the elbow-rest. That was the moment of death. Each of those present made a slight movement back, and only after that did everyone approach her while Armand, exclaiming "Marguerite, Marguerite!" fell to his knees before her. There the performance ended.

At one of the rehearsals Meyerhold was staging the episode from act two he called "The Count de Giray's Money." The tempo was *moderato secco*. Prudence, Marguerite's friend, has managed to talk Armand into returning to his beloved after their quarrel. He is already in the adjoining room and Prudence tries to leave him alone with Marguerite:

Prudence: Now, now, my dear. . . .
Marguerite: Don't leave me, please, not while he's here.
Prudence: Oh, no. You'll throw me out eventually
      anyway. I prefer to take my own leave, angel, and I'm
      leaving now.

The actress Remizova who played the role of Prudence blew a kiss to Marguerite and disappeared on the spot, behind a curtain.

Meyerhold stopped the rehearsal and said that in that scene the words should be matched with movement. Since Prudence was saying that she was "leaving" the house, she should not simply disappear into the nearest wing. The audience must remember exactly how Prudence left the lovers to themselves. It was very important for the development of the dramatic action. Meyerhold asked the prop men to bring a glass holder with cigarettes and put it on the trumeau table at the diagonally opposite corner of the stage. Then, just before her exit line: ". . . angel, and I'm leaving now," Meyerhold inserted a line for Prudence: "Marguerite, let me take a couple of cigarettes," and made the actress go and get the cigarettes. Then, in order to leave the room, she had to cross almost the entire length of the stage.

The episode was repeated once more, and this time Meyerhold was satisfied. "Now," he said, "the actress is able not only to state that she is leaving the house but to act it out as expressively as possible."

Meyerhold always attributed great significance to moments of exit and entrance, especially where the main characters were concerned. "The actor's first appearance on the stage is his calling card," he would always say. With Marguerite Gautier's very first appearance on stage, Meyerhold completely destroyed the conventional image of the character.

Gone were the feverish flush, the shivering, the coughing—all the tokens of disease and doom. Instead there was recklessness, joy, enthusiasm, energy, no hint of illness.

One thinks involuntarily of Meyerhold's dictum: "In order to shoot a bow you must first draw the bowstring."

Marguerite's first entrance was preceded by a static scene, during which Marguerite's companion Nanine and the Baron de Varville conversed. They exchanged cues without looking at each other from opposite ends of the stage. Their conversation was strained. Nanine was knitting, Varville was playing the piano. This staging gave this purely expositional scene the aloofness and coldness that it required. Marguerite's sudden entrance made a sharp contrast, and was staged with extraordinary dynamism. She was returning from the opera surrounded by a group of young men she had invited to a masquerade at her home. Shouting phrases in Italian, Marguerite dashed across the full diagonal of the stage pulling at reins to which two of her young admirers were harnessed. The young men lifted their top hats high in the air while Marguerite waved an improvised whip.

By staging this stunningly unexpected entrance, Meyerhold laid out the path the actress was to follow in the course of the play, from illness to death. And to give a hint of the heroine's illness from the very beginning, Meyerhold instructed the actress playing the role of one of Marguerite's friends to follow her closely holding a warm scarf in her hands as if prepared to prevent Marguerite from catching cold.

The "reject" device was contained in the very tempo of the heroine's entry, but Meyerhold elaborated it in the staging as well. When the doorbell announced Marguerite's return, Varville got up from the piano and walked downstage diagonally opposite the door, while Nanine began to walk toward the door but stopped stage center and retreated to make way for the galloping group. And then it was only after a pause which kept the audience in suspense that Zinaida Raikh as Marguerite, with actors Konsovsky and Shorin, made her entrance.

The famous scene in *The Inspector General*, in which Khlestakov and the city officials make their drunken way to the house of the mayor after lavish libations, was staged entirely with movement along the balustrade as its basis. This movement went back and forth in two directions: now toward the house, now away from it. It was his masterly skill at using the "reject" technique that enabled Meyerhold to stage this classic parade with an unforgettable expressiveness.

Meyerhold knew Russian classical literature well and valued it highly. But Pushkin occupied a special place for him. Meyerhold was constantly rereading and studying Pushkin. He could quote from memory not only Pushkin's poems, but his articles, letters, and draft notes as well.

Meyerhold used to tell his disciples that the art of directing should be learned from Pushkin. He particularly stressed that one could learn from the great poet the art of *mise en scène*. "*Mise en scène* above all! You should study not only the texts and stage directions of Pushkin's works for the theater, but his poems and stories as well. There you'll see how he analyzes the actions and behavior of his characters and what *mises en scène* he invents for them. Pushkin as theater director—this is a most important theme that has so far never been investigated."

We were all constantly captivated by Meyerhold's ideas, and began a close study of Pushkin from this new purely directorial point of view. I too was very interested in the task Meyerhold had set, and it seemed to me after much careful study that I had discovered in Pushkin's texts a morphology and syntax of theater. Moreover, I was constantly struck by the amazing similarity of approaches between these two great theater directors: Pushkin and Meyerhold.

Once, analyzing "Count Nulin," I examined closely the stanza where Pushkin describes the count making his way at night to Natalya Pavlovna's room. Here is the stanza:

> The lovesick count in total darkness
> Has to grope to find his way;
> Aflame with passionate desire,
> Scarcely can he draw a breath,
> Trembling when the floor suddenly
> Cracks beneath him. Now he reaches
> The longed-for bedroom door and lightly
> Moves the latch of the bronze lock;
> The door swings softly, softly in;
> He looks: the lamp is barely burning
> And feebly throws its pale light.
> Peacefully his hostess drowses—
> Or at least pretends that she's asleep.
> He enters, hesitates, draws back—
> And sinks down suddenly at her feet.

If this scene had been staged not by Pushkin but by Meyerhold, he would surely have produced it according to the same scheme. He also would have made the actor entering the bedroom first of all hesitate ("retard") then draw back ("reject") and only after that make the decisive move—to kneel before her. In a single line of Pushkin: "He enters, hesitates, draws back," we find expressed the two principles of Meyerholdian composition and style!

Like Oscar Wilde's Dorian Gray, Meyerhold possessed the secret of eternal youth. He was young when he played the role of Chekhov's Treplyov, he remained young in the period of his passion for Symbolism, he kept the enthusiasm and vigor of youth even after twenty years' work in the theater when, after October, he became the leader of the young revolutionary art.

In the thirties I often used to hear Meyerhold say that it
bored him to be with people who had been born in the nineteenth century. I never saw him in the company of Igumnov
and Goldenweiser, whereas the pianists Oborin and Sofronitsky were his regular guests. His close friends were not Vasi-
lenko and Glière but Shostakovich and Shebalin. Meyerhold's
friendly ties to many of his great contemporaries were established when they were still very young: he staged the plays of
the young Blok; he gave to the young Prokofiev the idea for
the opera _Love for Three Oranges_; he created with Mayakovsky, then twenty-five years old, the first revolutionary theater
work, _Mystery-Bouffe_; and he treated as a colleague his disciple Eisenstein—when Eisenstein was only twenty-three.

It was always fascinating to be in the presence of Meyerhold. One could spend hours listening to his stories and improvisations. He loved all kinds of practical jokes and hoaxes.

But one had always to be on the lookout with him for all
sorts of surprises. Once he came to pick me up in his car, we
drove off, and it was only in the car that I learned that he had
been invited to give a talk about theater at the Red Army
Club to the commanders of the Moscow Military Region, that
he had not prepared the talk, and that he had decided instead
to do it in the form of a dialogue—a Socratic dialogue. "We
shall come out onto the stage," Meyerhold said, "and will talk
with each other, and if need be with the audience as well."
I must confess that I was absolutely dumbfounded, but as
we were approaching the Red Army Club I had no other
choice but to consent. I still keep as a relic the issue of _Ogo-
nek_ which contains a detailed description of this classical
improvisation.

Meyerhold's friendship turned eventually, and quite regularly, into its diametrical opposite, and the rejected friend
had to suffer in succession his indifference, coldness, suspicion, dislike, hostility, and hatred.

Meyerhold's attitude toward me developed exactly according to this pattern. His last letter to me, from Foros,
dated September 1935, was so harsh and unjust that it did
not even give me a chance to respond to its host of absurd
charges and reproaches. He concluded his letter by writing:
"The doctor who is treating me has forbidden me to work.
That is why I ask you not to answer this letter, since this
would force me to enter into a correspondence with you, and

corresponding is very, very fatiguing for me. We can discuss everything in detail in Moscow, where I hope to return in good health. . . ."

Needless to say, I did not reply to his letter and I never spoke with Meyerhold in Moscow. I simply left his theater and handed over all my archives, material accumulated during three years of work there, to a research institute.

Leonid Varpaxovskij, "Zametki prošlyx let," *Vstreči s Mejerxol'dom* (Moscow, 1967), pp. 464–479.

Lev Snezhnitsky

After work on *One Life* had been dropped, Meyerhold proposed that I start rehearsing *Camille* onstage.

Zinaida Nikolaevna Raikh had gone through all of Armand Duval's scenes with me, first during the tour in Leningrad and then at home in Moscow.

"The way Meyerhold sees him, Armand Duval is a provincial, a poet," Raikh told me. "He is more natural, his feelings are more sincere than those of the young men described in French literature of the period. Armand has been brought up on the philosophy of Rousseau and Voltaire. His attachment to Marguerite is based on love for her, not for himself."

I have to admit that my rehearsals didn't go too well.

The shape of the role that Meyerhold had found for Tsarev wasn't working for me.

But one day I did manage to have a good rehearsal of the episode "The Meeting"; the scene took place in Marguerite's sickroom.

The first declaration of love turned out to be the crucial point.

"Why are you so devoted to me?" Marguerite asks Armand. "When did it begin?"

"For two years now, from the very first moment I saw you," Armand answers. "It was at the Opera. I remember, you passed me there . . . and ever since that moment I have silently watched you from a distance. . . ."

I realized that this was one of the most significant speeches in my part and I tried to be passionate. But the only way I could express my love was by saying my lines in a constrained voice as if I were choking.

Zinaida Nikolaevna stopped me and said: "You know, when we were rehearsing this scene with Tsarev, Meyerhold scattered a boxful of matches on the carpet before him and asked him to pick one of them up. He suggested that Tsarev say his lines while breaking the match into little pieces. Try it. It may help you."

Zinaida Nikolaevna dropped some matches in front of me and went back to her place. Without much hope, I picked up a match and began speaking while I broke it into little pieces.

Suddenly I felt free. My inhibitions vanished. I concentrated on breaking the match. My voice came out not loud, but full of emotion and excitement.

Our work was interrupted by Meyerhold's arrival. Zinaida Nikolaevna told him we were having a good rehearsal and asked him to watch the scene we had done. Rehearsing in front of Meyerhold was much more difficult. Again I felt self-conscious and somewhat inhibited.

"It's sincere, but not poetic enough," said Meyerhold. "The secret of this scene is that it has to come out somewhat Ibsenesque. The problem here is the overflowing of emotion. . . . The words express only a small part of what he feels inside. . . . The words mustn't come out all at once, but with pauses. . . . Keep breaking the match, but don't let yourself get totally absorbed in it. When you tell Marguerite about your first sight of her, you ought to be seeing her in a haze of memory, as it were. . . ."

And Meyerhold demonstrated the way the scene ought to go. He kept breaking the match in an absent-minded way, the way people in love tear petals from a flower or leaves from a branch. When he spoke about meeting Marguerite he lifted his head, his eyes gazed pensively into the distance, and his voice was full of emotion, of poetry. Then, as if overcome by shyness, he lowered his head again, broke off a piece of the match, and absent-mindedly dropped it on the carpet.

"Try it," said Meyerhold when he had finished his demonstration. I repeated the scene.

"It's better, but still it's not quite what it should be.
. . . Declaim it a little. . . . Don't forget about the match,"
prompted Meyerhold.

I repeated the scene again, continuing to break the help-
ful match.

"All right, you've got it!" said Vsevolod Emilievich and,
turning to Raikh, he laughed and added: "Zinochka, he's
biomechanical!"

One evening Zinaida Nikolaevna and I were rehearsing a
scene from the fourth act. Vsevolod Emilievich was at home.
When we had finished the scene he came out of his study.

"I heard you in the next room," Meyerhold said to me.
"There's one drawback in what you're doing: the way you say
your lines, all of them sound the same, they all sound equally
important. As a result you begin to sound too cerebral. Instead, we should hear a difference between the main word or
phrase and its embellishments. The embellishments ought to
be swallowed, so to speak. . . . Well, that's not an exact definition, but you understand what I mean, don't you? The embellishments should be moved into the background."

Meyerhold was free that evening. I decided to take advantage of the fact that it was he who started the conversation about my part, and I asked him how one should start
work on building a character.

"It's difficult to say, in general," replied Vsevolod Emilievich. "All actors are different. Some of them see the role first,
while others hear it. Those who hear it first begin by working
on speech characteristics. Those who see it, delineate from
the very start the external appearance of the character. With
one actor, it'll be, for instance, a vulgar and snobbish way of
speaking, while another will put the accent on sloppy man-
ners. That is why it's impossible to give general recommen-
dations for all possible cases. Actors need practical help.
Abilities have to be balanced and deficiencies taken care of, in
case someone is lacking some quality or other, so that everything will be in harmony."

Vsevolod Emilievich slapped the pockets of his jacket
and, finding no tobacco and pipe, went to his study to get
them. I went along.

"The main thing in acting is imagination," continued
Meyerhold. "You must first develop a clear picture of the role
and then make yourself at home in every fiber of it. When

acting, an actor has to feel his character in every joint. And for that, an enormous imagination is indispensable."

After lighting his pipe, Meyerhold sat down at his desk and motioned me to sit opposite him.

"Imagination can be developed," Meyerhold went on. "Some people, for instance, can't visualize in detail what an author has described in a book, while others may see things in it that have not been specifically described. If we can train ourselves to read fiction regularly, we develop our imagination. There was one period when I had a passion for Oscar Wilde. I used to go around all day being elegant and stand-offish."

Without rising from his seat, Meyerhold began to take on the appearance of a stiff Englishman. His neck sank down into his soft shirt collar until it looked as if it were encircled by a stiffly starched wing collar. When Meyerhold turned from side to side, his head, the chin raised high, turned together with his body. His face assumed the expression of a person bored with life. He looked so comically important that I could not help laughing.

"A dandy, damn it all! A dandy!" Meyerhold said cheerfully. Then the stand-offish image vanished and Meyerhold leaned easily forward, his elbows on the desk. "An actor must keep in training all the time," he said, puffing at his pipe. "One day he puts on the rags of a vagabond and behaves like a bum, and the next day he must wear a tail coat and act like a perfect gentleman."

"It is hard to say exactly where work on the role should start," Meyerhold said on his way to the dining room. "It all depends very much on the actor's personality. Some actors rely more on physical factors, others on psychological ones. Our system of acting is often presented as the opposite of the Art Theater's system. That's not correct. According to James' psychological theory, if you smile broadly you may cheer up inside as well. But it isn't James' theories that matter here; one can always dispute them. What matters is correct observation. Work on the role can start with whatever psychological factors will lead to the right physical patterns. Or it can start with those physical elements which make it possible to find the needed inner content." . . .

In order not to interrupt my account of work on *Camille* I'll take some liberty with the chronological presentation of events, and describe a rehearsal that Vsevolod Emilievich conducted some time later.

The rehearsal was conducted onstage with the main cast.

After the episode "In Marguerite's Room" had been rehearsed, Meyerhold called all the actors to the auditorium. There was an ordinary school notebook lying on his table and Vsevolod Emilievich had been making some notes in it. "I shall start with details and then make some general conclusions," said Meyerhold, consulting his comments in the notebook. "Armand should not glance to the right when he says, 'You are killing yourself.' The whole point here is that you should feel how depressed Marguerite is made by her illness. Keep looking at her. When you ask her, 'What is happening to you?' do not turn your head away, just nod slightly. If you understand the state Marguerite is in you'll feel sympathy toward her, and there's only a single step from sympathy to love. Armand is very distressed to see a woman like this, a human being pure as Marguerite, surrounded by all this filth and depravity. He wants to take her away from it all. There is inner tension in this scene already. Marguerite makes fun of Armand's intentions, she does not trust them. This awakens the young man's masculinity.

"Armand is modest but he's not timid, not weak-willed, not inclined to melancholy. Even in the preceding scene we must feel Armand's hostility toward the bohemian element that surrounds Marguerite, all those idle chatterers he does not understand, toward the entire behavior of this lot he is so repulsed by. This is why Armand keeps so much to himself. But he mustn't be indifferent to the life around him; we must remember Armand's hostile attitude in the preceding scene to Marguerite's guests, who are now carousing in the adjoining room. So, in this scene, when he realizes that Marguerite is ill, Armand heads energetically for the door to quiet her guests, and then tries to persuade Marguerite to give up a way of life that he, being a provincial, can't comprehend or accept.

"In this episode we must already begin to feel the strength of Armand's masculinity, because we know what he'll be capable of doing later on. Armand is modest. He's different from Gaston Rieux, he doesn't go after one woman after another, he's not voracious. But we must feel the tremor of his love, his nervousness, his desire to be close to Marguerite, to breathe the scent of her perfume. And your performance lacks this love, this anxiety; it doesn't have what I'd call the subtle atmosphere of love. That's why you give the impression of being her cousin or her doctor. . . . You must absolutely find this atmosphere of love, you can't do without it; without it we get pure formalism. For instance, you touch the flowers in the vase on the table, but instead you should either tear off their petals, or else bury your face in them, the way people do when they are nervous. When people are overcome by emotions they tear things like flowers, orange peels, always groping for words. . . ."

As he spoke, Meyerhold tore off a piece of his notebook cover and demonstrated Armand's behavior as he tries to persuade Marguerite to give up her mad social life. Vsevolod Emilievich concluded: "The look on your face has to say: 'tell me to jump out the third-story window, I'll do whatever you want!'"

Then Meyerhold said he wanted to go through the entire episode again, and asked me and Zinaida Nikolaevna to go up onstage. It seemed to me that we had rehearsed the episode carefully enough at home. But Meyerhold made me go to work all over again, in a difficult and fascinating way. The scene with Marguerite turned out to be woven with a multitude of subtle motivations which kept forcing Armand to act, to move energetically toward his objective. Each of these psychological motivations was to be made clear in the young man's behavior, each of them was fixed by a chain of physical devices. Some of these devices were obvious to the spectators, but many others were simply to aid the imagination of the actor and were never visible to the public. Raikh had been concerned that we should find the right approach to the scene as a whole, and failed to notice that I did not understand Armand's inner motivations and that I was simply executing much of the blocking and many of the physical movements purely formally.

Vsevolod Emilievich now made clear to me the inner motivations of Armand Duval, helped me to realize the latent possibilities of each piece of blocking, taught me to make use of physical movement. Throughout the rehearsal he guided me up a ladder, as it were, making me go higher, using every device to help me climb onto the next rung. At the end of the rehearsal Vsevolod Emilievich tore a page covered with notes from his notebook, handed it to me, and told me to study it carefully when I had time. That sheet of paper has helped me to recall Meyerhold's instructions, his requirements, and the way the rehearsal proceeded.

My problems began the moment I appeared in Marguerite's room. I was making my entrance as if I expected to have plenty of time for a leisurely talk; I wasn't taking into account the noisy company in the adjoining room.

Meyerhold let me do only the very beginning of the scene without interruption:

Marguerite: Monsieur Duval?

Armand: Are you feeling better? Tell me, are you feeling better?

Marguerite: Oh, yes, thank you, I feel marvellous.

Armand: You are killing yourself! I want only to be a friend to you, a brother, to keep you from destroying yourself.

Marguerite: And you would never manage. What is the matter with you? (She picks up a glass of wine.)

Armand: It is very painful for me to see you like this.

Marguerite: Ah, you are kind. Look at the others—they don't care what happens to me.

At that point, after the words "Ah, you are kind," there was a burst of laughter from the adjoining room. This laughter was Armand's cue to walk across the room to the door to quiet the noisy guests. Meyerhold never let me get to the door.

"There, you see," came his voice from the auditorium, "you think about the guests only when they get noisy. But you should be on the alert all the time. You know very well that someone might come in and interrupt you any minute. You've got to keep that in mind from the very first moment you enter Marguerite's room, otherwise the blocking will look purely formal."

The blocking in question was as follows: hearing Armand's steps, Marguerite, who was lying on the sofa, sits up and leans against the back of the sofa, facing the audience.

"Monsieur Duval?" she asks.

"Are you feeling better? Tell me, are you feeling better?" asks Armand in turn, standing behind Marguerite and bending down over the back of the sofa to see the invalid's face.

After the words "Oh yes, thank you, I feel marvellous"

Armand walks around the sofa and comes closer to Marguerite on the line "You are killing yourself!"

Meyerhold climbed onto the stage and demonstrated the entrance. The way he did it, a certain theatricality in the blocking (dialogue while looking straight at the audience) seemed totally justified. After he entered the room, Vsevolod Emilievich made a movement toward the sofa, as if not quite believing he was now able to speak to Marguerite in private. The back of the sofa kept him from seeing her face; the obstacle it occasioned forced him to make a quick movement closer to Marguerite on the line "You are killing yourself!" The agitation of the staging was to help the actor playing Armand, so that his entrance into Marguerite's room appeared agitated and nervous.

What helped further to increase the passion of the scene was the business with the wine glass that Marguerite picked up on the line "And you would never manage." Zinaida Nikolaevna spoke in mockery of Armand's ardor, as if not yet trusting his love. It was the glass of wine at her lips that made Armand move toward her on the line: "It is very painful for me to see you like this."

A device that helped the actor to climb yet one step higher was the cross to the door behind which the guests were having such a noisy good time. After demonstrating how Armand should cross the room in order to bring the noisy company to order, Meyerhold told me aside that the energy of this unfinished movement—unfinished because Armand's cross was stopped by Marguerite's line: "Look at the others— they don't care what happens to me"—was to be preserved, to be used in the next scene. In this way Armand's reply: "The others do not love you as I do," was delivered from "the height of a third step."

"Oh yes, of course, I had forgotten—I had completely forgotten about this great love," Marguerite says somewhat absent-mindedly, picking up a book that was lying on the sofa. Marguerite's failure to understand Armand, stressed by the physical gesture, served as a pretext for Armand to change his position. "You are making fun of me," he says, returning to the table by the sofa.

"I am sorry, but I have to listen to the same thing every day. It's no longer amusing," Marguerite answers, laying the book aside.

"Yes, but my love is different. And I think I am justified in hoping for some promise from you," Armand insists.

With this line began the scene Meyerhold had spoken about when he reprimanded me for merely touching the flowers. Armand urges Marguerite to leave society and to go with him to the country, to restore her health. Marguerite does not trust Armand and does not want to answer him directly, so she teases him.

Vsevolod Emilievich demonstrated how I should be standing at the table, leaning on it slightly with one hand, and tearing at the petals of the camelias with the other. Here and later Meyerhold constantly reminded me about "asymmetry of movement," telling me never to "stand at attention" with both hands at my sides. This notion helped me to find expressive body positions. But the essential point was not only outer expressiveness. Far more important was that all these physical devices helped to free me of inner inhibitions by getting rid of muscular tension. That was why a requirement that seemed merely formal had in fact a profound purpose.

Demonstrating what he meant by "asymmetry of movement," Meyerhold kept finding various positions for his hands. For example, one hand reaches out toward Marguerite, as if to stop her, while the fingers of the other grope in a vest pocket for the button of his beloved's glove. Or, again: Meyerhold held the lapel of his coat with his left hand while picking up a glass of wine with the right one. As I watched Meyerhold I saw that his hands were always at different heights, that he kept changing his movements, searching for the most expressive postures, the precise gestures. The amazing thing was that the correctly executed physical device or the precisely discovered movement helped the actor to come alive on the stage. The line "Yes, but my love is different. . . ." began to sound quite different once I had succeeded in fulfilling Meyerhold's requirements.

All the blocking in *Camille* was constructed on diagonals that ran from the footlights far upstage. Every cross an actor made described figure-eights of varying dimensions. Vsevolod Emilievich attached great importance to this principle of blocking that he had discovered, working with long diagonals. It made it possible for him to place two partners in a "duelling position," where one of the actors was standing half-turned toward the spectators while the other was facing directly front. In this way both actors were clearly visible to the spectators. In intimate scenes the diagonal arrangement made it possible for the actors to move very close to each other, almost touching, without either blocking the other from the spectators' view. That was the point of the blocking to which he kept referring in his notes to me.

On the line: "Why was it that when I was ill . . . you inquired so persistently after my health?" Raikh took two or three steps toward the audience, a glass of wine in her hand. It was as if she were enticing Armand to follow her. Waiting for him to answer she stopped, looking straight out into the audience. Armand was to follow her and stop somewhat behind her, slightly to her right. Both performers stood facing the audience, without in any way destroying the absolute naturalness of the whole scene. It was a very expressive piece of blocking, and made it possible to convey to the spectators all the nuances of the feelings the young couple was beginning to experience.

Demonstrating this scene, Meyerhold reminded us once again that it was to sound "Ibsenesque." The difficulty lay in the fact that the blocking was calculated to the inch. If I carelessly made as little as half a step to the side or back, Zinaida Nikolaevna would no longer be able to clink her glass against mine while still looking out at the audience. If that happened, then all the subtle coloring of the scene would be wasted because of a tiny inaccuracy. At the same time Meyerhold kept telling us over and over that this scene must express "the overflowing of feelings, when one is at a loss for words." Vsevolod Emilievich repeated this tiny scene several times until he got the results he wanted.

After the rehearsal was over, Meyerhold asked me: "What sort of make-up are you thinking of doing?"

I confessed that I hadn't even thought about make-up yet.

"I shall look for a photograph I used to have at home, Ingres' portrait of the Duc d'Orléans," said Vsevolod Emilievich. "It might be of some help. I know you young leading men don't usually think too much about period styles. You prefer to show off your own pretty faces," he grinned. "But I'll bring you the picture anyway. You'll see what to do with it."

Lev Snežnickij, "Poslednyj god," *Vstreči s Mejerxol'dom* (Moscow, 1967), pp. 554–562.

Meyerhold to Vissarion Shebalin

Vinnitsa
June 24, 1933

Dear Vissarion Yakovlevich,

Please forgive me: after I'd promised to talk with you about the music for *Camille*, about what exactly we needed from you for the Dumas play, I didn't even manage to set aside a half-hour in my schedule, which was quite heavily laden in Moscow with work and business, but still not so much as to exclude a half-hour so important for us both and so necessary for our work.

So I'm writing now. And I must ask you to forgive me once again—I should have written this letter from Kharkov, where I'd gone right after we'd agreed in principle on your music for *Camille*, and now I'm writing two weeks later from Vinnitsa.

Down to business anyway.

We are shifting Dumas' play from the forties and fifties to the end of the seventies. We see the characters of this remarkable play through the eyes of Edouard Manet. This phase of bourgeois society seems to us more appropriate for the expression of the author's ideas—ideas we have sharpened and intend to pursue in the composition of our production.

In the music then, it is not Weber's "Invitation à la Valse" that can excite Marguerite, nor Rosellen's fantasia.

We choose the age of the *can-can*.

And the waltz—slow, flowing, limpid, modest, even naive (Lanner, Glinka, Weber)—becomes voluptuous, heady, impetuous (Johann Strauss). Open decadence. The cabaret flourishes in a corrupt Paris (the great traditions of Flaubert, Stendhal, and Balzac are long since gone; a lonely Maupassant flees from Paris and the Eiffel Tower), and spawns a sea of off-color songs. *Diseurs* and *diseuses* are found in salons as well as onstage; they scatter among their audiences indecencies devoid of lyricism. (Flaubert: "Any indecency is permitted, so long as it is lyrical.")

The reign of Mistinguette. The morality of the new family requires the presence of a "friend." "Kept woman" is the going term for a new kind of Parisienne. Young people display all their attractions at the Quatz' Arts Ball, where private debauch grows into a general orgy.

This is the atmosphere in which Marguerite Gautier perishes.

So far the first act is laid out for your work.

In the copy of the play we are sending under separate cover, all the places in the first act where we need music are indicated, along with the exact timings.

Here are some details and comments for your information.

Varville we play as in the military, a major or something similar, obviously an habitué of the music halls, a balletomane, a cynic beneath his good breeding. He plays the piano.

Music for the first act:

1. "Madame Nichette, Madame Nichette. . . ." Varville finds a rhyme for Nichette, improvises a couple of ambiguous lines, and sings them to the tune of a vulgar song, while accompanying himself at the piano.

2. Varville sits down at the piano and plays a fragment of a military march.

3. Instead of the Rosellen fantasia, Varville plays the melody of some off-color cabaret hit song (Mistinguette in the seventies).

Note: Our choice of music has been pretty limited, so during rehearsals we've been using something danceable, a kind of *pas de quatre* in 12/8 time.

4. Two waltzes:

    a. A crude waltz, rather upbeat. St.-Gaudens sings (perhaps in the style of an Italian tenor) the name Amanda, weaving it into the song and then sings it out, taking a melody from whatever Varville plays.

    b. A very limpid waltz, tender and sweet. Much more elegant than the first. Armand's theme (see the text). As if the pianist had captured the very moment when love dawns for Armand and Marguerite.

5. A little song for Prudence—frivolous, actually off-color, in fact, very short. I'm asking Mikhail Kuzmin to write the words.

6. A little song for another of the guests (she may be a professional *diseuse*).

7. A musical background (melodramatic) for Prudence's rendition of a scene from a "blood and thunder" tragedy (Vol-

taire or Racine). Prudence will be in a purple cloak with a dagger in her hand; she pretends to stab one of the good-looking young men at the party.

8. Gaston (a cabaret regular, an intimate of Camille's) strums a polka (trying out the piano). Very short. Five measures.

9. He plays a hot little song, off-color lyrics, short couplets with a refrain. (Very vulgar!)

10. A waltz *con brio*, bravura, whatever, intended for a whirling dance in two figures.

11. First-act finale. This is a carnival scene in the spirit of the Quatz' Arts Ball. It has three phases:

a. Carnival "espagnole." Everyone in sombreros and cloaks, lots of flesh underneath. The Spanish feeling is in dry yellow colors, the parching heat of Toledo. Harsh music, in the spirit of Glinka's "Jota de Aragón." There is a sound-effects orchestra onstage—someone plays a guitar, someone blows into a bottle, another taps his glass, plucks at a string. And this orchestra onstage is accompanied by the real orchestra. Of course the sound-effects orchestra has to be organized, it must be contrapuntally connected with the strict musical background; the effect will be a web of cacophony. The orchestra does it all, the actors have only property instruments.

b. The Spanish carnival scene ends in a stormy, shocking, real French can-can. The cloaks are thrown off, lots of naked flesh gleams for a few seconds, everything is bare. Everything plunges into an orgy. The spectator must be left with the impression that an absolutely wild night is in store, a terrific orgy.

c. We need a little unison chorus of Norman or Breton peasants, almost in dialect. They sing a silly naive song which is the signal for the final scene. They come in wearing Spanish costumes, but they sing a country song.

As far as the music for the subsequent acts is concerned, I still can't give you anything but a tentative idea. As ideas for the music get clearer and more precise we'll let you know.

In act IV there is:

1. A can-can and a mazurka. Everyone is dancing so wildly offstage that you can hear the dishes rattling through the music.

2. A waltz.

In the third act we want to use an itinerant musician, someone who wanders from village to village, playing the bagpipes or some such country instrument. He may even appear onstage.

Very best,
V. Meyerhold

Meyerhold to Mikhail Kuzmin

Odessa
July 12, 1933

Dear Mikhail Alexeyevich,

Please help us (of course we'll pay you) with our work on the production of Dumas fils' *Camille*.

We must have, for several characters in the play—for Varville, Adèle (the author has her only in the fourth act, but we have put her in the first act as well), and Prudence—*words* for some couplets and songs they are to sing (in the first act):

1. Varville has a scene with Nanine (see the enclosed dialogue). After Varville says: "You mean *Madame* Nichette," he sits down at the piano and accompanies himself while singing something about "Kitty-cat" Nichette. Varville strings together in his couplets several rhymes on the word Nichette, so that we get a frivolous, ambiguous pun. It's a short bit, but very caustic and it shocks Nanine (we play her as a respectable old lady). And Varville, by the way, we play as in the military, a major.

2. The supper scene in act one. The guests pester Adèle (she does imitations of *chansonette* singers) and try to get her to sing something risqué. While they are talking to her, Prudence bounces up to show how well she can do that kind of song. Prudence sings four lines of some rollicking song, the kind of thing you hear in the Boulevard theaters or the cabarets around the Place Clichy. It could be some kind of satiric four-line refrain. After that Adèle gets up and belts out (in the style of the clown Milton or Mistinguette) a risqué couplet.

The music for your words will be written by Vissarion Shebalin. We're doing the play not in the period of the forties or fifties, but the end of the seventies.

We see the characters of this remarkable play through the eyes of Edouard Manet.

If you agree to undertake the job, please let me know when you can let us have the material.

If you do agree, let us know how much you want us to pay you.

Friendliest regards, dear Mikhail Alexeyevich.

V. Meyerhold

Meyerhold to Vissarion Shebalin

Odessa
July 16, 1933

Dear Vissarion Yakovlevich,

Here's the continuation of what we're sending you in separate pieces, as a guide to help you work out a plan for the music for *Camille*.

Act IV:

The act begins with music. The can-can (a gallop). As a build-up, before the lights come up ("before the curtain rises," as we used to say), an introduction (very short). The style of the music should recall the finale (traditional) of some operetta. The stuff our accompanists Pappe and Muskatblit have been playing for us at rehearsal follows this scheme:

8	measures	*forte*	
16	"	*piano*	major
8	"	*f*	
16	"	*p*	
8	"	*f*	minor
8	"	*p*	
8	"	*f*	
16	"	*p*	major
8	"	*fff*	

The music is playing offstage and the impression of the switch from *f* to *p* should be that of doors opening and then closing, the doors between the two rooms (the onstage room and the one offstage).

Length: 1 minute, 10 seconds.

The music serves as background to the first scene of act IV (see p. 84 of the copy of the play we sent you). Gaston is dealing at the gaming table: "Ladies and gentlemen, place your bets" (the beginning). That musical number ends on p. 85 after the doctor's line: "That's a disease of youth, it passes as you grow older." So that's musical section no. 1 for act IV.

No. 2: see p. 86. After the line: "Give me ten louis d'or, St.-Gaudens, I want to play a little longer" there's a short pause; then before Gaston's line "Your soirée is charming, Olympe," we hear a mazurka (*brillante*). Something "chic," suitable for dancing, and so of course the rhythm of the dance must be sharply marked in it.

Length: 1 min., 30 sec. It ends on p. 87 after Gaston's line: "It's a good thing you're the last of the Arthurs."

No. 3: A waltz. Animated, *nervous, impetuous*. Length: 1 min., 50 sec. See p. 88 where it's marked "scene 2, the same and Armand." Dialogue to music: Gaston: "When did you arrive?" Armand: "An hour ago." Small pause. The waltz begins. The scene between Armand and Prudence plays over the waltz. The waltz ends at the beginning of Dumas' "scene 3" after the two lines of Armand and Gustave—first: "So you finally got my letter"; second: "Of course, since I'm here."

No. 4: A second waltz. Length: 2 min., 50 sec. A softly lyrical waltz, somewhat like a barcarolle, intensely moving.

It begins exactly at the end of Gustave's line: "An insult to a woman is the equivalent of cowardice." The waltz ends after Varville's speech to Marguerite which ends with the words: "We are at the party and we are going to stay."

No. 5: Music to accompany supper. "Dessert music." Very graceful. They are probably being served ice-cream cake decorated with bon-bons and candied fruit. You almost want to say: "Are they playing a scherzo? No. Yes, it is a scherzo! . . . No, it's something different. More expressive. Sober, almost, but beneath the ground of the music there's a lyric impulse." Oh, how expressive music can be!

Length: 3 min., 10 sec. Divided somehow into sections. This is a play all by itself. An expressive tension (saturated with erotic agitation). It mustn't defuse the scene—on the contrary, it must strain forward so that at the end it weaves into the strong scene of the finale, when Armand throws Marguerite to the floor, shouts: "Come here, all of you," and then in the presence of the company throws the money into Marguerite's face. The finale is no longer a scherzo at all. Everything is rampant. Someone has put his foot in the ice-cream cake.

Dear Vissarion Yakovlevich, you know what's needed better than I. No one ever pleases us the way you do. We love you very much, as a composer and as Vissarion Yakovlevich.

Zinaida Nikolaevna sends her best.

Our best regards to both of you.

V. Meyerhold

Mikhail Kuzmin to Meyerhold

Leningrad
July 22, 1933

Dear Vsevolod Emilievich,

Of course, I am most eager to take part in *Camille* and delighted at the prospect. I shall most likely send you several variants for both Prudence and Varville. Your idea for the production is convincing and fascinating. In other words, the seventies, just before the Franco-Prussian War, the period of Offenbach, the eve of the Paris Commune?

I believe I can send you the material by August 10, but if it's necessary I can get it done earlier.

As for payment, of course, it should be a flat fee without getting involved in an honorarium, since for such a small job I could get only, say, twenty percent. So I think about 150–200 rubles. Anyway, whatever the theater thinks suitable. If any rewriting or a new text is necessary, the same payment will of course take care of that.

I'm very anxious to do something that will be exactly what you have in mind.

Thank you for remembering me (that is very, very important to me). I embrace you and remain

Very sincerely yours,
M. Kuzmin

Mikhail Sadovsky

Once while I was still with the Ermolova Theater, I was playing in *Kabal und Liebe* at the summer theater in Aquarium Park. After the performance an usher brought a note to my dressing room, a small scrap of paper that seemed to have been torn out of a lady's notebook. There was a laconic phrase on it: "Sadovsky! Call me. Meyerhold."

The next day, trembling with excitement, I lifted the receiver and gave the operator the number. A masculine voice answered the call.

And this was the conversation:

"Could I speak to Vsevolod Emilievich, please?"

"Speaking."

"Vsevolod Emilievich! It's Sadovsky."

"Ah! Hello! Will you join my theater?"

I was speechless. A small pause ensued. Meyerhold went on:

"What are you doing now? Are you free? Come over and let's talk."

In response I mumbled something like: "I'm free. . . . I'd love to. . . ."

"Where are you?"

"At home."

"Give me your address, I'll send a car to pick you up."

I gave him my address and within fifteen minutes a car was waiting at the entrance to the house where I lived. I dressed frantically, dashing about the room, scattering ties and shirts and shoes in every direction.

"This Meyerhold has turned your head," my father observed skeptically. "You're crazy if you're thinking of working for him. You know everything he does is topsy-turvy."

I paid no attention and continued to dress as fast as I

could. How could I make him wait for me? In the car at last. And then on Brusov Street.

"That way," the chauffeur pointed. "Second floor, the door to your left."

I pushed the door wide open and dashed up the stairs two steps at a time. There were two doors on the second-floor landing. Following my instructions, I pushed the bell on the left. At the same moment the door on the right opened noisily behind me. I made an involuntary turn and there was Meyerhold. What had happened? Had I made a mistake? Did I ring at the wrong door? . . . Naturally, I was quite embarrassed.

"That's all right," said Meyerhold with a smile. "That's the way we do it here: you ring at one door and enter at the other!" (I remembered my father's words: "topsy-turvy"!)

Later I learned that he occupied two adjoining apartments that had been connected to each other. Regular visitors knew the trick and would ring the bell at the left door, then wait for the right door to open. But novices like myself were astonished at the arrangement and their reaction obviously amused the mischievous host.

Meyerhold was cheerful and amazingly hospitable. He shook my hand with both of his and continued: "You made it here quickly! Good boy! Come on in!"

He led me to a large yellow room.

There were two people in the room. A woman was sitting in an armchair by the balcony. It was Meyerhold's wife, Zinaida Nikolaevna Raikh. Her hairdo reminded me of the head of "The Italian Boy" in Brullov's well-known painting. I was dazzled by her large shining chestnut eyes and her extremely attractive, open smile.

"Zinochka!" Meyerhold said, and brought me over to Raikh. "Meet our guest! This is the Ferdinand we saw at the theater yesterday."

There was fruit and cognac on the table. A thin young man in a gray suit was sitting next to it. "And this is Sofronitsky!" Meyerhold went on. "No one plays Scriabin better than he does!"

Meyerhold loved music and was its discerning connoisseur. He often entertained the most distinguished musicians and composers. It was at his home that I met the pianist Oborin. He was then only twenty-three or twenty-four but had already become famous both at home and abroad.

At Meyerhold's I also met Vissarion Shebalin, who was at that time composing music for _Camille_.

"Do sit down!" said Meyerhold. "Would you like some cognac?"

And there we were, the four of us, sitting at the table.

Sofronitsky was telling jokes, and Meyerhold and Raikh were laughing delightedly.

Soon Meyerhold invited me to an adjoining room, sat me in an armchair, and began to talk to me about the interesting work in store for me at his theater. He concluded the short conversation by handing me a blank sheet of paper and suggesting that I write an application for admission to his theater.

I wrote the application. Meyerhold wrote his approval in the corner of it. My fate was sealed.

"Come to rehearsal tomorrow at eleven," said Vsevolod Emilievich. "Go directly to the auditorium and sit next to me."

I told him that I was still working at the Ermolova Theater and I wasn't sure they'd let me go just like that, right away. . . .

"It will be all right," he interrupted me. "Everything will be all right. I'll help you arrange things, if need be."

I felt both tremendously excited and uneasy. How could I have agreed so readily? But I felt that I had done the right thing—or, rather, that I could not have done otherwise. It was impossible to resist the strong will, the temperament, the charm of Meyerhold! I felt as if I had been hypnotized. I was uneasy, too, about this unexpected invitation to join the Meyerhold State Theater, because it seemed to go contrary to my expected plans.

Since my childhood I had been aware that when the time came I was to continue the tradition of our family, a family of actors that had been associated with the Maly Theater since 1839, generation after generation. And Meyerhold's theater was fundamentally opposed to the Maly Theater. But I never regret what happened; on the contrary, I am grateful to fate for bringing me close to an incredibly interesting director, an incredibly interesting man—Vsevolod Emilievich Meyerhold.

The portentous morning came. December 25, 1933. By ten-thirty I was already at the theater on Gorky Street (where the Ermolova Theater is now located). I took off my coat and went into the lobby, which was very long, high-ceilinged, and shabby. Three doors led to the auditorium; I glanced inside through one of them. The auditorium was even more lacking in comfort than the lobby. It was undecorated—a large white construction, that was all. Although the ceiling was quite high there were no balconies, just a long auditorium with rows of simple wooden chairs, the kind you find in cheap moviehouses.

I looked at the stage—it was exposed. As everyone knew, there was no curtain in Meyerhold's theater. Some fabrics were hanging on the stage, a few pieces of furniture and props—everything was ready for the rehearsal.

Since I did not know where Meyerhold's regular seat was, I decided to wait for him at the back of the auditorium. Soon the actors began to appear on the stage wearing their street clothes. A number of seats in the auditorium began to fill. Then came Meyerhold, accompanied by a host of assistants. They were saying something to him, interrupting each other. And Meyerhold, turning from one side to the other, was walking so quickly it seemed as if he wanted to escape from them.

In the middle of the ninth row Meyerhold stopped and looked around. When he saw me he raised his hands in welcome and called: "There you are! Hello! Come sit over here." He gave a brisk order to the assistants: "Let's begin!" and then began to ask me about something.

Soon came the sound of a gong. The lights went out for a moment, then went on again, brightly illuminating the stage.

The rehearsal began. They were doing the first and second scenes of _Camille_.

Meyerhold did not stay sitting next to me for very long. He jumped from his seat, took off his jacket, and rushed to the stage. He made a few comments, then ran back into the auditorium just as quickly, bent over someone there, and whispered something in his ear. A moment later he was at the opposite end of the auditorium and only his sharp voice was heard calling: "All right! Bravo! Terrific!"

I had a hard time trying to follow the action on the stage and Meyerhold's movements; he was never still for a moment, but would appear now here, now there.

When the two young actors rehearsing the parts of Armand Duval and Gaston Rieux appeared on the stage, Meyerhold ran up to me, pointed at the second one, and whispered: "Watch his part."

I was glad that I was to be given a role, and obviously a good one, but it left a rather bad taste in my mouth; I found something unpleasant in all this whispering.

The rehearsal continued. Meyerhold kept running back and forth between the stage and the auditorium. One could only admire his energy. At that time he was over sixty.

The actor I was watching more attentively than the others rehearsed his part very well, without any corrections from Meyerhold.

Vsevolod Emilievich was at his best. He kept saying the most interesting things, gave splendid demonstrations. He staged a brilliant entrance for Zinaida Raikh as Marguerite Gautier at this rehearsal.

Marguerite's maid Nanine and the Baron de Varville are onstage. The Baron is waiting for Marguerite and chatting with Nanine. The doorbell rings. Marguerite has arrived home from the Opera. Nanine and Varville go out to meet her. The stage is empty. Judging by the sound of voices coming from backstage, we assume that Marguerite has brought along a large group of people. One can hear bursts of laughter and applause. And then, all of a sudden, two young men in tails, with top hats in their hands, harnessed like horses, dash from the wings upstage right diagonally across the stage to the proscenium. Small bells jingle on their reins. And after them, holding the reins in one hand and a long whip in the other, runs Marguerite Gautier, in a red velvet dress and wearing a top hat. Following Marguerite, all her noisy retinue pour into the drawing room. This entry invariably made the audience gasp. It was beautiful, it was daring, it was chic!

Suddenly I felt someone's hand on my shoulder. I turned and saw a gray-haired man with kind gray eyes standing near me.

"Are you Sadovsky?" he asked.

"Yes," I replied.

"Let me introduce myself," he said. "My name is Mikhail Mikhailovich Korenev. Vsevolod Emilievich asked me to give you the text of your part." He handed me a rather thick notebook.

I thanked him, and my attention was once again absorbed by the stage. There was a torrent of fun on stage—singing, dancing, pounding music, and Meyerhold, high above it all, like a maestro, conducting a symphony in a creative ecstasy.

After the rehearsal ended, Vsevolod Emilievich came to me.

"Well, did you like it?" he asked.

"Oh yes, very much," I answered.

"The rehearsal tomorrow will be at eleven as well. Come and sit next to me."

I smiled in response. Meyerhold understood my smile, laughed, and said: "Yes, yes, you're right. It is rather difficult to sit next to me at rehearsal. I just wanted to arrange about how we'll meet."

The next day I came to the theater, sat in "my" seat in the ninth row, and began to wait.

Everything started in just the same way as the day before. The actors in their street clothes appeared on the stage at the appointed time. The seats in the hall filled with people.

Meyerhold came with his assistants. But it was a different Meyerhold, not the one that I saw yesterday, sparkling and sunny. This Meyerhold was gloomy and sullen, like a cloud before a storm. He said hello to me, but very drily; it was not the welcome of the previous day.

"Shall we start?" asked one of the assistants.

"Yes, start. With the entry of Armand and Gaston," growled Meyerhold. He sat down in front of me and lit a cigarette. (He smoked a great deal, and almost always had a cigarette in his mouth.)

The gong sounded, the lights went off and on again. The rehearsal began.

From his very first step, his very first words, Meyerhold began to pick on the actor who was playing the part of Gaston. Everything was wrong! His posture was wrong, his manner of speaking was wrong, his way of laughing was wrong, and on and on in the same vein. To make it worse, Meyerhold expressed his criticism in very rough language.

I sat back in my chair, trying to make myself invisible, trying to avoid Meyerhold's stare, and thought: "Oh my God. Why did I join this theater in the first place? Maybe I can still go back to the Ermolova Theater. . . . This actor is doing his part beautifully. I could hardly do it better. . . . And if he's getting it in the neck, what's in store for me? . . ."

None of the actors made any attempt to speak up for the actor who was being torn to shreds. He did not defend himself either.

"It's absolutely impossible!" shouted Meyerhold. "You cannot play this part! I am taking the part away from you! Leave the stage immediately!"

The actor turned and left the stage. There was a pause. Everyone on the stage stood still, as if immobilized. The tension was broken by Meyerhold's furious shriek:

"Sadovsky!"

I rose from my seat, barely alive.

"Onstage! Begin with Gaston's entry," called Meyerhold. "Prompter, give him his cues."

The prompter wasn't necessary. I had a good memory, and had already memorized the episode just by listening to it, without consulting the text. The blocking I also knew fairly well because they had repeated the scene any number of times during the previous rehearsal.

And again, like yesterday, there was praise from the auditorium: "All right! That's good! Splendid!"

But I no longer believed all that praise.

After the rehearsal I went backstage. I saw a group of actors in one of the dressing rooms. A violent argument about something was going on in a thick cloud of tobacco smoke.

I approached them and addressed myself to the "victim"; I said that I had had nothing to do with the whole thing, that I had never asked for his part.

"That's all right. I know you have nothing to do with it. It's all because of my complicated relations with Meyerhold. If it hadn't been you, it would have been somebody else. I made up my mind to leave this theater long ago."

He did leave Meyerhold, and later occupied an important position in one of the large provincial theaters, and received the title of People's Artist of the RSFSR. . . .

Meyerhold needed good actors; he could not have existed without them. Not only could Meyerhold give a brilliant *demonstration* of the scene to an actor—he could just as easily *prompt* him into it.

In this connection I recall a rehearsal of *Camille*, act five, the scene with Gaston Rieux and Marguerite Gautier.

It is early morning in summer. Gaston has spent all night sitting at the bed of the sick Marguerite. At last she has awakened. She is feeling better, the sleep has done her good. Gaston is glad and suggests that Marguerite go out in the fresh air. He'll fetch a wheelchair right away, he says, and they'll have a lovely stroll through Paris in the spring. The stroll will amuse her. Marguerite agrees, and Gaston exits.

Meyerhold decided not to display the bed with the dying Marguerite on the stage, and he put it in the wings. That way Gaston remained alone on the stage at the open door to Marguerite's bedroom, and had to conduct the dialogue—or monologue, rather, interspersed with very brief and sparse remarks from backstage—alone with the audience.

Meyerhold made this scene even more difficult by demanding that Gaston communicate to the audience not only his own feelings and desires but what was taking place in the adjoining bedroom as well.

He said: "Now she is lying quietly in her bed and now she is tossing about, she tries to rise and falls back on the cushions again. . . . She is now distressed, then she is smiling!" The audience must see it all in Gaston's behavior.

I remember that I could not master this scene for a long time. It seemed difficult, it bogged me down. . . . My hands, legs, voice, all refused to function. And then at some point in the middle of the monologue Meyerhold ran up onto the stage. Without interrupting me he stopped behind me, extended his arms over my shoulder, and very gracefully, using both his hands, rearranged the handkerchief in the breast pocket of my morning coat. Then, giving me a light and encouraging slap on the back, as if to say "Go ahead! Enjoy yourself!" he ran back to the auditorium.

What happened to me after that is difficult to comprehend and still more difficult to describe. I became entirely transformed, as if a rock had fallen off my shoulders. I sensed that Meyerhold was presenting me, on a tray, as it were, to the audience. I realized the importance of every detail in my appearance, from the handkerchief in my breast pocket to the toes of my lacquered shoes. I saw that Gaston had to be cheerful, vigorous, confident, and even somewhat sly. I no longer tried to convey Marguerite's suffering through the expression on my face; on the contrary, I began concealing it. Could I permit Marguerite to guess from the expression on my face in what a poor state she really was? As I stood before her I was cheerful, and even reckless. It was at this happy moment of creative inspiration that I heard Meyerhold's famous "All right!" from the auditorium.

After the rehearsal Meyerhold called to me: "So long, Sadovsky! See you on opening night! We'll leave this scene as it is!"

He felt certain that I would not stray away from what I had achieved. He trusted his actors and did not like to drill a scene endlessly once it had become lucid, organic, and alive.

Meyerhold used to say: "The actor must not rivet his role tightly, like a bridge builder with his metal construction. He must leave some slots open for improvising."

I want to speak of one more example of how Meyerhold valued actors, of his awareness that without actors, without the living spark of their presence, his own work as a director would have been lifeless.

It happened at a rehearsal of the second scene of _Camille_, the scene that Meyerhold called "One of Those Nights." This scene was intended to present the reckless merry-making, the drunken debauchery, through which Marguerite sought to escape from her illness. All of us who were engaged in this scene, about eleven actors, followed the instructions of the director precisely. We sang, recited poetry, clinked our glasses, smoked, danced all kinds of dances, from the waltz to the can-can. Some of the participants wore masks, paper streamers were being flung from one corner to another. Shebalin's music fit the scene splendidly. But the main element— genuine merriment, mischievousness, creative inspiration, the spark—was somehow missing.

The scene had been created but it remained without a life of its own.

Meyerhold was standing before us like Pygmalion before Galatea, not knowing how to inspire life into us.

He realized that no instructions, demonstrations, or repetitions would be of any use at that time, especially since he had no complaints against anyone in particular. What was to be done?

And then one day we were informed that after that evening's performance of _The Forest_ a night rehearsal had been scheduled. "You never know what Meyerhold will think of next," we were saying, as we came to the theater after midnight.

We entered the auditorium. The sets of _The Forest_ had already been replaced by the set-up for *Camille*. Meyerhold was sitting in the auditorium, a basket full of bottles of champagne at his feet, a table with glasses by his side. He greeted us cheerfully and said: "Rouget de Lille created the great "Marseillaise" in one night, and we are required to do much less. . . ."

Jokes and witticisms were the reaction. Corks popped out of bottles, we filled our glasses and emptied them. Meyerhold ordered them to switch off the electric lamps and light candles instead. Huge candelabra appeared on the grand piano, on chests of drawers, on the floor.

We went up on the stage. And I can't explain what happened, whether it was the fact that we were rehearsing at night without the daily worries that must occupy our subconscious during daytime rehearsals, or whether we were under the spell of the burning candles and champagne— anyway, a miracle happened: the scene we were rehearsing came alive at once. Everything went along as it had at the previous rehearsal, and yet everything was different. "Jeanette," a racy song by Béranger that Remizova sang so well, suddenly acquired some special charm. Some discoveries were made too: while singing the last words of her song, Remizova stumbled on something and fell on the polar-bear skin spread on the floor.

"You fall down next to her too!" Meyerhold called to me from the auditorium.

Amid general laughter and the applause of the actors, I threw myself down on the bearskin.

This episode gave the scene some wonderful piquancy.

Although Meyerhold always had a clear vision of the production in advance, and a precisely detailed plan of the staging, he always liked it when the unexpected came up in the process of work, and he knew how to utilize it.

During the same rehearsal the actors started to throw paper streamers too high, and some of them accidentally caught in the flies and dangled from them.

Meyerhold applauded and at once expanded this accidental mistake into a wonderful show. Some additional wires were stretched immediately and the stagehands from backstage together with the actors began to throw paper streamers onto these wires. In a moment the stage was flooded in motley colors. The scene became even more festive. Naturally, the new look of the stage could not fail to affect the mood of the actors.

The Verlaine poem, so well recited by Tsarev as Armand, became tinged with some special emotion:

I often have a sacred dream—
An unknown woman, cherished and beloved. . . .

He read these first two lines in almost a whisper. It was unusual, unexpected, and fit very well into the general pattern of the scene.

The lighted candles were of much help to us. They brought to the stage warmth, comfort, an atmosphere of mystery and fantasy. Our shadows on the backdrop and wings changed in size, now growing large, now disappearing altogether.

This accidentally discovered lighting was retained in the performance as well, enhanced by the masterful lighting of set designer Ivan Leistikov.

What a wonderful rehearsal that was! It was not even a rehearsal—it was a party. We felt we were Marguerite's guests, we felt free and easy, we were having a really good time and played with abandon. Meyerhold was enjoying it with us.

I remember that we rehearsed for a very long time with great enthusiasm. When we went home it was almost morning, and nobody felt tired at all. Working with Meyerhold could be difficult, but it was always fascinating and never boring.

If we can compare the art of a theater director with the art of a chef, then Meyerhold did not belong to the category of those who prepare cold entrées. Meyerhold the chef needed a hot stove. He cooked only hot dishes. He needed sizzling skillets and flaming coals. His first concern at rehearsal was to set his actors on fire, to make the atmosphere red-hot.

I do not remember that he was ever dispassionate, I do not remember him solemnly sitting at a table, making notes, stressing one thing, clarifying another. Even when everyone else was sitting at the table Meyerhold was not—he was standing in front of us, jacket off, hair disheveled, speaking passionately, gesturing energetically. That is exactly how I picture him when I think of him at rehearsals. . . .

It was always interesting to be invited to the Meyerholds', especially on some festive occasion, for example a birthday party for Zinaida Nikolaevna. It was a day Meyerhold celebrated with particular affection.

Let me try to describe one of those parties.

By the time I got to Meyerhold's a fair number of guests had already arrived. Kerzhentsev was there, and Eisenstein, Olesha, Shebalin, and Mikhail Svetlov. There were actors from our theater—Tsarev, Starkovsky, Zaichikov, Kuliabko-Koretskaya. There was also a black actor, Wayland Rudd, who had emigrated from America and had been taken by Meyerhold into his theater.

I was surprised not to see the traditional festive table, which usually took up all the space in the room. Instead there was a smaller table in the corner, crammed with hors d'oeuvres and lots of bottles. Next to it was a small table with plates and dishes.

As soon as I arrived Meyerhold introduced me to his guests and then dragged me to the table. In an instant I had a full glass and a plate of food.

"To Zinochka's health!" announced Meyerhold loudly. "Drink up, and remember where this table is!"

The table was rarely deserted. You could tell by the flushed faces of the guests, their loud voices, the laughter and jokes. And new guests kept arriving. There were already about thirty people there, perhaps more. Each time the bell rang, Meyerhold himself hurried to open the door, greeted the new arrival, introduced him, and then dragged him to the table.

One more surprising thing: there wasn't a single chair in the room, absolutely nowhere to sit.

"Meyerhold!" called Kerzhentsev, trying to make himself heard amid the general noise. "Come on, give us at least a couple of chairs. We'll take turns on them."

"I can't," replied Meyerhold. "They're gone. The Ostrogradskys borrowed them all."

Fyodor Ostrogradsky lived in the same building but his apartment was in another entry.

"If anybody's tired, use the floor. There's the carpet and here are some cushions," the mischievous host went on.

"Well, *I'm* tired," exclaimed Eisenstein, and he settled himself down on the carpet. A number of other people followed his example.

"There's another carpet," said Meyerhold. "Bring it over here! Put it down there! That's the way! This is the lying-down area and that's the dancing area!"

The carpets created a special atmosphere. Titles and rank lost their significance. Everyone was at the same level, and everyone was having a good time.

"Wayland, would you sing for us?" asked Meyerhold. "Do sing, please! Attention everybody: Wayland is going to sing!"

Everyone became quiet, and the room filled with the tender sounds of a Negro spiritual, accompanied by the piano.

People started dancing; there were constant jokes and laughter. The bottles and plates began to stray down onto the carpets.

"Misha!" called Meyerhold again, addressing Tsarev. "Recite 'Mtsyri' for us, will you? I love the way you do the fight with the snow leopard!"

"I don't think I can remember it at this point," Tsarev answered bashfully.

"Never mind! You can do it with the text, can't you? I'll get you everything you need; wait right there," said Meyerhold, and he disappeared into the adjoining room. He returned in a moment—carrying a chair.

Shouts and applause followed.

"This isn't a chair, it's a throne," said Meyerhold. "And he gets it."

A huge candelabrum was brought in with the candles burning and the lights were turned off. Meyerhold settled Tsarev on the chair, and the recital began.

Tsarev began timidly and uncertainly, as if measuring up his audience, and then gradually turned his energy loose. . . .

The morning sky was already blue outside when we began to leave. But it was a party that everyone talked about for a long while afterward. . . .

My notes are coming to an end. I have only a few more pages to write, and they are difficult and painful ones. I have to tell the story of the last days of Meyerhold's theater, the story of its liquidation.

It's a time I have difficulty remembering; it all seems to have happened in a thick fog. I remember that newspaper articles began to appear, attacking the theater and Meyerhold personally. I remember a meeting taking place, resolutions

being adopted. The atmosphere surrounding Meyerhold became very tense. All of us were expecting some changes in
regard to the theater. There was no more talk about an American tour of the Meyerhold State Theater which had been
scheduled some time before. New crates for costumes and
props, with the inscription "Moscow–New York" sat idly in
the theater as if they had nothing to do with us any more.

But events took a swifter turn than anyone could have
predicted, and we were stunned by their unexpectedness.

On Saturday, January 7, 1938, I went to the theater as
usual to perform in *Camille*. As usual, there were people outside trying to buy last-minute tickets. This was the 725th performance, and things were proceeding very much as they
always had. As usual, the house was sold out, as usual Meyerhold was wandering, cigarette in mouth, from one dressing
room to another. While I was changing for the third act I
heard Zaichikov and Starkovsky, who were in my dressing
room, talking about something in hushed tones. Evidently
by that time the rumor about closing the theater was being
discussed.

Was it possible to check the rumor? Whom could we call?
Who was there to ask? Everyone was upset, but nobody dared
ask Meyerhold, and his calm look betrayed nothing.

The performance was going admirably. Zinaida Nikolaevna Raikh was wonderful. It was her best performance. I
had never seen the depth of feeling, the warmth that she displayed that night.

Then came the fifth and final act. It was short, only about
twenty to twenty-five minutes. The finale of the play—let me
describe it—was staged in this way: Marguerite Gautier goes
to the window and with a sweeping gesture draws the heavy
curtain to one side. A breeze blows into the room, swaying
the light under-curtains. Marguerite starts away from the
window, her back to the audience, and then falls back into a
large wing chair. Armand hurries to her across the entire
stage, grasps her hand, and presses it to his chest. And then,
from the look on Armand's face, and Marguerite's hand as it
slips from between Armand's, the audience realizes that Marguerite is dead.

After that Armand backs away from the armchair and
sits in front of Marguerite on the low windowsill, while Marguerite's friend Nichette slowly approaches, her wedding

dress rustling, and kneels slowly in front of her. Gustave, Nichette's bridegroom, stands at a distance, bewildered. A gong sounds, the lights go out. Then the lights go up again, and we take our bows.

When I ran up to Marguerite in this performance (by that time I had switched from the part of Gaston to the part of Armand) and pressed her hand to my chest, I saw that Zinaida Nikolaevna's face was distorted and her throat was twitching spasmodically. I sensed she was about to become hysterical. I had to do something to prevent it; there was less than a minute until the end of the act. I pressed her small hand with all my strength—I wanted the physical pain to distract her from her anguish. The pain was so strong that Zinaida Nikolaevna turned to me with frightened eyes, but the imminent hysterics were averted.

We managed to finish the act. Gong. Darkness and then the lights again. I raised her in my arms, lifted her from the armchair, and we bowed to the audience.

When we got backstage Zinaida Nikolaevna fainted. The stagehands and I lifted her and carried her to her dressing room. On our way we met Meyerhold.

"Zinochka!" he was practically shouting. "What happened?" He took her from me and began carrying her himself. The public was applauding and calling insistently: "Meyerhold! Meyerhold! Meyerhold!"

"What shall we do, Vsevolod Emilievich?" I asked.

"Go out and tell them Zinaida Nikolaevna is sick and that I am not in the theater."

"Meyerhold! Meyerhold! Meyerhold!" the public went on calling.

I came to the stage, raised my hand, and repeated the announcement Meyerhold had instructed me to make.

And then something extraordinary took place. Everyone in the audience began heading toward the stage, looking for the quickest way backstage. Everyone who was onstage at that moment, the actors, stagehands, property men, firemen, all formed a chain and did everything in their power to stop the avalanche. But we couldn't manage to keep everyone out—hordes of people did make it backstage.

It turned out that many people had learned by that time that our theater had been closed and that we were performing for the last time.

The decision to close the theater had been made in the late afternoon, and it was evening before the news became known all over Moscow. Naturally, Vsevolod Emilievich and Zinaida Nikolaevna had known all about it, but had done what they could to keep people from finding out. And it was only at the end of the last performance of *Camille*, the last performance of her life for Zinaida Nikolaevna Raikh, that her strength failed her. What happened then?

Zinaida Nikolaevna recovered soon. She lay on a small sofa in her dressing room and smoked a cigarette. Meyerhold was sitting in the armchair in front of her; he also smoked. Her dressing room, the greenroom, and our dressing rooms were full of people. I remember the atmosphere well; it resembled the mood in a family where somebody everyone loved had just died: people were standing around in groups, smoking, saying nothing, thinking about things. If they broke the silence, it was to talk about something irrelevant. There were no words that could explain what had happened. It was comforting to realize that the friends of our theater stood by us at that bitter moment. Their very presence made us feel their friendly support. I remember that we all stayed very late; it must have been after three in the morning when we all went home. Despite the common knowledge that the theater had been closed, we received no official document to that effect. *The Inspector General* was scheduled for the matinée next day and all the tickets had been sold out. Meyerhold announced that as long as he had received no official order to close the theater it would continue to function.

The matinée did take place. But by then it had been officially announced that our theater was liquidated. Everyone knew that *The Inspector General* was being performed for the last time. The part of Anna Andreevna was played not by Raikh, but by Bagorskaya.

They had already scheduled a performance for that same night by a ballet troupe, directed by somebody called Victorina Krueger, on our stage. Somebody else's sets were already being carried into our theater.

The Inspector General began, and each scene as it was played disappeared forever.

The play concludes with the well-known dumb scene; Meyerhold had replaced the actors in this final scene by life-size dummies. Each dummy was costumed and made up to resemble the character it replaced.

The dummies were put in place in darkness. The sound of a gong. The lights went up. And those dead dolls, which Meyerhold had conceived of as a final image of deadness and petrifaction, were especially terrifying that night, in that last performance of *The Inspector General*.

The sound of the gong again. Darkness.

End of scene. End of theater.

Mixail Sadovskij, "Teatral'nyj čarodej," *Vstreči s Mejerxol'dom* (Moscow, 1967), pp. 504–509, 511–515, 524–528.

News Item from Literaturnaya Gazeta, January 12, 1938

The Committee for Artistic Affairs of the Soviet of Peoples' Commissars of the USSR recognizes that the Meyerhold Theater has fallen definitively into a position alien to Soviet art and has become alien to Soviet spectators.

In its decree the Committee for Artistic Affairs made an evaluation of the Meyerhold Theater, which during the entire course of its existence has been unable to free itself from profoundly bourgeois, formalist positions, alien to Soviet art. The Meyerhold Theater has shown itself totally bankrupt where the production of Soviet playwrights is concerned.

The Committee for Artistic Affairs of the Soviet of Peoples' Commissars of the USSR has resolved:

1. To liquidate the Meyerhold Theater as alien to Soviet art;

2. To relocate members of the theater company in other theaters;

3. To discuss separately the matter of the participation of Vsevolod Meyerhold in any further theatrical activity.

VII.

■ The Lost Theater

There is, finally, one enormous absence, the last of the images we must try to reconstruct. This is perhaps the most poignant task of all, since we must reconstruct something never constructed: the theater building that Meyerhold dreamed of, planned, and began to build, but which he never saw.

The space of theater and the arrangement of spectators and spectacle within that space is at the heart of any conception of theater, and anyone with a vision of theater must eventually have a space of his own, within which his vision can be absolute.

Theater is one of the most conservative of the arts. Plays are produced from year to year within highly conventionalized spaces, and these spaces remain fixed; the world without changes, as do the plays within that mirror that world, but the buildings themselves rarely change. Yet any serious attempt to reconstruct theater must come to the massive task of constructing a theater building.

All of Meyerhold's spectacles were in some sense makeshift, for they were all produced in theaters that did not correspond to his vision but were, rather, remnants of the vision of theater he was attempting to overcome. His were productions designed to test theater and its boundaries. The best-appointed of the traditional theaters Meyerhold worked in were the Alexandrinsky and Mariinsky theaters in Petersburg, yet his two great prerevolutionary productions at the Alexandrinsky, Molière's <u>Don Juan</u> and Lermontov's <u>Masquerade</u>, were exciting precisely because they were attempts to arrange or rearrange the space of the theater, to reorder the relationship of spectator to spectacle.

After the Revolution Meyerhold worked in Moscow, in the former Sohn Theater on Triumphal Square. He first occupied it in 1920, and it was this theater building which he planned to redesign in order to create an environment that would accommodate the theater of the future. The reconstruction was begun in 1932 but never completed, and after his theater was liquidated plans for the building were altered. It is now Tschaikovsky Hall, on what is now Mayakovsky Square.

Sergei Vakhtangov and Mikhail Barkhin were the architects who worked with Meyerhold on the building. Their description of the project is the clearest image we have of what might have been one of the world's most powerful theaters. But it too, for us, is nothing but memory and imagination.

Mikhail Barkhin, Sergei Vakhtangov

Not many spectators today still remember a small theater with seating in the orchestra, two semicircular balconies, and a bare, open stage with exposed brick walls, upon which were once performed those legendary productions that now make us envy those who saw them.

But it was precisely that old-fashioned theater, with the spectators on one side of an archway and the actors on the other, its entire design supporting theatrical illusion, that exasperated its director.

He had long since gotten rid of naturalistically painted backdrops, teasers, and wings, and had banished the curtain. He hated the orchestra pit that physically divided actor and spectator; he thought that a purely frontal view of the stage action, a point of view that annihilated any construction in depth of *mise en scène* or blocking, was a stupid idea. (He himself liked to watch his productions from the niche of a side door in the auditorium down front, close to the stage, or from a seat in the side balcony.) The twelve hundred seats of the former Sohn Theater on Triumphal Square in Moscow were not enough for him; he felt constrained in the enclosed box of a traditional theater. He needed a new theater, a spacious one, in which to realize projects that were impossible within the boxy confines of a makeshift building.

And so it became of the utmost importance to reconstruct that box.

Vsevolod Meyerhold enlisted us to work with him on the project. We had worked with him in the past as stage designers/constructors for several productions, and we were familiar with his ideas about theater.

Thus began a rather extensive collaboration on a series of designs for a new theater, designs which are still published today, thirty years later, in architectural journals here in the USSR and abroad.

We cannot, of course, remember all the long interesting conversations during which we discussed directorial requirements and structural possibilities, the needs of the theater, and the means of implementing them; conversations where we investigated creative perspectives, weighed the purposes of art and the function of the director, spoke about the role of theater and the history of its architecture, about Shakespeare and about the Greek chorus, about Roman amphitheaters and Wagnerian opera, about Mayakovsky, Olesha, and Bezymensky, Corbusier and Tatlin, Reinhardt, Van de Velde, Ehrenburg—about acoustics and optics, about descriptive geometry and mechanics, about cranes and automobiles, about all the things that might possibly be part of a new theater—and all the things that faced architects who had agreed to think about a theater for Meyerhold.

Where does the director want to place his actors, to arrange the action? _In front of_ the spectators? _Around_ the spectators? Or will he _surround_ the action with the spectators?

In Greek theaters the orchestra (the space for the chorus) was surrounded by an amphitheater of seats that could accommodate up to thirty thousand spectators. A small stage (the skene) was open and viewed from the front. In essence, this system combined two methods of perceiving the action. It is only after many centuries that we again find a similar solution, in Renaissance England, at Shakespeare's Globe. Finally, in our own time, this conception has been realized in the theater by Poelzig in Berlin (the Max Reinhardt Theater, 1919). In all these instances there were two stages: a rear stage and in front of it a strong thrust stage (forestage, proscenium, or "orchestra").

Throughout history, however, the system of the Roman theater has had a wider and stronger influence. In the Roman theater the audience already sat in the orchestra—as they do today in what are called "orchestra" seats. The action was intended to take place only on the frontal stage, much expanded and developed. From this system all European theaters derive, right down to present-day theater buildings. And it was precisely in this system that we see the separation of the stage and the auditorium, of actor and spectator. From this system derives the proscenium arch, the orchestra pit, and eventually the curtain.

But innovative directors had grown disenchanted with it. By 1912 Van de Velde, and shortly after him Auguste Perret, decided to construct not a frontal stage with a single proscenium arch, but a so-called tripartite stage with three proscenium arches which took in the front part of the orchestra. This idea was developed still later by Piscator and Gropius, who surrounded the entire auditorium with a circular stage, where the action could take place on all sides of the spectator.

Meyerhold conceived this crucial problem differently. He wanted to give the spectator the possibility of seeing the actor in all the complex richness of his movement, and the action in all the richness of its spatial progression—movement flowing not merely from left to right before the spectator's eyes, but forward and back, penetrating the auditorium.

During conversations like these—studying the rich experience of previous productions, estimating future requirements, dreaming of future productions—certain basic premises began to take shape, the theoretical prerequisites of a new theater, for which we would have to discover the necessary form.

These ideas shook theater to its very foundations. How was the theatrical action to be deployed? Would it remain flat, frontal, or would it embrace the entire auditorium, its entire spatial structure? Would the frame of a proscenium arch remain, dividing stage from auditorium, and establish two-dimensional action? Or would actor and spectator somehow, by some means, be brought together? How was the actor best perceived—always from the front? Or were there yet other interesting ways to look at him: from the sides, from above, from below? How would an actor act best: with the dark aperture of the traditional proscenium arch in front of him, working only in one direction, "to the house," protected on three sides? Or acting as he might in a circus, surrounded by spectators, "unprotected"? Or was it necessary to leave him at least one side for his own, a back wall, a background, a support? How was the actor to be linked physically to the acting area? Was he to sit by himself in a dressing room miles away from the stage, and run, when his cue came, to the spot he was to enter from, and then on his entrance line begin "his part"? Or would it be better for him to have a place very near the stage, so that he could then move naturally, easily, organically into the action when required? Should the auditorium be illuminated with natural light, so that the actors could rehearse under the same conditions that obtained in other places of production? During certain productions should daylight flood the theater? And so on and on and on.

Until then no one had ever formulated such questions, let alone provided ready answers.

One by one, we worked out some guiding principles for the new theater:

1. Unity of stage and auditorium;
2. Spectators surrounding the action on three sides;
3. Blocking and *mise en scène* in depth, and axonometric perception of the action from above and from the sides;
4. No curtain, proscenium arch, or orchestra pit to separate actors and spectators;
5. Natural light to illuminate the auditorium;
6. The closest proximity of actors to the playing area.

For all of that, a reconstruction of the former Sohn Theater would hardly suffice. What was quite frankly required was to tear it down and build something new in its place. But at that period only "reconstructions" were permitted and, for that reason, unfortunately, the exterior walls had to be preserved—rigid limits, a stiff box, that determined the nature of our construction plans.

After we had ripped out the old interior, including the proscenium arch and the balcony, and designed a single space for both stage and auditorium, we had somehow to situate the stage area. An elongated, off-centered area that thrust strongly into the auditorium was surrounded on three sides by places for thousands of spectators. Thus were the spectators assured a view of action staged in depth. It was further necessary to assure the perception of that action more advantageously—from above, that is, in all the three-dimensional variety of the staging.

We have spoken already of the advantages of perceiving the actor and the entire stage action from above and from the side, axonometrically. For this it would of course be possible to have recourse to tiers and balconies, so familiar from old-style theaters. But it seemed better to us to arrange the spectators' seats in an amphitheater of steeply rising levels. Only the amphitheater (Greek, Roman, Palladian) provided the best conditions for viewing: a broad, complete, all-embracing perception of the spectacle. It made it impossible for people seated in front to block the view. And, most importantly, it would be a theater without rows, without orchestra and box seats for a few and distant balconies for everybody else. It would thus be really new, truly for a mass audience, a democratic theater building.

All that was for the spectators. But great attention had to be paid to the actors as well. We wanted to move the actors closer to the stage (specifically, their dressing rooms and the places where they waited for their entrances). This was a matter Meyerhold considered of the greatest importance. The actor should not be forced to run panting down from the fifth floor, and then arrive onstage only mechanically aware of what had gone on before he made his entrance. On the contrary, the way Meyerhold conceived the matter, an actor who was not involved in a given scene could wait for his entrance right onstage, only at a distance, outside the lighted area, totally aware of the tempo and rhythm of the performance, its dynamic, and then in two steps he could appear in the midst of the action.

Some of Meyerhold's previous productions, as we have said, yielded a great many ideas that helped shape the architecture of the new theater. For example, the question of how to situate the actors' dressing rooms. In *The Inspector General* there was a marvellous scene where Khlestakov took the bribes from the town officials. The scene was played in front of a semicircular wall, made up solely of doors. And just such a semicircle of doors became the background, the fourth wall of the stage area, now part of the building itself, in the form of two rows of dressing rooms for the principal actors. In the production of Selvinsky's *Commander of the Second Army* a semicircular wall was built to surround the entire stage. In *A List of Benefits* by Yury Olesha special panels ran from the depth of the stage out into the hall, thus uniting the stage and the auditorium.

After a number of experiments onstage, a place for the orchestra was found, set in a space high in the back wall above the actors' dressing rooms. The orchestra could remain in view or could be hidden.

The matter of mechanization continued to occupy a central role, although flies and hanging decorations were omitted. The stage area comprised two revolving circles, placed on the longitudinal axis. This determined the shape of the stage. But mechanical devices might be required above as well. For this purpose we proposed to hang diagonally from the ceiling a kind of monorail, by which the stage areas could be raised to various heights and moved to various points in the theater. All this greatly enriched the possibilities for changing scenery and for utilizing the entire space of the theater. When an act had ended, the lights would be disconnected and the stage revolves would descend into a double pit, and then be raised again when they were cleared of scenery (or scenic constructions, as we called them then).

Finally—and this might have been most interesting—we intended to let the audience occupy the stage during intermissions. Besides going into the lobby they could descend the steps of the amphitheater and mount the great stage area, now cleared of sets and scenery. Here they would once again experience the unity of the theater space, and themselves provide something unexpected, a brilliant spectacle of rhythmic movement and color for those who had remained in their seats.

For a number of previous productions it had been necessary to provide a passage for automobiles through the auditorium and onto the stage. Meyerhold considered it absolutely necessary to incorporate this connection between exterior space and stage space into the new building as an organic part of the structure, as one of the fundamental characteristics of his theater. We managed to find room for this through passage, despite the cramped space.

This requirement of Meyerhold's was incorporated many times into plans for subsequent theater buildings, as one of the most typical features of a modern theater. And, in fact, if the Bolshoi can bring on horses for performances of _Don Quixote_ or _Khovanshchina_, then it seems only natural to be able to bring on automobiles in contemporary works. . . . How many people who saw _The Earth Rampant_ will ever forget the moment when the doors at the back of the house were thrown open and a truck drove through the audience toward the stage, bearing the body of the slain hero?

We talked at great length with Meyerhold about open-air performances. He was anxious that his theater should include a roof that could be rolled back when necessary, which might have been very effective on summer evenings. Today, of course, such a roof might be constructed, but in 1930 it seemed to pose insuperable problems. Nevertheless our engineer Artyushkov was enthusiastic about the idea, and tried to work out a retractable roof for the entire auditorium as well as for the stage.

If not a retractable roof, we managed at least to bring daylight from overhead into the theater by means of an opaque glass ceiling. And we intended to install the lighting instruments above this ceiling.

Meyerhold had thought not only about the actors' space, but also about space for the director, the designer, the construction builder, the composer. Our restrictions had already led to an unusual arrangement of the space in the building. So we conceived the idea of constructing a "tower of creativity."

What troubles that tower cost us! The unusual notion of introducing a tower into the design of a theater building, whose forms had been conventionalized for hundreds of years, occasioned more than one difficult argument during the long process of getting the necessary authorities to approve the project.

But the work continued.

Beginning in 1930 and for the next several years, our work group made three different designs, incorporating the various ideas discussed above.

The first variant (1930–1931) kept a major part of the previous building: vestibule, lobby, staircase, even a little theater room tucked away behind the main theater. In general we reworked only the main auditorium and the stage area, where we ripped out everything and were to build a new auditorium. Its shape was essentially rectangular with semicircular corners. The stage area was similarly backed by a single curved wall. Both revolves were the same size.

The second variant (1931–1932) offered a more radical solution. This was an entirely new building which preserved only the foundations of the place and wholly ignored the old building. The strongly elongated ellipse of the auditorium contained a narrowed stage area with revolves of very different diameters. Plans were made for two thousand seats. In order to present earlier-style productions, which depended on a shallow box stage and on the presence of orchestra seats, it was intended that the smaller forward revolve and the part of the fixed stage space in front of the larger rear revolve could be transformed into orchestra seating by using portable chairs.

The third variant (1932–1933), finally, was the most realistic. It preserved the exterior walls and made maximum use of the entire interior volume of the box-like building. The ellipse was not so elongated, and the seats were thus closer to the stage. The auditorium seated sixteen hundred people. And this variant we did indeed build, in concrete and brick.

But construction was subsequently halted. Further work and changes to the structure were undertaken without our participation. The theater was finally opened to the public as Tschaikovsky Concert Hall.

We had no further connection with the project nor its realization.

We still recall one conversation with Meyerhold. He intended to open the new theater with a production of *Othello*. Meyerhold was always able to describe things so that we could see exactly what he wanted, and how he envisaged it. . . .

The forward revolving stage, thrust powerfully toward the audience, is covered in black velvet. The house is dark. And then one, and then another, and then a third spotlight hits that stage, illuminating it clearly for even the spectators at the top of the house. The stage is empty, and on the black velvet lies one single, blindingly white, object—Desdemona's handkerchief. . . .

We knew then that things which in an ordinary theater remain unperceived would, in this theater, become the pivot of the action.

And that would be true for more than just a handkerchief.

Mixail Barxin and Sergej Vaxtangov, "Nezaveršennyj zamysel," *Vstreči s Mejerxol'dom* (Moscow, 1967), pp. 570–578.

Mikhail Sadovsky

In 1930 Vsevolod Emilievich began to work on a project for a new theater building.

He worked on this project himself, together with two young architects, Mikhail Barkhin and Sergei Vakhtangov.

The plan, as we know, was to redesign the building of the former Sohn Theater on Triumphal Square (now Mayakovsky Square). The building was eventually converted into what is now Tschaikovsky Concert Hall. Those who have been inside it can easily imagine what the theater that Meyerhold planned would have looked like, since the theater had already been finished in its rough form and the subsequent conversion changed almost nothing of its auditorium, lobby, or beautiful broad staircase.

Picture to yourself, then, Tschaikovsky Concert Hall, and imagine the following: the audience is seated in the amphitheater, there is neither a stage nor orchestra seats. Where the orchestra seats are now located was to be the "minor arena" or "the small circle," according to Meyerhold's plan, and the place that is now occupied by the stage was to contain "the major arena" or "the large circle." These circles could either be clearly separated from each other—say, through their being on different levels, or through lighting, etc.—or they could be connected, in which case the action would have taken place on an enormous scenic area incorporating both what is now the orchestra and the stage.

In such a scenic area no box sets, backdrops, or hanging sets would have been possible. They were to be replaced by constructions, furnishings, and carpet.

A spacious glassed-in terrace was to open onto the corner of Gorky Street and Mayakovsky Square. This terrace was to serve as a lobby, and could be opened wide on hot Moscow nights.

"Our theater," Meyerhold said, "will have the maximum in comfort for both the spectator and the actor. When Zimin and Strisky were building their theaters in Moscow the only thing they were concerned about was having as many seats in the auditorium as possible, so that it would yield the most profit. They had no consideration for the actors. Their dressing rooms were tiny stuffy closets, situated fifty miles from the stage."

Meyerhold planned to locate the dressing rooms in the semicircle of the "major arena." Their doors were to open directly into the auditorium. The actor's walk from the door of his dressing room to his place in the scenic area and the few seconds that he would spend waiting for his cue were to take place in full view of the audience. And, naturally, this walk and this wait were to be directed. This walk would be performed not by actor X in the make-up of Othello, nor by the "real" Othello, but by actor X about to play the part of Othello. Not only was Meyerhold intent on destroying the conventional stage, but he wanted also to take the audience almost backstage, to show it some of the tools of the trade.

The facade was to be decorated with large mosaics showing various scenes from Meyerhold Theater productions. Several artists (I can't recall their names now) worked on the designs, which were done first in oils and then sent to Leningrad where the mosaics were to be made. The mosaics were completed as well, but after the Meyerhold Theater was closed and the construction work on the theater suspended they were donated to the Leningrad Academy of Arts.

Meyerhold wanted to have the following quotation from Pushkin carved across the pediment of the new theater: "The spirit of the age demands major changes on the dramatic stage as well."

Mixail Sadovskij, "Teatral'nyj čarodej," _Vstreči s Mejerxol'dom_ (Moscow, 1967), pp. 519–520.

News Item from <u>Sovetskoe Iskusstvo</u>, January 26, 1938

FUTURE PLANS FOR THE NEW THEATER BUILDING
ON MAYAKOVSKY SQUARE

The great theater building now being constructed in Moscow on Mayakovsky Square had been intended for the Meyerhold Theater—now liquidated, as everyone knows. The task of converting the projected theater to a concert hall has been assigned to architect D. N. Chechulin.

"The building," said Chechulin, "was previously being constructed according to plans by architects Vakhtangov and Bakhrin, as well as by Meyerhold himself. The latter's views played a decisive role in the planning and design of the building as a whole. The planners had reduced the theater to a naked Constructivist scheme without the slightest regard for elementary architectural requirements. Beginning with the lobby and the service accommodations and ending with the auditorium, everything was calculated for external, unjustifiable, and totally unnecessary effect. During the planning and the actual construction the interests of neither spectators nor theater workers were taken into consideration. The actors' dressing rooms were planned for some back corner and were totally unequipped, uncomfortable little closets. In the auditorium Formalist extravagances were carried to such a point that, for example, special little wagons filled with props, etc. were to pass on suspended rails or wires over the spectators' heads during the intermissions. Beyond their understandable feelings of fear, the spectators would also undergo the danger of dripping oil, which the little wagons and rails would require in order to function noiselessly. . . . In Meyerhold's opinion, the spectators were no more than 'raw material', and during performances lighting effects would even be aimed at them. . . ."

In the external design of the building no attention had been paid to the complex of buildings to be constructed eventually on Mayakovsky Square.

Even while it was being built the project had occasioned sharp criticism, and many parts of it had to be modified during construction, or even eliminated.

The possibility presented itself of utilizing the building, after reconstruction, as a concert hall for approximately two thousand people. According to the new plans the stage area will be divided from the auditorium by a specially built proscenium arch, which, together with the orchestra pit, will make it possible to present a combined orchestra and a chorus of up to one thousand individuals. Besides this, the stage arrangement will permit the presentation of mass theatrical productions.

The external plans for the building will harmonize with the architectural ensemble of the square. The facade of the theater facing the square will be decorated with a tall six-columned portico with statues. Within, the building will contain a normal-type lobby, a bar, a coat-check, comfortable seats for the spectators, spacious recital halls, etc.

The new edifice is scheduled for completion by the middle of the current year.

VIII.
Epilogue

Meyerhold to Stanislavsky

Moscow
January 18, 1938

Dear Konstantin Sergeevich,

Nikolai Gogol, trying to describe an occurrence in one of his stories, felt how hard it was to express on paper something that had just happened in the story; he suddenly stopped writing and exclaimed:

"No, I can't! Give me another pen! This pen is dead, it's worn out, it has too fine a point for this picture!"

I have been trying to write you a letter on your birthday, and I find myself in Gogol's predicament.

My feelings for you—my dear teacher—are so strong that any pen I use will be too dead, too worn out, to express them on paper.

How can I describe how much I love you?

How can I describe how thankful I am for all the things you have taught me about the enormously difficult art of directing?

If I have strength enough to surmount all the difficulties that have come my way during the last few months, I will come see you, and you will be able to read in my eyes my joy at seeing you recovered from your illness, seeing you again hale and hearty, seeing you again at work in the service of our great country.

My warmest congratulations! I embrace you.

Very best to your family, especially to Maria Petrovna.
My warmest greetings to your granddaughter, who moved me
to tears by her courtesy to me when I asked her about you.

Devotedly yours,
V. Meyerhold

Meyerhold to Zinaida Raikh

Gorenki
October 15, 1938

My dearest Zinochka,

I miss you the way a blind man misses his guide. It's the
work. When I don't have my work to worry me I miss you the
way a green apple misses the sunshine.

I came to Gorenki on the thirteenth, looked at the birchtrees and caught my breath. What was it? What Renaissance
jewel-maker had set out all that splendor on invisible cobwebs? Surely those leaves are made of gold! (You remember
when we were children, those fragile leaves of gold we used
to cover the rough shells of walnuts with, to make Christmas-
tree decorations?) Look: those leaves, scattered in the air.
Scattered, and still as if they were frozen—in a veil? On
glass? On what? Still, and yet they seemed to be waiting for
something. Who is lying in wait for them?

I could count the last seconds of their life like the pulse of
a dying man. Will I find them still alive when I come again to
Gorenki—in a day, in an hour? As I stood that day looking at
the golden fairy-tale world of autumn, at all those wonders, I
kept whispering to myself: Zina, Zinochka, look at these wonders and do not leave me, _I love you_, you are my wife, my
sister, my mother, my friend, my beloved, golden as this wonder-working nature!

Zina, do not leave me!

There is nothing in the world more terrible than loneliness!

Why do the wonders of nature always bring me thoughts
of terrible loneliness? It isn't really, after all! I mean, it—this
loneliness—is only temporary, isn't it?

All right, but why is it the wonders of nature never make me rejoice, but terrify me? No, more precisely: make me rejoice and then immediately after terrify me?

When I was a child it was the same way: my wonder at nature immediately turned to a feeling of terror, always, always terror!

I don't know why, but it was like that, always like that.

My beloved Zina, take care of yourself. Rest. Get well. We are all managing here. And we will manage. I miss you *ineffably*, but it must be endured. And this separation is only for a month, isn't it? Soon we'll be together again like two halves of a single sweet ripe apple, a delicious apple.

My beloved, I embrace you.

Regards from Kostya. He's well. His studies are going well.

Regards from Lydia Anisimovna.

Warmest regards from Mayakovsky's sister Ludmilla. (She phoned today.)

I kiss you.

Vsevolod

News Item From the <u>New York Times</u>, July 18, 1939

ACTRESS SLAIN IN MOSCOW IN CHAIN OF COINCIDENCES

MME. MEYERHOLD WAS FORMER WIFE OF SERGEI YESSENIN

Moscow, July 17 (AP). The brutal slaying of Zenaida Reich, actress wife of the former Bolshevik stage producer Vsevolod Meyerhold, shocked Moscow today. Found in her apartment with eleven knife wounds in her body, her eyes put out and her throat cut, she was rushed to a hospital, but died four hours later. Burglars were suspected.

Her death continued a train of tragic coincidences. Her first husband, the poet Sergei Yessenin, hanged himself. Yessenin's second wife, the American dancer Isadora Duncan, was strangled in a freak automobile accident at Nice, France, in 1927. Her scarf became entangled in one of the wheels and pulled her out of the machine.

Zenaida Reich was reported taken in custody by secret police last Wednesday for unexplained reasons.

Her arrest followed that of her internationally known husband, who had stood high in Bolshevist circles only a few years before, but whose theater was closed in 1938 when the Communist party organ "Pravda" denounced the "anti-Soviet" tinge of some of his later productions.

Glossary of Names

Aksyonov, Ivan (1884–1935). Poet, translator, critic. He translated Crommelynck's *Magnanimous Cuckold* for Meyerhold's production in 1922, and taught in the Meyerhold workshops.

Amaglobeli, Sergei (1899–1946). From 1933 to 1936 artistic director of the Maly Theater.

Andreyev, Leonid (1871–1919). A popular but superficial Symbolist playwright of the turn of the century. Meyerhold staged the first productions of his *Life of a Man* and *To the Stars* in 1907.

Andreyeva (Zheliabuzhskaya), **Maria** (1868–1953). A member of the original company of the Moscow Art Theater, she created the roles of Irina in *Three Sisters* and Varya in *The Cherry Orchard*. From 1918 to 1921 she was in charge of theaters in Petrograd and head of the division of theaters and spectacles of the Commissariat of Education of the Union of Communes of the northern region. In this position she was frequently in conflict with Meyerhold in his role, from 1920 to 1921, as head of the Theatrical Division of the People's Commissariat of Education (TEO Narkompros).

Anisimovna. Lydia Anisimovna Charnetskaya, the Meyerholds' housekeeper.

Asafyev, Boris (Igor Glebov) (1884–1949). Composer and musicologist, People's Artist of the USSR. He chose and arranged the music for Meyerhold's production of Griboyedov's *Woe from Wit*.

Aseyev, Nikolai (1889–1963). Poet. With Sergei Gorodetsky and Sergei Tretiakov he wrote *Verturnaf*, an agit-spectacle which Meyerhold rehearsed in 1922, but never opened.

Averkiev, Dmitry (1836–1905). Playwright and theater critic. Meyerhold staged his play *Kashirskaya Starina* in 1902, and cited his studies of Shakespeare and Pushkin in *O Teatre* (St. Petersburg, 1913).

Babanova, Maria (b. 1900). Actress, People's Artist of the USSR. A student at the Meyerhold workshops, she worked at the Meyerhold Theater until 1927. She played Stella in *The Magnanimous Cuckold*, Maria Antonovna in *The Inspector General*.

Bakst, Leon (Lev Rosenberg) (1866–1924). Artist, stage designer. He and Meyerhold collaborated on two productions: Oscar Wilde's *Salomé* in 1908 (the production, rehearsed at the Mikhailovsky Theater, was canceled a month before its opening); and d'Annunzio's *Pisanella*, commis-

sioned by Ida Rubinstein (opened June 11, 1913, at the Théâtre du Cha-
telet, Paris).

Barkhin, Mikhail. Architect. Barkhin and Sergei Vakhtangov designed
the theater that Meyerhold planned to build on the site of the former
Sohn Theater in Moscow, and which was subsequently converted into the
present Tschaikovsky Hall.

Bely, Andrey (Boris Bugaev) (1880–1934). Novelist (*Petersburg*, *The Silver
Dove*), poet, critic. Bely was an admirer and supporter of Meyerhold's
work.

Blok, Alexander (1880–1921). Poet and playwright. Meyerhold's first his-
toric production was Blok's *Balaganchik* (variously translated as *Farce*,
The Puppet Show, *The Fairground Booth*), which he first staged for Vera
Kommissarzhevskaya's company with sets by Sapunov and music by
Kuzmin (opened December 30, 1906). From 1914 to 1916 Blok was poetry
editor of Meyerhold's journal *Love for Three Oranges*.

Briusov, Valery (1873–1924). Poet, playwright, translator, and critic. Associated with Meyerhold in the Moscow Art Theater's abortive Theater
Studio in 1905.

Bulgakov, Mikhail (1891–1940). Author, playwright.

Butorin, Nikolai (1893–1961). Director, actor at the Meyerhold Theater.
From 1924 to 1926 he was head of the teaching program at the Meyerhold
workshops.

Chaliapin, Fyodor (1873–1938). Singer and actor. Meyerhold admired
Chaliapin enormously, and felt that he had solved the problem of incorporating rhythm into acting. He speaks of Chaliapin at length in his important essay on Wagner, "On a Production of *Tristan and Isolde* at the
Mariinsky Theater" (translated in Braun, *Meyerhold on Theater*, pp. 80–
98): "Chaliapin's acting is always true—not true to life, but theatrically
true."

Chekhov, Anton (1860–1904). Writer and playwright. Meyerhold created
the roles of Treplyov in *The Sea Gull* and Tusenbach in *Three Sisters*.

Chekhov, Mikhail (1891–1955). Actor; nephew of the playwright. He directed the Moscow Art Theater's Second Studio from 1924 to 1928.

Dolmatovsky, Evgeny (b. 1915). Poet. A protégé of Meyerhold's.

Dovgalevsky, Valerian (1885–1934). Soviet plenipotentiary in France.

Ehrenburg, Ilya (1891–1967). Novelist, playwright, memoirist. Meyerhold's agit-spectacle, *D. E.* (opened June 15, 1924), was based on his novel
The D. E. Trust.

Eisenstein, Sergei (1898–1948). Film director, theoretician. He studied in
the Meyerhold workshops from 1921 to 1922.

Ekk, Nikolai (b. 1902). Actor and film director. He studied in the Meyerhold workshops in 1921.

Erdman, Nikolai (1902–1970). Playwright. Meyerhold staged his *Mandate*
(opened April 20, 1925), and began extensive work in 1932 on a production of *The Suicide*, which was abandoned.

Fadeyev, Alexander (1901–1956). Writer.

Faiko, Alexei (b. 1893). Playwright. Meyerhold staged two of his plays:
Lake Liul (opened November 7, 1923) and *Bubus the Teacher* (opened January 29, 1925). *Bubus the Teacher* was one of the most significant of Meyerhold's productions from a theoretical point of view, but had little

success with the general public, and Faiko generally resented Meyerhold.
Fokine, Mikhail (1880–1942). Dancer and choreographer. Fokine's greatest work was done for Diaghilev's company, but he collaborated with Meyerhold on numerous productions, including Oscar Wilde's *Salomé* in 1908, Gluck's opera *Orpheus* at the Mariinsky Theater (opened December 21, 1911), d'Annunzio's *Pisanella*, and *Jota de Aragón* to Glinka's music (opened January 29, 1916).

Garin, Erast (b. 1902). Actor and director. He joined the Meyerhold workshops in 1921 and later became a member of the Meyerhold Theater. He played the title role in *The Inspector General* (opened December 9, 1926), Guliachkin in Erdman's *Mandate* (opened April 20, 1925), and Chatsky in the first version of Griboyedov's *Woe from Wit* (opened March 12, 1928).

Germanova, Maria (1884–1940). Actress at the Moscow Art Theater.

Gladkov, Alexander (1913–1976). Playwright and critic. He worked as Meyerhold's assistant from 1934 to the closing of his theater, and made stenographic transcriptions of Meyerhold's remarks and rehearsal notes.

Glière, Reinhold (1874–1956). Composer. He wrote music for Meyerhold's abandoned production of Hauptmann's *Schluck und Jau* at Stanislavsky's Theater-Studio in 1905, but Meyerhold had no high opinion of his work, and parodied his famous ballet *The Red Poppy* in his 1930 production of Mayakovsky's *Bathhouse* (opened March 16, 1930) and Vishnevsky's *Last Decisive Battle* (opened February 7, 1931).

Gogol, Nikolai (1801–1852). Author and playwright. Meyerhold's version of his *Inspector General* (opened December 9, 1926) is perhaps his most famous production, and the great exemplar of modern staging of classic texts. Meyerhold had the highest regard for Mussorgsky's opera *Marriage*, a setting of Gogol's play of the same name, as a treatment of the fundamental theatrical problem of combining musical rhythm and natural speech.

Gorbunov, Ivan (1831–1895). Actor, *diseur*, writer.

Gorky, Maxim (Alexei Peshkov) (1868–1936). Writer. Meyerhold created the role of Pyotr in his play *Philistines (Meschchane)* at the Moscow Art Theater. Gorky's plays were widely performed in the Soviet Union in the 1930s and 1940s and were considered models of Socialist Realism. They still are.

Griboyedov, Alexander (1795–1829). Playwright. Meyerhold staged his famous comedy in verse, *Woe from Wit* (retitled *Woe to Wit*), in two versions. The first opened March 12, 1928 (this is the version Pasternak saw on March 25, 1928). The second version, much revised, opened September 25, 1935.

Grigoryev, Boris. Painter. He painted a famous double portrait of Meyerhold in 1916.

Gvozdev, Alexei (1887–1939). Theater historian and critic. He was a strong supporter of Meyerhold's work, and wrote numerous articles devoted to it.

Hofman, Josef (1876–1957). Pianist and composer.

Ilyinsky, Igor (b. 1901). Actor, People's Artist of the USSR. He studied at the Meyerhold workshops in 1921, and joined the Meyerhold Theater the following year. He worked for Meyerhold from 1921 to 1935, and created the role of Bruno in *The Magnanimous Cuckold* (opened April 25, 1922) and the title role in _Bubus the Teacher_, among others. After leaving the Meyerhold Theater he worked at the Maly Theater, and made numerous films.

Isakov, Sergei (b. 1900). Set designer. He worked with Meyerhold on the unrealized production of Pushkin's _Boris Godunov_ at the Vakhtangov Studio from 1924 to 1926.

Ivanter, Benjamin (1904–1942). Writer. He studied at the Meyerhold workshops in 1921.

Kachalov, Vasily (1875–1948). Actor at the Moscow Art Theater, People's Artist of the USSR.

Karatygin, Vasily (1802–1853). One of the great Russian actors of the nineteenth century. Meyerhold often referred to him as a source of traditional acting techniques.

Kellerman, Bernard (1879–1951). German writer; his novel _Tunnel_ was a source for some of the material in the agit-spectacle _D. E._ (opened June 15, 1924).

Kerzhentsev, Platon (1881–1940). Theater critic and journalist. As president of the Committee on Artistic Affairs of the SNK of the USSR, his article in _Pravda_ ("An Alien Theater," December 17, 1937), sharply critical of Meyerhold's theater, marked the beginning of the official opposition that resulted in the closing of the theater in 1938.

Kiligin, Sergei. Actor. He joined the Meyerhold Theater in the thirties, and rehearsed the part of Pimen in _Boris Godunov_.

Kirshon, Vladimir (1902–1938). Playwright. Associated with the Organization of Proletarian Writers (RAPP), he wrote plays with titles like _Bread_. Meyerhold had a low opinion of his work.

Kommissarzhevskaya, Vera (1864–1910). Actress. She created the role of Nina in the première performance of Chekhov's _Sea Gull_ at the Alexandrinsky Theater in St. Petersburg on October 17, 1896. A superb actress, she founded her own theater company in 1904. In 1906 she invited Meyerhold to join the company as director, and it was for her he did his first remarkable Symbolist productions (Ibsen's _Hedda Gabler_, opened November 10, 1906; Maeterlinck's _Sister Beatrice_, opened November 22, 1906; Blok's _Balaganchik_, opened December 30, 1906). The two artists were never comfortable with each other (". . . you don't talk to me enough. You only half-hear what I say," Meyerhold wrote her), and on November 8, 1907, Kommissarzhevskaya asked Meyerhold to leave her company. He did, under protest.

Konchalovsky, Pyotr (1876–1956). Painter. He painted a portrait of Meyerhold in 1938.

Korenev, Mikhail (b. 1889). Director. He studied at the Meyerhold workshops, and later worked as a director in the Meyerhold Theater.

Korin, Pavel (1892–1967). Painter, People's Artist of the USSR.

Kornilov, Boris (1907–1938). A young poet whose work Meyerhold much appreciated.

Kotlyarevsky, Nestor (1863–1925). Literary historian.

Kritsberg, Lazar (1899–1950?) Director. He studied in the Meyerhold workshops in 1921.

Kuliabko-Koretskaya, Anna. Actress. She began work with Meyerhold in the Theater-Studio in 1915, and continued in his company until the Meyerhold Theater was closed in 1938.

Kuzmin, Mikhail (1875–1936). Poet, translator, composer. He wrote the music for Meyerhold's production of Blok's *Balaganchik* (opened December 30, 1906), as well as for a few smaller studio productions.

Lazarenko, Vitaly (1890–1936). Circus performer. Meyerhold and Mayakovsky, among others, valued his use of political satire in his work.

Leistikov, Ivan (1892–1963). Painter. He worked on the sets for Meyerhold's productions of Olesha's *List of Benefits* (opened June 4, 1931); Dumas fils' *Camille* (opened March 19, 1934); and Erdman's *Suicide* (never opened). He also designed the sets for German's *Prelude* (opened January 28, 1933).

Lensky, Alexander (1847–1908). Actor, director, teacher. A member of the Maly Theater company, Lensky was the actor of the generation preceding his whom Meyerhold most admired.

Lermontov, Mikhail (1814–1841). Poet and playwright. Meyerhold's production of his play *Masquerade* (opened February 25, 1917) was the most famous of his prerevolutionary productions. The production stayed in the repertory of the Alexandrinsky Theater for almost thirty years.

Loginov, Andrei (1877–1943). Actor. He played Khlopov in Meyerhold's production of Gogol's *Inspector General* (opened December 9, 1926).

Lokshina, Hesia (b. 1902). Director. A student in the Meyerhold workshops, she later worked as a director in the Meyerhold Theater.

Loyter, Naum (1890–1966). Director. A student in the Meyerhold workshops in 1921.

Lunacharsky, Anatoly (1875–1933). Playwright, critic, public official. Lunacharsky served as Commissar of Education for the Soviet government from 1917 to 1929. He greatly admired Meyerhold's work and, although he often criticized specific productions, he constantly defended Meyerhold against attack. In 1920 he appointed Meyerhold head of the Theater Section of the People's Commissariat of Education (TEO Narkompros), which Meyerhold directed until the following year.

Martinson, Sergei (b. 1899). Actor. He joined the Meyerhold Theater in the thirties, and played Khlestakov in the *The Inspector General*, among other roles.

Martynova, Klavdia. Costume mistress of the Meyerhold Theater.

Mayakovsky, Vladimir (1893–1930). Poet, playwright. Personal friendship, as well as artistic accord and unswerving commitment to the Revolution, bound Meyerhold and Mayakovsky. Meyerhold staged all of Mayakovsky's plays: *Mystery-Bouffe* in two versions (opened November 7, 1918 and May 1, 1921); *The Bedbug* (opened February 13, 1929); and *The Bathhouse* (opened March 16, 1930).

Michurin, Gennady. Actor in the Meyerhold Theater.

Mochalov, Pavel (1800–1848). Actor. A member of the Maly Theater, Mochalov was one of the most famous—and most melodramatic—Russian actors of the nineteenth century.

Mologin, Nikolai (1892–1951). Actor. He studied in the Meyerhold workshops, then joined the Meyerhold Theater. He reworked Podgaetsky's script for the agit-spectacle *D. E.*

Morozov, Saava (1862–1905). Manufacturer, patron of the arts. One of Stanislavsky's major supporters and one of the directors of the Moscow Art Theater from 1902 to 1905.

Moskvin, Ivan (1874–1946). Actor, People's Artist of the USSR. A member of the Moscow Art Theater, he created the roles of Rohde in _Three Sisters_, and Yepikhodov in _The Cherry Orchard_.

Muskatblit, Anatoly (b. 1905). Musician. He was concertmaster at the Meyerhold Theater.

Muzil, Nikolai (1839–1906). Actor.

Nemirovich-Danchenko, Vladimir (1858–1943). Playwright, director. Founder, with Stanislavsky, of the Moscow Art Theater. Meyerhold first studied theater in his acting class at the Moscow Philharmonic Society, and through him joined the original company of the Art Theater in 1898.

Nesterov, Mikhail (1862–1942). Painter. One of the group called the Wanderers; a painter of historical genre scenes and landscapes.

Oborin, Lev (1907–1974). Pianist, People's Artist of the USSR. A protégé of Meyerhold, who dedicated his first production of _Woe from Wit_ to him.

Ostrovsky, Alexander (1823–1886). Playwright, associated with the Maly Theater. Meyerhold's production of his _Forest_ (opened January 19, 1924) was one of his most successful and best-known productions.

Pappe, Anatoly (b. 1908). Musician. Conductor of the orchestra at the Meyerhold Theater.

Parnakh, Valentin (1891–1951). Poet and translator.

Podgaetsky, Mikhail. Playwright. He compiled the agit-spectacle _D. E._

Polivanov, Lev (1832–1899). Literary historian.

Popov, Gavrila (b. 1904). Composer. He wrote the music for Olesha's play _A List of Benefits_ (opened June 4, 1931) and the unfinished production _One Life_.

Popova, Lyubov (1889–1924). Painter and set designer. Associated early with the Jack of Diamonds group, she designed the Constructivist set for Meyerhold's production of Crommelynck's _Magnanimous Cuckold_ (opened April 25, 1922).

Prokofiev, Alexander (b. 1900). Poet.

Prokofiev, Sergei (1891–1953). Composer, People's Artist of the USSR. Meyerhold was a great admirer of his work, especially his opera _The Gambler_, which he made numerous attempts to stage. Prokofiev composed the music for Meyerhold's unfinished production of Pushkin's _Boris Godunov_.

Pushkin, Alexander (1799–1837). Poet and playwright. The work of Pushkin is a constant reference in the work and theories of Meyerhold. Although he never staged any of Pushkin's plays, Meyerhold expended much of his creative energy on plans for a production of _Boris Godunov_.

Pyast, Vladimir (1886–1940). Poet and translator. Meyerhold had him prepare "a score of the playtext of _Boris Godunov_ for the actors involved in the production, in which he [was] to note all the particularities of Pushkin's meter . . . and departures from the canonic form."

Raikh, Zinaida (1894–1939). Meyerhold's second wife. Formerly married to the poet Sergei Esenin, she was a student in the Meyerhold workshops and later one of the leading actresses of the Meyerhold Theater.

Remizova, Varvara (1882–1951). Actress in the Meyerhold Theater.

Rubinstein, Ida (1885–1960). Actress-impresario. Brought to Paris by Diaghilev in 1909 as a dancer in his company, the wealthy Ida Rubinstein stayed in France, and commissioned from an extraordinary range of artists a number of dance-mime-dramas which she performed. The number and scope of her commissions rival those of Diaghilev. Meyerhold directed her in d'Annunzio's *Pisanella* (opened June 11, 1913).

Sadovsky, Mikhail Mikhailovich (b. 1909). Member of a famous family of actors, he played Armand Duval in Meyerhold's production of *Camille* (opened March 19, 1934).

Samoilov, Evgeny (b. 1912). An actor at the Meyerhold Theater, he played Chatsky in *Woe from Wit* and rehearsed the role of the pretender in *Boris Godunov*.

Scriabin, Alexander (1871–1915). Composer and pianist. Meyerhold greatly appreciated his music and his various theoretical projects for combining music with color and odors in mass performances.

Seifullina, Lydia (1889–1954). Writer and playwright. Meyerhold planned to stage her play *Natasha* in 1937.

Selvinsky, Ilya (1898–1968). Poet, playwright. Meyerhold staged his play *Commander of the Second Army* (opened July 24, 1929).

Serov, Valentin (1865–1911). Painter. He did many portraits of theater personalities of his time.

Shchukin, Boris (1894–1939). Actor, People's Artist of the USSR. He rehearsed the role of Boris Godunov with Meyerhold at the Vakhtangov Studio.

Shebalin, Vissarion (1902–1963). Composer. He wrote the music for Meyerhold's production of Selvinsky's *Commander of the Second Army*, Mayakovsky's *Bathhouse*, Vishnevsky's *Last Decisive Battle*, German's *Prelude*, and Dumas fils' *Camille*.

Shostakovich, Dmitry (1906–1975). Composer, People's Artist of the USSR. He worked as pianist and music director for the Meyerhold Theater in 1922, and wrote the music for the production of Mayakovsky's *Bedbug*.

Shtraukh, Maxim (1900–1974). Actor, People's Artist of the USSR. He worked with the Meyerhold Theater from 1929 to 1931, and created the role of Pobedonosikov in Mayakovsky's *Bathhouse*.

Snezhnitsky, Lev. Actor. He joined the Meyerhold Theater in 1937, its last year, and played Armand Duval in *Camille*.

Sobinov, Leonid (1872–1934). Opera singer, famous for his elegant tenor voice. Meyerhold directed him in Gluck's *Orpheus* at the Mariinsky Theater (opened December 21, 1911).

Sofronitsky, Vladimir (1901–1961). Pianist. A musical protégé of Meyerhold's, married to Scriabin's daughter. Meyerhold dedicated to Sofronitsky his production of Tschaikovsky's *Queen of Spades* (opened January 25, 1935, at the Maly Opera Theater in Leningrad).

Stanislavsky (Alexeyev), Konstantin (1863–1938). Actor, director, People's Artist of the USSR. Founder, with Vladimir Nemirovich-Danchenko, in 1898, of the Moscow Art Theater. Meyerhold was one of the actors in the original company, but he left in 1902. Relations between the two men were complicated, as Meyerhold's letters to Stanislavsky in 1902 (included in this book) bear witness. (Stanislavsky had accused Meyerhold of organizing a demonstration against Nemirovich-Danchenko's play *Dreaming*, and refused to speak to him.) Although, throughout their careers, the two directors represented opposed conceptions of theater, they had great respect for each other's work, and when Meyerhold's theater was closed in 1938, Stanislavsky immediately invited him to direct his opera studio.

Starkovsky, Pyotr (1884–1964). Actor. He worked with the Meyerhold Theater from 1924 to 1937, and played the mayor in Gogol's *Inspector General*.

Sukhovo-Kobylin, Alexander (1817–1903). Playwright. Meyerhold staged his trio of plays (*Krechinsky's Wedding*, *The Affair*, and *The Death of Tarelkin*) in several versions.

Sulerzhitsky, Leopold (1872–1916). Director, artist, writer. A disciple and friend of Leo Tolstoy, assistant and private secretary to Stanislavsky, he worked with Meyerhold in the Theater-Studio in 1905. Although Sulerzhitsky's influence on those around him was often not specifically theatrical, he became an enthusiastic proponent for Stanislavsky's system for training actors.

Tairov, Alexander (1885–1950). Director. He directed the Chamber (Kamerny) Theater in Moscow from 1914 until it was liquidated in 1948. Stylistically, theoretically, and temperamentally, he and Meyerhold were in constant opposition.

Tiapkina, Elena (b. 1900). Actress. She worked at the Meyerhold Theater from 1924 to 1936.

Tolstoy, Alexei Konstantinovich (1817–1875). Poet and playwright. Meyerhold played the title role in his *Death of Ivan the Terrible* at the Moscow Art Theater in 1899.

Tretiakov, Sergei (1892–1939). Writer and playwright. He wrote the scenario for the agit-spectacle *The Earth Upside Down* (opened March 4, 1923). Meyerhold planned to stage his play *I Want a Child*, with sets by El Lissitsky. The play was rehearsed in 1927, but never opened. The Meyerhold Theater staged his play *Roar, China* (opened January 23, 1926), but the major work of directing was done by Meyerhold's assistant Vasily Fyodorov. It was through Tretiakov that Bertolt Brecht became acquainted with Meyerhold's work.

Tsarev, Mikhail (b. 1903). Actor, People's Artist of the USSR. He worked in the Meyerhold Theater from 1933 to 1937, and played Chatsky in *Woe from Wit* and Armand Duval in *Camille*.

Vakhtangov, Evgeny (1883–1922). Director of the Art Theater's Third Studio. Meyerhold valued highly the work of Vakhtangov, and after his death continued to assist the work of Vakhtangov's theater. The work of the two directors had a common theoretical basis.

Vakhtangov, Sergei (b. 1907). Architect and designer. The son of Evgeny Vakhtangov, he designed several productions for Meyerhold and, with Mikhail Barkhin, designed Meyerhold's new theater.

Varpakhovsky, Leonid (1908–1976). Director. He worked as secretary to the Meyerhold Theater and as one of Meyerhold's assistants.

Vishnevsky, Vsevolod (1900–1951). Playwright. Meyerhold staged his *Last Decisive Battle* (opened February 7, 1931).

Yakhontov, Vladimir (1899–1945). Actor. Worked at the Meyerhold Theater from 1924 to 1925.

Yermolova, Maria (1853–1928). Actress, People's Artist of the USSR. One of the famous actresses of the Russian stage, a member of the Maly Theater.

Zaichikov, Vasily (1888–1947). Actor. He studied in the Meyerhold workshops, and stayed with the theater as an actor until 1938.

Zakhava, Boris (b. 1896). Actor, director, People's Artist of the USSR. A member of Vakhtangov's theater and Vakhtangov's close assistant; from 1923 to 1925 he acted at the Meyerhold Theater.

Zlobin, Zosima (1901–1965). Actor and choreographer. He was a student in the Meyerhold workshops in 1921 and remained with the Meyerhold Theater.

Zoshchenko, Mikhail (1895–1958). Writer. Meyerhold had intended to produce his play *Dear Comrade* in 1930, but abandoned the project when he learned that Zoshchenko had submitted the script to another theater at the same time.